Suffragist Artists in Partnership

Edinburgh Critical Studies in Victorian Culture
Series Editor: Julian Wolfreys
Volumes available in the series:

Visit the Edinburgh Critical Studies in Victorian Culture web page at www.edinburghuniversitypress.com/series/ecvc

Also Available
Victoriographies – A Journal of Nineteenth-Century Writing, 1790–1914, edited by Julian Wolfreys
ISSN: 2044-2416
www.eupjournals.com/vic

Suffragist Artists in Partnership

Gender, Word and Image

Lucy Ella Rose

EDINBURGH
University Press

Edinburgh University Press is one of the leading university presses in the UK. We publish academic books and journals in our selected subject areas across the humanities and social sciences, combining cutting-edge scholarship with high editorial and production values to produce academic works of lasting importance. For more information visit our website: edinburghuniversitypress.com

Edinburgh University Press Ltd
The Tun – Holyrood Road,
12(2f) Jackson's Entry,
Edinburgh EH8 8PJ

First published in hardback by Edinburgh University Press 2018

Typeset in 11/13 Adobe Sabon by
IDSUK (DataConnection) Ltd, and
printed and bound by CPI Group (UK) Ltd,
Croydon, CR0 4YY

A CIP record for this book is available from the British Library

ISBN 978 1 4744 2145 4 (hardback)
ISBN 978 1 4744 5245 8 (paperback)
ISBN 978 1 4744 2146 1 (webready PDF)
ISBN 978 1 4744 2147 8 (epub)

Published with the support of the University of Edinburgh Scholarly Publishing Initiatives Fund.

Contents

Series Editor's Preface

'Victorian' is a term, at once indicative of a strongly determined concept and an often notoriously vague notion, emptied of all meaningful content by the many journalistic misconceptions that persist about the inhabitants and cultures of the British Isles and Victoria's Empire in the nineteenth century. As such, it has become a by-word for the assumption of various, often contradictory habits of thought, belief, behaviour and perceptions. Victorian studies and studies in nineteenth-century literature and culture have, from their institutional inception, questioned narrowness of presumption, pushed at the limits of the nominal definition, and have sought to question the very grounds on which the unreflective perception of the so-called Victorian has been built; and so they continue to do. Victorian and nineteenth-century studies of literature and culture maintain a breadth and diversity of interest, of focus and inquiry, in an interrogative and intellectually open-minded and challenging manner, which are equal to the exploration and inquisitiveness of its subjects. Many of the questions asked by scholars and researchers of the innumerable productions of nineteenth-century society actively put into suspension the clichés and stereotypes of 'Victorianism', whether the approach has been sustained by historical, scientific, philosophical, empirical, ideological or theoretical concerns; indeed, it would be incorrect to assume that each of these approaches to the idea of the Victorian has been, or has remained, in the main exclusive, sealed off from the interests and engagements of other approaches. A vital interdisciplinarity has been pursued and embraced, for the most part, even as there has been contest and debate amongst Victorianists, pursued with as much fervour as the affirmative exploration between different disciplines and differing epistemologies put to work in the service of reading the nineteenth century.

Edinburgh Critical Studies in Victorian Culture aims to take up both the debates and the inventive approaches and departures from convention that studies in the nineteenth century have witnessed for the last half century at least. Aiming to maintain a 'Victorian' (in the most positive sense of that motif) spirit of inquiry, the series' purpose is to continue and augment the cross-fertilisation of interdisciplinary approaches, and to offer, in addition, a number of timely and untimely revisions of Victorian literature, culture, history and identity. At the same time, the series will ask questions concerning what has been missed or improperly received, misread, or not read at all, in order to present a multi-faceted and heterogeneous kaleidoscope of representations. Drawing on the most provocative, thoughtful and original research, the series will seek to prod at the notion of the 'Victorian', and in so doing, principally through theoretically and epistemologically sophisticated close readings of the historicity of literature and culture in the nineteenth century, to offer the reader provocative insights into a world that is at once overly familiar, and irreducibly different, other and strange. Working from original sources, primary documents and recent interdisciplinary theoretical models, Edinburgh Critical Studies in Victorian Culture seeks not simply to push at the boundaries of research in the nineteenth century, but also to inaugurate the persistent erasure and provisional, strategic redrawing of those borders.

Julian Wolfreys

Acknowledgements

First and foremost, thank you to the University of Surrey and Watts Gallery Trust for awarding the three-year doctoral studentship (their first collaboration) that enabled me to conduct my research for this book. I would like to extend my gratitude particularly to Gregory Tate, Marion Wynne-Davies, Diane Watt, Mark Bills and Nicholas Tromans for this opportunity and their guidance throughout. My thanks goes to everyone at Watts Gallery, particularly Desna Greenhow and Beatrice Bertram, and to the Trust for kindly permitting my use of treasured archival materials and images. I am immensely grateful to the De Morgan Foundation for its support and generous provision of dazzling images, and specifically to Claire Longworth for patiently allowing and guiding my archival research.

I would like to thank all the academics and researchers who helped in various ways, including my anonymous readers, Lindsay Smith, Adeline Johns-Putra, Elise Lawton Smith, Irene Cockroft, Jan Marsh, Elizabeth Crawford, Trev Broughton, Felicity James, Elaine Cheasley Paterson, Veronica Franklin Gould, Ann Laver, Sarah Sullivan, Louise Boreham, Gail Naughton, Harvey Pitcher, Felicity Cain, Chloe Ward, Rhian Addison, Kerri Offord, Mary McMahon, Iain Cameron, Martin Kenig, Brian Butterly and Kathy Atherton. I am extremely grateful to the team at Edinburgh University Press, especially Julian Wolfreys, Michelle Houston, Adela Rauchova and James Dale. Thanks also to my ever-supportive friends, especially Lyndsey Jenkins, Zoe Thomas, Nathan Ashman and Tom Selby.

Thank you to the libraries, museums, galleries, archives and collections that were rich resources for research, including the British Library, National Portrait Gallery, V&A, Women's Library, Birmingham Museum and Art Gallery, Surrey History Centre, Guildford Institute, Godalming Museum and Standen House. Thanks also to the British Association for Victorian Studies, Pre-Raphaelite Society, the Society for the Arts and Crafts Movement in Surrey and the International Centre for Victorian Women Writers.

Some material in Chapter 3 and Chapter 6 is extracted from an article published in *Journal of Victorian Culture* 21.1 (2016): 74–91, copyright Taylor & Francis. Chapter 4 is derived in part from an article published in *Life Writing* 14.2 (2017): 217–31, copyright Taylor & Francis. Part of Chapter 5 builds on an article published in *Visual Culture in Britain* 17.1 (2016): 47–74, copyright Taylor & Francis. I am grateful to the readers for assisting the development of my work, and to the editors for allowing me to reprint this work in a revised and expanded form here.

A special word of thanks goes to my family – Jill, George, Eve and Harry – for their constant love and encouragement, and to my inspiring 'conjugal creative partner' Sam. This book is dedicated to Jill, my first feminist icon, without whom none of this would have been possible.

Abbreviations

ASL	Artists' Suffrage League
DMF	De Morgan Foundation Collection / Archives
HAIA	Home Arts and Industries Association
NUWSS	National Union of Women's Suffrage Societies
PRB	Pre-Raphaelite Brotherhood
TWL	The Women's Library
WG	Watts Gallery Collection / Archives
WGA	Women's Guild of Arts
WSPU	Women's Social and Political Union

'Woman is Now Beginning to Take Her Place'

'The hope of the future lies greatly in the fact that woman is now beginning to take her place', wrote Mary Watts in her diary (1893: 4 April). A year later, feminist writer Sarah Grand coined the term 'New Woman' and wrote, 'women generally are becoming conscious that some great change is taking place in their position' (Grand 1894: 707). An increasing preoccupation with woman's place – and specifically, the evolving role and shifting socio-political position of women – is perceptible in much art and literature of the later nineteenth century, the period that engendered active feminism in the form of the women's suffrage movement. Woman's place was a primary focus of Victorian–Edwardian feminist discourse, and remains central to present-day feminism. This book shows how neglected nineteenth-century women writers and artists transgressed traditional female spheres and restrictive feminine norms in their professional creative practices and unconventional creative partnerships with men, and how their literary and visual texts can be read as sites of struggle against – rather than submission to – patriarchy. These marginalised Victorian women, traditionally defined as subordinate gender 'others' in relation to their famous husbands, can be seen as 'significant others' who were not passive and peripheral but rather active and influential in their creative partnerships as well as in contemporary debates, through which they achieved and promoted greater personal and political empowerment and freedom.

This book explores the role of women in the artistic and literary professions, the representation of women in art and literature, and the rise of feminism through these discourses. It focuses on two conjugal creative partnerships of artists, writers and suffragists: Mary Seton Watts (1849–1938) and George Frederic Watts (1817–1904); and Evelyn Mary De Morgan (1855–1919) and William Frend De Morgan (1839–1917).[1] Collectively their lives coincided with the rise of the women's movement, from its embryonic stage in the mid-nineteenth century to the later phase of militant suffragism preceding the First World War; Evelyn saw the franchise extended to certain women in 1918, while Mary lived to see citizenship rights granted to women on the same terms as men in 1928. Witnessing such advances inevitably impacted their lives and works. I aim to show how literary and visual texts produced by the Wattses and the De Morgans can be re-read in relation to more recent feminist and gender theory; how these figures and their works were influenced by, and contributed to, contemporary gender debates and early feminist discourse; and how the female figures worked within traditionally masculinist structures (marriage; the traditional gender binary) and male traditions (art; literature) in order to achieve greater social, political and economic equality, empowerment and emancipation. Overall, my aim is to show how Victorian women redefined themselves in relation to masculinity, femininity and society, and forged the key to their freedom through creative practice, profession and partnership.

This book focuses predominately on the female figures who have been historically overshadowed by, and more critically neglected than, their husbands. Very little has been written about Mary and Evelyn, who are primarily known only as the wives of famous Victorian artists; despite their notoriety in the nineteenth century, they have since been largely forgotten along with their vast *oeuvres*. Existing scholarship on these women has tended to focus on a particular (aspect of their) work for which they are best known (that is, Mary's ceramic work and Evelyn's spiritualist paintings) at the expense of exploring their many lesser-known works of cultural importance and feminist significance, and the dominant critical focus has been on religion or spiritualism in both their works. This is the first study of their literary and visual works, creative practices and partnerships specifically in relation to feminism. Mary and Evelyn have hitherto never been appraised as literary as well as artistic figures, and one of this book's original contributions is its feminist analysis of unpublished and (until now) untranscribed writings by Mary and Evelyn that reside in the fascinating archives of Watts Gallery and the De Morgan Foundation. This book thus brings previously unseen material to light, offering alternative perspectives on the (supposedly submissive or subordinate female) figures and new readings of their works.

This introductory chapter will discuss the Wattses and the De Morgans as interconnected creative partnerships, with similar or shared aesthetic and socio-political views, situating them in biographical, historical and socio-political contexts. It will explore the couples' connections and collaborations as well as their interactions recorded in Mary's diaries in order to illuminate parallels in their lives and works, before comparing them to other marital and familial creative partnerships of the Victorian period to show how they were unconventional as individual creative partnerships and unique as a double creative partnership. It will then discuss how early feminist ideas were expressed and promoted through artistic and literary discourses in the nineteenth century, and explain the inextricable link between art and literature in the works of the Wattses and the De Morgans, laying the groundwork for the chapters which will analyse them in more detail. However, the lack of available biographical material on these figures makes it necessary to briefly introduce them here before continuing.

George Frederic Watts (OM, RA) is widely considered to be the greatest painter of the Victorian period, dubbed 'Signor' and hailed 'England's Michelangelo' (W. Blunt 1989). The son of a piano-maker, he was home-schooled before entering the Royal Academy aged eighteen. He was a symbolist, portraitist and sculptor, famed for his visionary allegorical works, and his later paintings anticipate abstract art. He donated much of his work to the nation, including the portrait collection of his famous contemporaries, the 'Hall of Fame'. He married the young English actress Ellen Terry in 1864, but they separated within a year and he later married Mary; both Ellen and Mary participated in suffrage marches. He had residences, at various times, in London, the Isle of Wight, Surrey and Brighton. He refused the baronetcy offered to him by Queen Victoria but accepted the Order of Merit in 1902. By the end of his long life, he was one of the most famous painters in the world.

Mary Watts (née Fraser Tytler), whose life spanned the reign of five monarchs, was a painter, symbolist craftswoman, designer and pioneer of Liberty's Celtic style. She was an active member of, and campaigner for, the Home Arts and Industries Association (HAIA), and became a famous name in the field of Arts and Crafts. The daughter of a civil servant, she was born in India and brought up in the Scottish Highlands, before embarking on formal art training in London, where she became acquainted with George Watts. Believing in the moral potential of art, she set up a clay-modelling class for shoeblacks in the East End, and later taught Surrey villagers to produce terracotta bricks and tiles for her Watts Cemetery Chapel; she subsequently founded her own pottery business. After George's death in 1904 she became more politically active in the women's suffrage movement.

William De Morgan, artist, potter, designer, inventor and novelist, was born in London to educated and enlightened parents.

He was one of the most significant ceramic artists of the Arts and Crafts movement of the late nineteenth century. His work, along with that of William Morris and Walter Crane, laid the foundation for the Victorian regeneration of the Arts and Crafts, and he helped to organise the first exhibition in 1888. While he achieved fame as a novelist in later life, and studied fine art in his earlier years, he spent most of his life as a potter and craftsman. He attracted attention among artists for his experiments in shimmering lustre pottery. He lived in Cheyne Row, Chelsea – also home to Thomas Carlyle, and close to Dante Gabriel Rossetti and Algernon Charles Swinburne in Cheyne Walk (all of whom George Watts painted for his 'Hall of Fame') – where he built a kiln in the garden and completed the tiles commissioned for the Arab Hall at Leighton House. His distinctive, decorative tile panels were thereafter requested by P&O for twelve ocean liner cabins, the Czar of Russia for his yacht and Lord Debenham for his London home.

Evelyn De Morgan (née Pickering) was perhaps the most accomplished female painter of the second phase of Pre-Raphaelitism and one of the most visionary of the late nineteenth-century British symbolist painters. Nonetheless, she is often marginalised in accounts of late Victorian painting, and especially the avant-garde Pre-Raphaelite and Aesthetic movements. Born into a wealthy family in London, she was educated first at home and then at art schools, and she became the pupil of her uncle, the artist John Roddam Spencer Stanhope (himself a pupil of George Watts). Her work – rooted in Italian Renaissance art and inspired by mythology and literature – combines ideas about spiritualism and (increasingly) feminism. She was a spiritualist medium who experimented with automatic writing and a pacifist who produced war paintings. Her work thus offers fascinating insight into a turbulent, evolving Victorian–Edwardian world.

Collaborating Couples

And in the present case both husband and wife are artists, and what is more rare, two artists who are of just the same mind concerning their ideals of art. (Hulda Friederichs 1895: 74)

It is unusual to find two people, so gifted and so entirely in harmony in their art, who acted and re-acted on each other's genius. (Anna Maria Wilhelmina Stirling 1922: 12)

These contemporary descriptions of the Wattses and the De Morgans respectively are strikingly similar. Both portray a mutually beneficial marital creative partnership of like minds, a reciprocity rare for the period, and (what writer Charles Lamb, describing his creative partnership with his sister Mary, called) 'a sort of double singleness' (qtd. in Aaron 1991: 2): two distinct individuals brought together by art and a shared worldview. A friend of the De Morgans observed that they 'were absolutely *one*: one in sympathy, in intelligence and its direction, one in tastes, and in perfect companionship. . . . He believed in her Art and she in his' (Richmond qtd. in Stirling 1922: 11). While they retained their own individual personalities in marriage, their coupling 'united them as one' (Barrington *c*.1922: 37), and William was 'made even more highly finished by the remarkable woman he married' (Richmond qtd. in Stirling 1922: 11). A 'spirit letter' from the De Morgans' automatic writing experiment describes the couple's 'spirits in the flesh' as 'the strangest, most miraculous turn-out; both separate, yet united' (1909: 9).

In her diaries, Mary records her 'oneness' with her husband in a productive artistic partnership, rather than her 'otherness' as merely the dutiful housewife of an artist: 'My dear one is pleased to find that we are of one mind upon these things which concern us both so much. [. . . He] added "now we are one"!' (1887: 24 January). She continues, 'He says we have an affinity with each other which is very unusual' (1887: 22 May), and concludes, 'marriage [is] a completion of self that none but happily married people could understand' (1891: 5 October). Mary also recalls a letter from British feminist Josephine Butler saying, 'I have you & your husband often, together, in my minds [*sic*] eye & my heart' (1896: 26 August). The equality and reciprocity of the Wattses' partnership – in which they, like the De Morgans, established individual artistic identities while working together and alongside each other – seems symbolised by the plaster cast of their clasped left hands (1886) (Fig. I.1), which they had made on their wedding day. Mary refers to this cast in her diary as the 'dear blessed symbol of our double yet one life' (1891: 18 August). While one purpose of Victorian marriage was to 'construct a purportedly unified conjugal gaze so that . . . members of the couple would see things literally the same way . . . with one pair of eyes . . . belong[ing] to the husband' (Michie 2006: 12), these marriages were unusual in the sense that their unified conjugal gazes were egalitarian rather than patriarchal, underpinned by progressive socio-political and suffragist views.

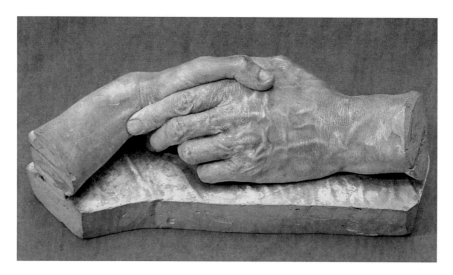

Figure I.1 *Plaster Cast of the Left Hands of Mary and George Watts*, 1886, Watts Gallery Trust.

The Wattses and the De Morgans are connected in various ways that are not widely acknowledged. They were two of the most eminent and prolific conjugal creative partnerships of the Victorian art world, although – due to Victorian art falling out of fashion and into obscurity in the twentieth century – they are only just beginning to be re-recognised as such. They were key participants at the beginning of the Arts and Crafts movement (which rejected mass production and industrialisation, prioritising skilled hand-production methods), part of the Pre-Raphaelite circle, and supporters of the early women's suffrage movement. They became Victorian celebrities over the course of their lifetimes, were much admired by their forward-thinking contemporaries (artists, writers, intellectuals and suffragists), and were part of an emergent feminist community. Their mutual friends included the Burne-Joneses, the Rossettis, the Morrises and the Holidays. Each couple represents a marriage of arts and crafts, consisting of a symbolist painter or fine artist (George; Evelyn) and a ceramicist or designer (Mary; William). Yet while Mary and William are primarily perceived as pioneering decorative artists, they both had a background in fine art; George and Evelyn also produced sculpture, and all of these four figures were writers. Thus the married figures' aesthetic interests remained complementary without clashing.

There are also striking similarities between the lives and works of Mary and Evelyn. They both trained at the same art school, painted and modelled, and created gesso angels carrying symbols in a church or chapel.[2] They both joined the Women's Guild of Arts (WGA) and actively supported the women's suffrage movement in petition, paint or procession. They were also both prolific (if predominantly private) writers who wrote diaries and poems, focusing on similar women-centred subjects, although their authorial roles are even less recognised than their artistic roles, and their (mostly unpublished) writings have never before been substantially explored. The Wattses and the De Morgans experimented with artistic and literary practices and techniques, and their works can be compared thematically, formally and stylistically. Elements of their discourses and iconographic vocabularies overlap, and this book presents them in conversation and collaboration, offering new perspectives on these figures and their works.

George said of Evelyn, 'She is a long way ahead of all the women and considerably ahead of most of the men. I look upon her as the first woman-artist of the day – if not of all time' (qtd. in Stirling 1922: 193). Such high praise suggests his immense respect and admiration for her as a talented pioneering professional woman artist. It also suggests his progressive perspective of women artists as equal if not superior to men at a time when it was a 'generally accepted principle' that 'women [had] no vision, talent or originality', and the notion of ever regarding women as equal to male artists was absurd, since they could only ever achieve 'partial success' in 'artistic mediocrity' (A. R. A. 1888: xxv). George had known Evelyn since her infancy, and before her marriage she regularly visited him at his London studio-home Little Holland House in the 'evening hours' when 'only the most intimate were admitted . . . and that but rarely' (Barrington 1905: 64), to discuss art and techniques. Evelyn's uncle, Pre-Raphaelite painter John Roddam Spencer Stanhope, had studied under George and frequently visited Little Holland House as a young man. Evelyn's palette knife was given to her by George (1893), and he was always interested in her work. When Mrs [Emilie Isabel] Russell Barrington met George in Italy she recalled, '[h]e wanted to know . . . especially what Mrs. de Morgan had been doing' (Barrington 1905: 176), and her garden in which the De Morgans' relationship blossomed was immortalised by George in a sunset landscape (Barrington *c.*1922: 37). The motto Evelyn's sister offers in summation of Evelyn's approach to art is George's own: 'The Utmost for the Highest' (Stirling 1924: 237).

The Wattses and the De Morgans were close friends and collaborators who sympathised with the aims of each other's art and actively supported each other's creative projects. The Watts

Memorial to Heroic Self-Sacrifice in Postman's Park (opened 1900 in central London, near St Paul's Cathedral where George's works were hung) was executed by George in collaboration with William, and continued by Mary after her husband's death.[3] George commissioned the production of tiled memorial plaques designed by William for a cloister to commemorate individual acts of heroism in everyday life. As well as being very important to the Wattses, this was itself a remarkable, unique project: unlike war memorials which honour almost exclusively the deeds of men, this memorial recognises men and women. The commemoration of self-sacrificing heroines challenged the 'prevailing belief that women were incapable of physical heroics' (Wingerden 1999: 104) and prefigured later tributes to suffragette heroism. The narration of tragic, heroic acts on decorated tiles not only stands testimony to those who died to save others but also to the passion, vision and skill of the artists who conceived and created it.

Mary records several visits from the De Morgans in her diaries, which offer insight into the interactions and relationships between the two couples. Her earliest mention suggests that she and George welcomed them as friends into their Surrey studio-home and enjoyed their company: 'Later came the de Morgans . . . How glad I am we have this gallery & the little house' (1893: 4 June). Another entry in the same year implies that Evelyn was privy to the Wattses' deep discussions about morality, society, philanthropy and spirituality:

> Mrs de Morgan here, our only visitor. Signor lay in the niche & talked of the change that might be wrought for mankind, were he but to realise that his present ideal is all for self, self advancement, & chiefly by money getting for self, & instead was to fix eyes upon the grand universal idea of helping all to reach a happier & better state of things. A heaven might really dawn upon earth. (1893: 20 August)

That George talks to Evelyn and Mary while he lays in the 'niche' – the Wattses' private reading alcove made by Mary, usually reserved for their evening readings together after visitors had left – suggests the level of intimacy between the three. They shared progressive social views and a deep concern about 'the downward descent of the nation in consequence of the universal mammon worship' (G. Watts qtd. in M. Watts 1891: 19 June), and Evelyn and George both produced works on the topic of Mammonism. Seeming to visualise George's idea of 'a happier & better state of things', many of Evelyn's paintings depict scenes of women entering, ascending to or envisioning a brighter world, and female angels descending on dark landscapes bringing light, which have both spiritual and socio-political significance.

Mary's final diary entry mentioning the De Morgans reveals their close friendship and mutual admiration for each other's work:

> A nice day of friends . . . the brougham met the de Morgans at 9.50 – [William] has become a celebrity as the author of [the novel] Joseph Vance – for indeed when later the door opened & Mrs. Francis Galton & her two nice nieces walked in, & were introduced, Miss Biggs went to her uncle who is slightly deaf & said 'The author of <u>Joseph Vance</u>' & the old man was enchanted & they sat together on the big sofa talking for some time. After tea we went to the gallery. . . . The De Morgans also I think loved their day & when they were leaving said all that my heart could wish about the shrine I have made for the pictures – (1907: August [no date])

The De Morgans continued to visit Mary at the Wattses' Surrey studio-home even after George's death, and admired her display of George's work at Watts Gallery. William greatly respected George and wrote to Mary soon after his death in 1904, 'My gratitude is great indeed to Signor, both for his Art and its teaching' (qtd. in Stirling 1922: 231). Evelyn's sister also corresponded with Mary.[4] Although there is no evidence that Mary read William's novels, she describes his newfound celebrity status in complementary detail, and is likely to have been aware of the basic plot and characters of his bestselling first novel *Joseph Vance* (1906), which 'took the novel-reading world by storm' (R. Blunt 1918: 190) and contains two of the most nuanced and sympathetic of William's female characters, Lossie Thorpe and Janey Vance. Mary later writes in an article that her Surrey kiln was 'built under the kind supervision of Mr. William De Morgan' (*c.*1892–5); she apparently realised that publicly acknowledging her famous friend's input could benefit her commercial pottery.[5] She also consulted William's business partner Halsey Ralph Ricardo on her terracotta work.[6]

Public interest in Mary Watts is on the rise, as evidenced by the appearance and discussion of her work, life and home in the BBC programmes *Flog It!* (2016), *Great British Railways* (2016) and *Sex and Sensibility: the Allure of Art Nouveau* (2015), as well as the display of her sculpture to critical acclaim at the Tate Britain's *Sculpture Victorious* exhibition (2015). The recent restoration of Watts Gallery itself and of the Wattses' studios at their Surrey home (a Grade II-listed Arts and Crafts building which is the last remaining nineteenth-century artists' studio with its collection still intact, now open to the public) is indicative of the considerable interest commanded by their work and the spaces in which they collaborated. Mary is largely responsible for the creation of this rare example of a Victorian artists' village and the endurance of their extraordinary legacy. The recent publication of *The Diary of Mary Watts 1887–1904* (Greenhow 2016b) has also significantly increased the visibility of Mary's work by bringing it into the public domain, and contributes to the growing body of scholarship on non-canonical nineteenth-century women writers. That the eightieth anniversary of Mary's death in 2018 coincides with the ninetieth anniversary of the Equal Franchise Act in 1928 (which gave women the right to vote at age twenty-one on the same terms as men) and the one hundredth anniversary of the Representation of the People Act in 1918 (which enabled all men and some women over the age of thirty to vote for the first time) highlights her largely unexplored relation to the suffrage movement.

The recent relocation of the De Morgan collection to the site of Watts Gallery in Surrey invites comparative study. The commemoration of both the bicentenary of George's birth and the centenary of William's death this year (2017) calls for a re-view of their works. With the recent resurgence of interest in Pre-Raphaelitism, the work of the lesser-known late Pre-Raphaelite Evelyn De Morgan – which featured in the recent *Botticelli Reimagined* and *Pre-Raphaelites on Paper* exhibitions (2016) – is also receiving renewed critical attention. In this book, I aim to contribute to the growing scholarship on these long-forgotten yet culturally important figures – and to the fields of English literature, art history, history, Victorian studies and women's and gender studies – by exploring their lives and works in the depth they deserve.

Nineteenth-Century Marriage and Partnership

This book's focus on the concept of the (double) creative partnership offers a broader context for, and opens up new ways of, studying and understanding nineteenth-century women writers and artists, their lives and works, their practices and relationships, and their socio-political positions. By placing the female figures in the context of their partnerships with eminent men – Britain's premier portrait painter (George), and one of England's most celebrated ceramicists (William) – their achievements are given important new perspectives. This book argues for the location of women writers and artists and their works not as marginal and insignificant, belonging to a sphere set apart from the male domain of work and business, nor merely exceptions in a male-dominated culture, but rather as an integral part of a period of momentous social, historical and cultural transformations.

A feminist re-view of the couples' marital relationships as creative partnerships radically challenges longstanding perceptions of them as representatives of the traditional gender binary in which man is the superior, dominant, active artist and woman is the subordinate, subservient, passive acolyte – of Mary as her more famous husband's 'nurse-companion-housekeeper' (W. Blunt 1989: 103) and Evelyn as merely the 'wife of William De Morgan' (Stirling 1922). These creative partnerships represented a progressive departure from, or radically different approach to, nineteenth-century gender politics: they were fundamentally founded on greater gender equality; they facilitated female activity in male traditions and female agency within traditionally masculinist structures; they represented a reciprocity and 'atypical merging of gender roles' (Aaron 1991: 3) in which both figures functioned as supporter and supported, professional artist and domestic partner; and they even to some extent embodied a gender-role inversion (in creative practices, economic positions and/or relationship dynamics) whereby women assumed positions of power and authority over men. These couples, which embodied a subversion and indeed inversion of traditional power relations between the sexes, represented a disruption of the patriarchal sex and gender binaries underpinning the Victorian society in which they lived.

In both the Wattses' and the De Morgans' relationships, the woman worked within the man/woman dyad as a fellow creator and cultural producer in an anti-patriarchal marital partnership where the figures facilitated, supported and influenced each other's careers, practices and works. These reciprocal creative partnerships demonstrated a way of woman giving and helping the male figure without being subservient in a hierarchical exchange, which, in a period governed by phallocentric values, was in itself revolutionary. Mary and Evelyn dispelled the prevailing myth that devoted wife and dedicated female artist were mutually exclusive and exemplified how these two competing visions of woman in the nineteenth century could successfully co-exist. The Wattses' and the De Morgans' creative partnerships subverted prevailing patriarchal assumptions and binaries that defined women in relation to men as inferior creators and subordinate gender Others. Although artistic women were more typically perceived and defined in relation to men as muses, copyists or professional helpmeets, Mary and Evelyn were respected creative partners, tough critics, intellectual companions and income generators. Their husbands never intentionally hindered – but rather wholeheartedly supported – their creativity in style and substance. These partnerships can be seen to reconfigure patriarchal power relations in their types of exchange and ways of relating based on love, respect and recognition of each other, escaping the patriarchal system which repressed and excluded women. An embracement of suffragist views inevitably played a part in the establishment and success of these two exceptional, mutually nurturing creative partnerships, which could not exist without elements of equality, encouragement and admiration.

These partnerships are particularly distinctive in relation to their immediate historical context and the 'strongly polarized gender system typical of the Victorian period' (Aaron 1991: 2) which dictated the male/female, active/passive, artistic/domestic, public/private, commercial/philanthropic patriarchal binaries. An awareness of how male domination and female dependency underpinned marital relations in this period is crucial to this book's exploration of how the Wattses' and De Morgans' partnerships were at variance with the masculinist culture considered characteristic of the Victorian period – which was in fact an age of transition. Indeed, women's formation of creative partnerships with men, transgression of traditional female spaces, participation in the male traditions of art and literature, and construction of professional artistic and literary identities blurred and broke down these apparently fixed and rigid binary boundaries and revealed them to be fluid and permeable. Through their creative practices, Mary and Evelyn disrupted the masculinist hierarchical order of these binaries, including the 'invidious division of creative categories' (Nunn 1987: 18) into 'masculine' fine art and 'feminine' applied art (or craft), since Evelyn was a painter and Mary combined the two in her career. While such categories served to sustain separate spheres and sexual difference, these women revealed such binaries to be socially constructed and thus potentially de/re-constructed to liberatory effect.

While the gender history of nineteenth-century Britain has been widely perceived as a predominantly patriarchal model which gave power and privilege to men, it can be re-viewed as a process of gradual but determined female challenge to women's exclusion (from the artistic and literary professions, from the right to vote, from expression) and to male supremacy, using the Wattses' and De Morgans' creative partnerships as case studies. A focus on the female figures within these couples (rather than in isolation) reveals not only how men and women interacted and worked together in familial or marital creative partnerships but also the power play, dynamics and tensions between male and female partners. Underpinned by feminist and gender theory, this book attends to the shifting balance of 'power relations inscribed in the areas patriarchal history treats as incidental: . . . private life and personal relations' between men and women. It addresses the inconsistencies in and instabilities of the patriarchal culture where they are found, which constitute evidence that 'existing power relations are always precarious' (Meaney 1993: viii, ix) and that those of the traditional gender binary can be destabilised or deconstructed from within. It analyses art and literature (artistic and literary representations of the female body as well as the artistic and literary professions, both being topics politicised by feminism) as sites where power is contested.

Mid-Victorian women artists were often the daughters, the sisters or the wives of artists, and in this sense the relationships of the Wattses and the De Morgans were typical of their time. However, the male artistic familial or marital connection was an 'important factor in the fate of aspiring women artists' (Nunn 1987: 30) which, crucially, either fostered and furthered or hindered and halted their creative careers; the Wattses' and the De Morgans' partnerships were atypical in their positive effects on the female figures' practices. While the artistic family connection gave women the advantage of an early familiarity with art, allowed them access to art without necessarily violating the limits of the domestic sphere, and made their artistic practices more socially respectable, women were invariably compared to and overshadowed by their male relatives, especially if they worked in the same medium, as they 'got caught in a much more typical familial role of lesser lights reflecting the greater glory of their [brother's or father's] talent' (Nunn 1987: 31). Significantly, the Wattses and the De Morgans predominantly did not work in the same media; they developed distinct practices or else focuses and styles, allowing each other to flourish in their own creative spaces rather than competing, which arguably strengthened their partnerships as well as their individual creative identities.

The shadow cast by the family connection is evident in press write-ups of women artists. As Pamela Gerrish Nunn points out,

> it seems that if there were so much as a hint of an artistic father, brother or husband in the woman's pedigree, he was brought forth by critics to stand . . . in front of her – and was used as a yardstick by which to measure her failings . . . the comparison was usually to the woman's disadvantage. (Nunn 1987: 33)

The constant emphasis on a woman artist's gender by mid-Victorian critics indicated and perpetuated the widespread perception and fundamental acceptance of the idea that art created by the 'second sex' was 'Other': it was 'necessarily different [from the norm that was male artists' work], and negatively so, and must be signalled as such' (Nunn 1987: 21). Women artists and writers were thus deemed doubly different as subordinate beings and abnormal, inferior creators. Women have historically been perceived (in men's eyes, including those of male critics) as the 'non-social, non-political, non-human half of the living structure; . . . they have [had] to acknowledge their fate as . . . relegation to the shadow thrown on them by patriarchy' (Foster 1990: 66).

As Deborah Cherry discusses, in Victorian Britain, men were 'not expected to rearrange their activities or reconstitute their sense of self on marriage . . . they expected their wives to adapt to them and to cater to their desires' (Cherry 1993: 40). A woman's artistic career was thus often effectively curtailed on marriage or took a secondary place in her life typically organised around the home, since 'social structures of sexual difference positioned married women in relation to their husbands, household management and motherhood' (Cherry 1993: 33). Anna Mary Howitt gave up painting for exhibition on her marriage to Alaric Watts in 1859; Mary Severn gave up painting on her marriage to Charles Newton in 1861; and Lucy Madox Brown's artistic career was effectively curtailed by her marriage to William Rossetti in 1874 (Cherry 1993: 33). Prevalent social expectations that wives of professional men did not work and were submissive and self-sacrificing not only reinforced the patriarchal institution of marriage as a 'relation of emotional and economic dependency' (Cherry 1993: 33) but also created an often irreconcilable conflict between a woman's creative identity and Victorian ideals of domestic femininity. For many women artists, marriage was the 'ultimate impediment' to their professional creative practices. Its demands and duties constituted the primary social pressures 'militating against women's achievement in the realm of art', and women's talent 'for the most part came to nought under the burdens of domesticity' (Harris and Nochlin 1976: 52) which for many were too heavy to bear.

Conjugal inequity was increasingly acknowledged and addressed by women writers and artists as the public debate surrounding marriage escalated in 1887–8 with the publication of early feminist Mona Caird's extensive critique of marriage. Caird described marriage being instituted 'on the foundation of bondage' (Caird [1905] qtd. in E. L. Smith 2002: 118), and artist Louise Jopling described marital duties as 'iron bars to [her] success' (Jopling [1873] qtd. in Cherry 1993: 34), drawing on the language of imprisonment, 'duty and dependency in which middle-class women often conceptualised marriage and wife-hood' (Cherry 1993: 34). Yet marital and familial relationships took many forms in the nineteenth century: creative partnerships formed between husband and wife shifted and subverted the traditional (im)balance in the power relations between the sexes.[7] The conjugal creative partnership of the 1870s and 80s – embodied by the Wattses and the De Morgans as well as William and Marie Spartali Stillman – was a 'revolutionary approach to marital politics' (E. L. Smith 2002: 27). It was a progressive if not radical departure from mid-Victorian mercenary marriage, and what Caird called that 'old tradition which for weary centuries [had] sacrificed the individual life of the woman for the husband' and caused love to be 'handcuffed and dragooned' (Caird [1905] qtd. in E. L. Smith 2002: 118).

Marriage to a practising artist and/or writer could facilitate a woman's professional creative practice and entrance into a creative and/or business partnership with her husband. Women artists who had established independent, successful careers prior to marriage 'often perceived marriage as an erosion or renunciation of their autonomy' (Cherry 1993: 33) – a view that Evelyn and Mary expressed before marriage.[8] Yet Mary and Evelyn demonstrated how marriage to a practising artist could make it possible for a woman to continue to work and to collaborate, to exhibit professionally and to achieve greater success as part of a professional creative couple. In such 'companionate marriages' where wife and husband worked together in the 'business of cultural production (literature or art)' (Cherry 1993: 33), both were active agents in a partnership that united artistic productivity and domesticity, kinship and capital. This is represented by the plaster cast of the Wattses' clasped hands, which is not just suggestive of a romantic holding of hands but also of a business-like handshake. This form of marriage can be seen as a career-enabling and self-empowering strategy for Victorian women writers and artists.

In addition to Mary and Evelyn's marriages (1886 and 1887 respectively) to practising artists, their relatively late entry into matrimony in their thirties (Evelyn at almost thirty-two and Mary at almost thirty-seven) at a time when the average age of marriage for middle-class women was twenty-five (E. L. Smith 2002: 26) is a good example of the 'strategy adopted by many women in the 1860s and 70s who wanted to pursue the increasing opportunities opening up to them in employment, education and politics' (Unwin 2004: 240).

They successfully reconciled the conflict between domestic matters and artistic careers, negotiating conventions and constraints in similar ways (late marriage; childlessness; establishment of partnerships) in order to pursue creative careers and develop professional identities. Significantly, the Wattses became guardians of the orphan Lilian (Lily) Mackintosh (1879–1972) when she was seventeen and less demanding of Mary's time than a small child. Although 'joint ventures were not uncommon' (Cherry 1993: 37) in the mid-to-late nineteenth century, the Wattses' and De Morgans' partnerships were unusual and unconventional in the sense that few Victorian women were professional artists, fewer continued to work and exhibit after marriage, and even fewer formed marital creative partnerships – especially those involving subversions of gender roles and gendered creative categories. Although neither Evelyn nor Mary married for money, their decisions to marry may have been influenced by the third of the Married Women's Property Acts in 1882, allowing wives to keep all the property they had before and after marriage.

There have been numerous specific studies of individual nineteenth-century partnerships, including Jane Aaron's focus on Charles and Mary Lamb in *A Double Singleness* (1991); Angela Thirlwell's book *William and Lucy: The Other Rossettis* (2003); and Mark Bills's focus on aspects of George and Mary Watts's life and works in *An Artists' Village* (2011).[9] The lengthening list demonstrates the continued interest in such studies. Building on Bills's focus on the Wattses (but challenging his interpretations), Aaron's study informed by feminist literary theory (but combining this with art history), and Thirlwell's discussion of a Victorian woman's relationship to early feminism (but showing how women's artistic careers were advanced rather than curtailed by marriage), this book's analysis of the Wattses' and the De Morgans' creative partnerships fills gaps in the currently available literature on these figures, engages with existing work on partnerships, and offers new perspectives on – and contributions to – this growing field of research. Discussing creative partnerships, Deborah Cherry points out,

> tantalising questions about the organisation of . . . partnerships remain as yet unanswered. It is not known how decisions were made or how the daily business of a joint enterprise was undertaken . . . What exchanges took place in a shared studio between . . . husband and wife? (Cherry 1993: 38)

Mary's and Evelyn's professional creative practices and collaborations can also be seen as the 'kinds of practices . . . which prompt a rethinking of our basic categories: what is gender, how is it produced and reproduced, what are its possibilities?' (Butler 1990: 113). This book aims to go some way towards answering these questions by exploring the Wattses' and the De Morgans' personal and professional relationships, and how they worked together as individual and interconnected creative partnerships, in interdisciplinary and innovative ways, in order to support and promote greater female liberation in the nineteenth century. It also focuses on moments of protest, struggle or gender-role inversion in their partnerships and works in order to trace the development of the female figures' creative identities and feminist voices, offering a more nuanced understanding of power relations between the sexes as well as of the relationship between feminism, art and literature in the period. This book reclaims and offers an original interpretation of the nineteenth-century partnership as a concept, identifying structures previously interpreted as straightforwardly patriarchal – that is, Victorian male/female conjugal relations – as sites of creative female agency.

Art, Literature and Feminism

A consideration of the creative partnerships within their historical context is crucial to an understanding of their roles in and relation to the emergent feminist discourse of the Victorian and Edwardian periods. The second half of the nineteenth century was a revolutionary period of socio-political change for British women: it was a 'boom time for women artists' (Nunn 1987: 21) which gave birth to a new species of female writers as well as feminism in the form of the women's suffrage movement. While Mary Wollstonecraft famously wrote *A Vindication of the Rights of Woman* in 1792, one of the earliest works of feminist philosophy promoting female education and positing women as companions (rather than servile wives) to their husbands, the demand for female suffrage had not yet been widely realised, and many of her proposed social changes did not come to fruition until the nineteenth century.[10] This is when women were offered formal art training and institutional education for the first time, and challenged their exclusion from the male traditions of art and literature through professional artistic and literary practices. The nineteenth century generated the professionalisation of the woman artist and the woman writer, and it was arguably women's move into professional creative practices that 'produced the greatest potential for change' (Nunn 1987: 2) in the (social, political and economic) place of women.

To highlight some landmarks in the progression towards gender equality and female empowerment specifically through women's increasing participation in the arts: the Society of Female Artists was founded in 1855; Laura Herford, a leading figure in campaigns for art education, became the first woman to be accepted as an art student at the Royal Academy in 1860 (obscuring her sex on the entrance exam by using only her initials); female friends and family members were employed in embroidery by the furniture and furnishings firm Morris, Marshall, Faulkner & Co., formed in 1861; the co-educational Slade School of Fine Art was established in London in 1871, with women students initially outnumbering men; women's work was accepted by the newly formed Arts and Crafts Exhibition Society under the presidency of Walter Crane in 1888; and female students at the Royal Academy were permitted to draw from the nude male model in 1893.

The literary professions also saw growth in female participation, and writing emerged as a profession for women although, unlike in the case of visual art, there were relatively few formal institutional and educational mechanisms through which to realise this change. Almost all colleges and universities only accepted men for most of the nineteenth century, but in the 1860s–70s Oxford and Cambridge opened colleges for women. William De Morgan's mother Sophia, who believed strongly in higher education for women, was a founder of the first higher education college for women in the UK, Bedford College in London (founded 1849), where she persuaded William's father, a mathematics professor, to give some of the first lectures. A photograph of the common room (*c*.1874–1913, Royal Holloway Archives) shows a print of George Watts's *Hope* hanging among other pictures. The establishment and opening of such institutions to women – in addition to growing mass literacy, a rising reading culture, girls' instruction by governesses and at private (boarding) schools – aided Victorian women's literary education, and fundamentally fed into changing female roles in the nineteenth century.

However, while women's access to formal training and institutional education which offered them new freedoms and opportunities was an achievement, and was undoubtedly helpful to the development of their careers, it was not necessarily essential to women's access to creative practices and professions. Despite the patriarchal institutions and social restrictions that made it difficult for women to embark on creative careers, women appealed to male family members and connections for aid and advice, developing artistic and literary careers for themselves with the help of relations and friends, and even taught themselves. For example, Mary designed and created the Watts Chapel despite receiving no architectural training, trained local villagers to be professional potters, and developed her own unique form of symbolic decoration; and Evelyn was taught by a drawing master at her family home as well as by her uncle, sought guidance from George Watts and later used a new process of painting invented by her husband. Individual talent, ambition and resourcefulness (in the use of family connections) – as well as institutional education – contributed to women's greater participation in artistic and literary practices and professions in the nineteenth century.

Whatever route they took, women's path to professional acceptance was not easy. Problems for aspiring artists included 'limitations in artistic training, conflicts with their domestic duties, restraints on their access to the art market and public galleries, and perhaps most insurmountably, their exclusion from the category of "genius"' (Unwin 2004: 246). Emily Mary Osborn's famous painting *Nameless and Friendless* (1857) portrays the prejudice and rejection faced by many Victorian women artists even as it stands testimony to her own success. Similar struggles were faced by aspiring women writers: some were forced to take unpaid roles; married women had no legal right to their earnings before the Married Women's Property Acts of 1870 and 1882; and women had to challenge and negotiate ideological prescriptions that constructed women as self-sacrificing, domestic goddesses or 'Angels in the House'. Yet it was arguably these 'difficulties [. . . that] made them feminists' (Cockroft 2005: 22). For Victorian women, becoming successful professional writers or artists necessitated departures from feminine norms or female spheres and participation in male traditions. Professional creative practice was arguably one of the key ways in which nineteenth-century women negotiated the apparently fixed boundaries between the polarisations at the centre of Victorian ideology and undermined masculinist binary structures in a subversive shaking-up of Victorian society; its patriarchal order was challenged and disrupted by women writers and artists.

The rise of the woman artist and of the woman writer coincided with and contributed considerably to the rise of feminism as both art and literature became increasingly interlinked with feminist politics over the second half of the nineteenth century. They became powerful mouthpieces for (historically silenced) women and were increasingly used as modes of expression, communication and contestation by early feminists. Vocational training in arts and crafts – as well as expanding education and employment opportunities – not only offered women greater creative freedom and financial security but also 'placed in women's hands weapons of mass propaganda' (Cockroft 2005: 6) to use in the fight for socio-political liberation. Artist-based suffrage organisations the Artists' Suffrage League (ASL) and the Suffrage Atelier were formed in 1907 and 1909 respectively, and the Women Writers' Suffrage League was formed in 1908. Women who had trained as artists and artisans supported and promoted the women's suffrage campaign with the design of political posters and postcards, distinctive jewellery and dress, the staging of banner parades and public events, combining word and image. Early feminist groups – suffragist and suffragette artists (including Ernestine Mills, Mary Lowndes and Sylvia Pankhurst) – created striking symbols, slogans and colourways with an awareness of the importance and power of both literary and visual imagery to promote their campaigns and reach a wide audience.

Technological developments in paper production, printing and photography began to transform the media, while women's suffrage newspapers, journals and feminist periodicals proliferated and provided the women's movement with spaces to organise and publicise their campaigns through a plethora of pictures and stories. These literary and visual texts significantly influenced ideas of gender during the later nineteenth century. In the mid-Victorian period and through the turn of the century, concerns began to be publicly expressed in the literary as well as the visual arts about the 'perplexities, dangers, and sufferings' springing from the relations between the sexes (work, marriage, sexuality, prostitution), heightened by 'the various publications and legal and political manoeuvres related to women's rights during these decades' (E. L. Smith 2002: 117–18).

It was no coincidence that the increasing involvement of women in the arts coincided with the growing momentum of the women's suffrage movement, represented by the 1866 Woman's Suffrage Petition that boasted 1,500 signatures (including Sophia De Morgan's) and revealed a network of intelligent women prepared to fight for women's rights. The female artist and the (proto)feminist had 'an overlapping if not shared agenda' (Cockroft 2005: 22) for gender equality. This affiliation was suggested by Edith Mason-Hinchley in an article from the *Vote* magazine of 1911 under the series title 'Why We Want the Vote: the Woman Artist', where she acknowledged the 'swift response of the woman artist to the Women's Movement' (qtd. in Cockroft 2005: 22). It was also suggested by the placement of the National Union of Women's Suffrage Societies (NUWSS) advertisements in the catalogue of the Society of Women Artists. While Pamela Gerrish Nunn argues that 'women who became artists were not necessarily progressive or radical people, never mind feminists' (Nunn 1987: 28), women artists striving to be accepted as successful professionals in the male-dominated Victorian art world necessarily embodied progressive social (if not political) positions. More than the profession of writing which could be carried out within the domestic sphere, artistic professions required a transgression of female spaces and a move into the traditionally male public and commercial domains.

Interdisciplinarity proliferated in the Victorian period, which saw a great fashion for paintings of literary subjects, illustrated books, imagistic prose and narrative pictures; these fundamentally involved a collaboration of word and image, and provided women with discourses and strategies in and with which to address their place in society. While the strong connection and parallels between art and literature, and particularly painting and poetry, long preceded the nineteenth century, the various forms of art and literature that were established, evolved and transformed during the Victorian period seem to invite, and are particularly well suited to, interdisciplinary approaches, methods of interrogation and textual analysis. Many critics acknowledge the Pre-Raphaelite enthusiasm for combining the disciplines of painting and poetry in the visual and verbal pairing of *ut pictura poesis*, and the strong bond between literary and visual texts can also be seen in the work of the Wattses and the De Morgans. This book offers a new understanding of these figures as writers as well as artists for whom literary and visual media were inextricably interlinked.

George Watts's paintings were often inspired by literature and accompanied by narratives, and Mary records him saying 'both the poet & the painter have to make use of figurative language to express ideas' (1887: 21 August); Mary likened her visual symbols to 'parable and metaphor' in that they had a 'fire of thought within them which has power to flash new light' (M. Watts 1905: 2.29) upon things. William De Morgan's second career as a novelist was facilitated by Evelyn, and most of her paintings have some literary reference. Mary Watts's illustrations for Richard von Volkmann's (aka Leander's) *Fantastic Stories* (1874) and her sister's *Sweet Violet, and Other Stories* (Fraser Tytler 1869) can be compared with William De Morgan's illustrations for his sister Mary De Morgan's book *On a Pincushion and other Fairy Tales* (1877), as well as Dante Gabriel Rossetti's more famous illustrations for his sister Christina Rossetti's poetry. The interdisciplinary nature of the Wattses' and the De Morgans' creative practices, outputs, discourses and partnerships – as well as of the movements in which they were interested and involved (the Arts and Crafts movement; the Pre-Raphaelite movement; the women's suffrage movement) – demands interdisciplinary interrogation, using a combination of literary and art historical analytic perspectives, criticism, techniques and concepts.

An analysis of a wide variety of un(der)explored, unpublished and in some cases hitherto untranscribed archival materials by the Wattses and the De Morgans is central to this book, which aims to bring new culturally important texts to light. It explores diaries, letters, newspaper articles and poems alongside paintings, designs, illustrations and photographs. These testify to the 'extraordinary richness and variety of women's contributions to nineteenth-century literary culture, their forays into an expanding range of discourses' (Shattock 2001: 3). A literary analysis of the figures' writings is presented alongside an art historical analysis of their visual texts, in which the couples' socio-political ideas – and the long nineteenth century's ideological and cultural upheavals – are registered. Artworks are approached from literary, and literature is approached from art historical, perspectives in this book: it explores the narrative aspects of, and the presence of or allusion to literary texts in, paintings; it also explores the visual imagery and artistic allusions or parallels in literature. This allows literary and visual texts to be read in relation to each other, illuminating otherwise unseen connections and (direct or indirect) correspondence between – as well as (latent and manifest) meanings in – them.

This interdisciplinary historicist-feminist study develops understandings of relationships between apparently disparate texts and figures who are generally perceived as occupying different discursive spheres, and by establishing the relevance of these figures in relation to historical and socio-political contexts, evinces the ways in which they dialogised with early feminist discourse individually and collectively. It shows how, in the late nineteenth and early twentieth centuries, art and literature served as powerful political media and important vehicles for feminist thought. The term 'feminist' itself was coined in the nineteenth century.[11] Although the early feminist movement was fragmented, and Mary and Evelyn never explicitly self-identified as such, my analysis of the ways in which they supported the women's suffrage movement and women's rights more generally shows how they can be reclaimed as influential (if forgotten) early feminists.

While an exploration of historical context is crucial to an understanding of how nineteenth-century figures and works engaged with early feminism, this book's use of late twentieth-century feminist and gender theory as a tool of textual analysis facilitates a radical and original re-view and re-reading of them, revealing their relevance to more recent perspectives. It employs aspects and concepts of feminist and gender theory – including Hélène Cixous's concept of *écriture féminine*, Judith Butler's theory of gender construction and performativity, and Judith Halberstam's theory of female masculinity – in order to illuminate (and expand an understanding of) the progressiveness, subversiveness and socio-political significance of these figures' lives and works.[12] An application of this theory to the wealth of understudied, unpublished and untranscribed texts by these figures produces entirely new perspectives on them. I will also respond to and engage with recent feminist or women-centred criticism, including Hermione Lee's and Linda Peterson's work on women's life writing; Deborah Cherry's and Jan Marsh's work on women's art and visual culture; and Lisa Tickner's and V. Irene Cockroft's work on the suffrage movement.

This book shows how the female figures in particular produced texts that subverted patriarchal Victorian ideologies and 'phallocentrism': the 'structuring of man as the central reference point of thought', of men's word as law, and of men as the 'origin of meaning' (Jones 1985: 80–1) always occupying the privileged position (while women and their works have been historically marginalised). Mary's and Evelyn's literary and artistic practices, texts and discourses can be seen as sites of political debate and resistance to phallocentrism, disrupting masculinist structures, challenging male supremacy and re-presenting women from specifically female and feminist perspectives. These women themselves represented a radical challenge to phallocentrism as active creators of meaning and cultural producers who achieved greater equality, empowerment and freedom through their professional creative practices and partnerships, asserting themselves in the male traditions of art and literature in defiance of any essential relation or synonymy between 'penis / phallus / pen' / paintbrush (Tong 1992: 225).

Cixous argues that the inscription of women's history through writing – and also, this book argues, art – can recast the prevailing order and power relations of the traditional gender binary, 'produce . . . radical effects of political and social change', and 'serve as a springboard for subversive thought, the precursory movement of a transformation of social and cultural structures' (1976: 882, 879). While women have historically been absent (because excluded) as subjects from the powerful public discourses of literature and art, this book explores how they became the very sites of resistance and liberation for women in the Victorian period. Literature and art offered women imaginative and intellectual spaces in which to formulate and promote their progressive ideas, and were crucial sites for the negotiation and contestation of patriarchal structures and ideologies. Women – historically 'caught in a world structured by male-centred concepts' with 'no way of knowing or representing themselves' – found forms of self-representation, self-expression and self-consciousness in art and literature through which they could reclaim and re-present female bodies and experiences which have been 'misrepresented in male discourse' (Jones 1993: 455). Cixous presents her concept of *écriture féminine* – a specifically 'feminine' antiphallocentric discourse – in 'The Laugh of the Medusa':

> Woman must write her self: must write about women and bring women to writing, from which they have been driven away as violently as from their bodies . . . Woman must put herself into the text – as into the world and into history – by her own movement. (1976: 875)

Mary and Evelyn inscribe the female body in their literary and visual texts despite Victorian women having been 'turned away from [their] bodies, shamefully taught to ignore them, to strike them with . . . sexual modesty' (Cixous 1976: 885). They challenge and surpass phallogocentrism by exploring and re-presenting the female body, telling the stories of silenced women, and prioritising specifically female experiences (such as motherhood and domestic captivity) in multiple media. This book traces the emergence and development of specifically female, antiphallocentric discourses in Victorian women's art and literature that embody or prefigure the revolutionary women's language of Cixous. To Julia Kristeva, 'woman' represents 'not so much a sex as an attitude, any resistance to conventional culture and language' (Jones 1993: 455), and thus men can also oppose phallogocentrism. Cixous similarly admires male writers who have produced antiphallocentric texts, acknowledging that 'there are some men (all too few) who aren't afraid of femininity' (Cixous 1976: 885). The idea that the enemy is not man but phallocentricity or patriarchy was apparently acknowledged by Mary and Evelyn, who constructed partnerships with men while challenging masculinist ideologies; their husbands similarly represented progressive socio-political positions and produced what can be read as feminist or antiphallocentric texts.

Each of this book's seven chapters offers a detailed discussion of the gender dynamics of the couples, whether in the context of their visual artworks, their socio-political interests, their reading practices or their writings. Collectively the chapters reassess connections between the works of both couples, along with their unconventional creative practices, in relation to the development of an early feminist discourse and iconography. The chronological limits of this book are largely determined by the Wattses' and the De Morgans' marriages which began these partnerships (1886 and 1887 respectively) and the deaths of the male figures which ended these partnerships (George's in 1904 and William's in 1917), although it also looks at the couples' courtships as well as the female figures' continued work and promotion of their shared causes after their husbands' deaths.

Chapters 1 and 2, focusing on the Wattses and the De Morgans respectively, explore the feminist dynamics of the couples' conjugal creative partnerships, their professional creative practices, and ways in which they supported the women's suffrage movement and women's liberation more generally. Chapter 3 continues this exploration by presenting alternative visions of these neglected Victorian figures through an analysis of their self/portraits (that is, self-portraits and portraits of each other as well as their famous female contemporaries); it focuses on their self-fashioning or conscious creation of artistic and feminist identities through the genre of portraiture. Chapters 4 and 5 are linked in their focus on artists' writings: Chapter 4 considers the diaries of Mary Watts and Evelyn De Morgan in conjunction and in relation to their emerging political positions, while Chapter 5 develops a discussion of the Wattses' and the De Morgans' (published and unpublished) writings in which they explore women-centred issues and inscribe the female body.

Chapters 6 and 7 are linked in their exploration of artists' readings, literary sources and subjects, and in their focus on paintings of women and water: from the drowned 'fallen woman' in George's work to the metamorphosing mermaids in Evelyn's work. Chapter 6 explores the Wattses' private library, their conjugal reading practice, and Mary's engagement with contemporary feminist writers and writings, before discussing George's series of female-focused social-realist paintings inspired by poetry, in order to show how the couple engaged with, were inspired by, and contributed to early feminist literary and visual culture. Chapter 7 explores Evelyn's series of symbolist paintings based on Hans Christian Andersen's popular fairy tale *The Little Mermaid* in relation to early and more recent feminism, and shows how she employed the mermaid as a model for socio-political transformation from captivity to liberty. Her paintings are compared with contemporary literary and visual texts in order to show how her work, often positioned in relation to male Pre-Raphaelite artists, dialogised with early feminist iconography. These two chapters reveal

George's and Evelyn's statuses as suffragist poet–painters and/or narrative painters who re-presented women to promote socio-political reform. Finally, the book's conclusion summarises its approach and key findings, and offers ideas for further study.

Notes

1. Contrary to conventional practice, for the sake of clarity and to avoid confusion between figures with the same surnames, these figures (that is, Mary Watts and George Watts, and Evelyn De Morgan and William De Morgan) will be referred to by their first names, except where it is necessary to distinguish them also by surname.

2. See Evelyn De Morgan's Angel Panels, All Saints Church, Cawthorne (1878), Mary's altarpiece for the chapel at Aldershot Cambridge Military Hospital (1916) and Watts Chapel.

3. See letter to *The Times* composed by Mary, 'Another Jubilee Suggestion' (5 September 1887). Although George personally selected the subjects from newspaper reports, the idea for the 'national memorial to all acts of heroism' was in fact conceived by Mary's sister Christina (see M. Watts 1887: 25, 29 August).

4. Stirling thanks 'Mrs. G. F. Watts' in the 'Author's Note' for contributing correspondence and information for her book; see letter from Mary Watts to Mrs Stirling (23 August 1912), DMF Archive Box 4, MS_0121.

5. Mrs G. F. Watts, 'A Village Pottery – A Developed Industry', *Village Life after the War, being Special Reports of Conferences on the Development of Rural Life convened by the Rural Organisation Council in 1917,* p. 100, WG; see Boreham 2013: 81 (date of kiln-building estimated by Boreham).

6. See Wilfred Mark Webb, 'The Potters' Art Guild at Compton', *Country Homes*, November 1911: 102, WG.

7. Other marital partners include Robert and Elizabeth Barrett Browning; William and Jane Morris; and George Eliot and George Henry Lewes (although they were not legally married). Sibling partners include Christina and Dante Gabriel Rossetti; Charlotte and Patrick Branwell Brontë; and William and Dorothy Wordsworth.

8. Mary 'intended to be the old Maid Aunt' and refused to accept 'a sort of medium happiness in married life' (Chapman 1945: 114, 120).

9. See also Lucy Newlyn's *William and Dorothy Wordsworth: 'All in each other'* (Oxford: Oxford University Press, 2013); David Elliott's *A Pre-Raphaelite Marriage: The Lives and Works of Marie Spartali Stillman and William James Stillman* (ACC Art Books, 2005); Mary Sanders Pollock's *Elizabeth Barrett and Robert Browning: A Creative Partnership* (Ashgate, 2003); and Phyllis Rose's *Parallel Lives: Five Victorian*

Marriages (Knopf, 1983). For more on Victorian artistic and literary networks, and on the professionalization of women, see Alison Chapman's *Networking the Nation* (Oxford: Oxford University Press, 2015); Jane Munro and Linda Goddard (eds), *Literary Circles: Artist, Author, Word and Image in Britain, 1800–1920* (Cambridge: The Fitzwilliam Museum, 2006); and Kyriaki Hadjiafxendi and Patricia Zakreski (eds), *Crafting the Woman Professional in the Long Nineteenth Century: Artistry and Industry in Britain* (Aldershot: Ashgate, 2013).

10. See Thirlwell 2003: 262–3. The commemoration of Wollstonecraft by a 1908 suffrage banner highlights her role as mother of the movement.

11. The *Oxford English Dictionary* (2nd edn, 1989) lists 1894 as the year of the first appearance of the term 'feminist' (used in the *Daily News*, meaning 'an advocate of feminism') and 1895 for 'feminism' (used in the *Athenaeum*, meaning 'advocacy of the rights of women'), available at <http://www.oed.com/oed2/00083535/36> (last accessed 10 August 2014). The term 'suffragette' was coined by the *Daily Mail* in 1906.

12. Mary's stand against restrictive female dress and her discussion of how women are rarely themselves in her diaries, and Evelyn's paintings of discontented women dressed in finery but striving for liberty, reveal their awareness on some level of the performativity and social construction of femininity. This is not solely a twentieth-century idea; it is also present, in some form, in the works of (for example) Mary Wollstonecraft and John Stuart Mill.

Part I
Practice, Partnership, Politics

The three chapters in this Part explore the Wattses' and the De Morgans' progressive socio-political positions as suffragist artists who actively supported and promoted the women's suffrage movement that gained momentum over the late nineteenth and early twentieth centuries. It shows how they achieved this through their anti-patriarchal conjugal creative partnerships; their professional creative practices; their involvement in suffrage societies and women's culture; and their works privileging female struggle, power and freedom. Most notably, Mary Watts convened suffrage meetings at the Wattses' Surrey studio-home; George Watts was close friends with – and his art was a source of inspiration for – early feminists; Evelyn De Morgan signed women's suffrage petitions; and William De Morgan wrote impassioned letters in support of women's suffrage. These chapters show how, for both Mary and Evelyn, professional creative practices and partnerships were liberatory strategies through which they achieved and promoted greater female emancipation and empowerment. The Wattses and the De Morgans had a shared agenda for greater gender equality and women's liberation, which they advocated in their visual and literary work. They can thus be reclaimed as early feminists with coinciding socio-political and aesthetic aims.

Chapter 1

Mary and George Watts

Practice and Partnership

Much has been written about the famous Victorian artist George Watts, and yet the life and work of Mary Watts, and the couple's progressive socio-political positions as conjugal creative partners and women's rights supporters, are comparatively neglected. Long-eclipsed by the dominant critical focus on her husband, and known primarily as the worshipping wife of a world-famous artist, Mary was a pioneering professional woman designer and ceramicist as well as a painter, illustrator and writer. Despite her prominence in her own lifetime, she is little-known today. The lack of critical and biographical material on her is disproportionate to the originality, high quality and multi-faceted nature of her *oeuvre*, encompassing fine art, gesso relief, sculpture, ceramic and textile design, and architecture.

Art historian Mark Bills's chapter on the Wattses in *An Artists' Village: G. F. Watts and Mary Watts at Compton* (Bills 2011: 9–23) incorporates the brief sections 'Married Life' and 'A Partnership', and yet they perpetuate rather than challenge traditional views of the couple. The former section presents Mary 'in awe of [George], overwhelmed by his reputation . . . as devoted and admiring as ever . . . in her subservient role' (2011: 14–15). Bills alludes to, without contesting, the popular public perception of Mary as George's 'nurse' and 'slave' who 'worshipped him blindly' (2011: 15–16). This partial and reductive view of Mary is reinforced by the latter section, beginning, 'The position of Mary as acolyte and servant to the genius of [George] was constant' (2011: 16). Although her involvement in the HAIA and her achievement as an artist in her construction of the Watts Chapel is acknowledged, Mary is severely undervalued here as in most existing scholarship. Building on the work of Veronica

Franklin Gould (1998), Melanie Unwin (2004) and Elaine Cheasley Paterson (2005), this chapter and book as a whole aims to rectify omissions and misconceptions of the Wattses: it develops a discussion of Mary's feminist activism and of the Wattses' partnership in unprecedented depth, showing how this subverted the relations they have long been seen to represent.

Mary's creative practices and progressive views were cultivated by her liberal upbringing in the Scottish Highlands and art education in London. Her father, himself a writer, encouraged her and her sisters to pursue their creative interests (Gould 1998: 20), and (unlike Evelyn De Morgan) she experienced no maternal resistance to her artistic career, since her mother died not long after her birth.[1] Both Mary and Evelyn were 'born just at the right time . . . the turn of the middle of the nineteenth century' (Jefferies 2006: 28) when debates about the status of women were already underway, and women were first offered the opportunity to undertake formal, vocational training in the arts and crafts. Mary and Evelyn were among the first wave of women to receive this training, upon which they embarked with gusto, carving out creative careers for themselves. Like many suffrage artists, they studied at the co-educational Slade School of Fine Art in London (established 1871), enrolling soon after it opened as two of its first female students.

Mary first met the world-famous painter George Watts as an awestruck pupil at (old) Little Holland House in Kensington in 1870, and 'embraced this opportunity to further her career – arguably the most significant step of her life' (Gould 1998: 22). Mary and George visited each other's studios before their engagement, when they would 'bemoan the stifling effect of the Machine Age on individual creative design and yearn for the revival of craftsmanship' (Gould 1998: 24). They believed in the transformative power of art – both personal and socio-political – and in 'art for all'. Mary greatly influenced George's support of the wider aesthetic aims of the Arts and Crafts movement that she personally promoted. While Mary 'looked towards [George] for her development as an artist' (Bills 2011: 13) when she was specialising in portraiture during the 1870s and early 1880s, and his influence on her early painting is evident, she had studied art formally, been a committee member of the HAIA and given clay modelling classes before her marriage. Although her reputation as an artist was advanced and sustained by her marital partnership, and George financially supported some of her artistic enterprises, her skills were not dependent upon – and her training and practice long preceded – this union.

Contrary to popular belief, Mary was not the docile and submissive 'wife in an unequal marriage . . . trapped in the dependent position in the hierarchies of personalized [patriarchal] power relations' (Aaron 1991: 27). The Wattses' affectionate correspondence in the lead up to their engagement and marriage in 1886 reveals their early relationship to be based on equality. Mary wrote to George, 'I grow when I am with you', and George wrote to Mary, 'I have come to feel for you the most profound and tender respect' (qtd. in Chapman 1945: 114, 116). George assured Mary that he would not limit her freedom in marriage, writing, 'the door of your cage shall be wide open and there shall be no wires' (qtd. in Chapman 1945: 120). He guaranteed her treatment as an autonomous equal and offered her an alternative to the conjugal bondage experienced by many Victorian women, which undoubtedly influenced her decision to marry him; her aversion to the 'moral wrong' of forced and loveless marriage is evident in her diaries (1891: 22 November). Mary consciously chose as her husband an artist she greatly admired who supported both her creative practice and her socio-political beliefs. As artists, symbolists, philanthropists and suffragists who supported greater female liberation and participation in the arts, the Wattses were partners who shared the same ideals in art and life, and 'suit[ed] each other . . . absolutely' (G. Watts qtd. in M. Watts 1887: 9 September).

In order to trace the development of Mary's creative partnership with George, an exploration of the place in which it was primarily initiated and facilitated – the marital home and artistic space of their Surrey studio-home – is essential. As Bills points out, if life had continued solely at George's London residence, Mary's art may never have developed to the extent that it did (2011: 16). George's studio-home that he had commissioned at the centre of an artistic community in Kensington had a stifling effect on her own work when they first married. She effectively stopped canvas painting thereafter, apparently to avoid being adversely compared with him and to dedicate herself to supporting him once she had been (as her brother wrote in a letter of 1886) 'give[n] . . . to the nation' (qtd. in Chapman 1945: 127) as his wife. Feeling artistically frustrated, Mary wrote in her diary while living in what was 'already a monument' (Bills 2011: 15) to George, 'instead of my <u>work</u>, I focus [on] <u>him</u>. . . . It will take me a little while yet to get over being under the shadow of his great work' (1887: 7 September).

Although Mary initially struggled to establish a distinct identity in her partnership with George, she found a form of liberation in the move from busy London to rural Surrey and fine art to decorative art, which was pivotal to her professional development. The Wattses' studio-home at Compton in the Surrey Hills, a winter residence that became the 'true centre of [Mary's] life' (Tromans 2016: 6) until her death, was built under her supervision in 1890–1. Mary transformed the interior itself into a work of art with her highly imaginative and ambitious schemes of symbolic decoration – including her intricately crafted plaster ceiling panels of stylised gesso symbols inspired by ancient cultures, her decorated reading alcove or 'niche', her Celtic fireplace surround designs and bed ends – thereby marking her territory and bringing a whole new meaning to Victorian homemaking. The Wattses worked together, sometimes in the same studio or alongside each other in adjacent studios, in this house and its grounds. They named it 'Limnerslease' – 'limner' being Latin for 'artist' and 'leasen' being the Old English word meaning 'to glean' – in the hope that golden years of creativity would be gleaned from this studio-home.

Together they established a work ethic within their shared domestic space, and Mary's diary writing reveals the happiness they found in a household routine that revolved around artistic productivity. Entries such as, 'I began my work when [George] did this morning . . . We had both a hard day of work' (1893: 13–15 May), pervade her diaries, and Mary records George exclaiming, 'How delightful it is to work together in this way!' (1891: 21 September). Contradicting critics' suggestions that 'the constant presence of [Mary's] husband in the home was somewhat restrictive' (Unwin 2004: 245), Mary writes, 'I am now doing what I purposed to do, at the beginning of my life with Signor & it makes it the most delightful work I have ever done' (1891: 12 March). Mary notes in her diary not long after their marriage, 'A lovely day, life seems like a dream . . . My loved one working . . . & I with my easel below him in the garden designing' (1887: 30 July). While Unwin claims that Mary was 'the wife of an artist forced to negotiate a "career" around her husband' (2004: 239), Mary's diaries suggest their facilitating roles in each other's creative practices, and show how she developed an artistic career within her marriage and in partnership with her husband.

Limnerslease represented a new lease of life for both artists – for George to refresh his artistic practice and for Mary to initiate a new course in her career – and their 'golden years' (M. Watts 1904: 31 December) of marriage here were the 'most productive and happy for both of them' (Jefferies 2006: 35). For Mary, 'a new home brought a new form of art' (Bills 2011: 16) in the form of terracotta modelling, and she dug the seams of clay in its grounds. Symbolic terracotta decoration and bas-relief design subsequently became her forte, and in it she found her niche as a remarkable artist in her own right. Her newfound creative practice necessitated a departure from feminine norms in the sense that, although 'well-bred women could study art, dabble in watercolours, and even exhibit, it was socially unacceptable to turn professional or to dirty their hands with clay modelling' (Gould 1998: 22). Building bricks, firing tiles and digging clay in the rural backwoods of the couple's Surrey home to make ceilings and fireplaces for Limnerslease, panels for the chapel and pots for Liberty's were not 'ladylike' activities. While seemingly reverting to a more 'feminine' position on marrying George by relinquishing fine art for decorative art practice, this was a strategic move that enabled her to explore new avenues available to her and to blur or break down traditional binary boundaries between art and craft, since she often combined the two in her works (such as her painted gesso decorations). Mary held terracotta modelling classes for villagers (as part of the HAIA scheme) to help her build the chapel, and established her commercial Compton Pottery at Limnerslease (for which she designed well into her eighties). Thus the site of the studio-home itself permitted a deconstruction of traditional binary boundaries between art/craft, artistic/domestic, public/private, work/leisure and commercial/philanthropic.

Unwin argues that Mary, ever-mindful of propriety and what was socially acceptable in a Victorian artist's wife, facilitated a position of social 'safety' away from fine art because it would infringe on and invite comparison with her husband's artistic practice, and because 'the world of applied and decorative arts was, in comparison, far less restrictive' (Unwin 2004: 239, 246). While both undoubtedly motivated Mary's move from fine art into decorative art, this move itself – as well as the innovative and 'far less restrictive' nature of her decoration – involved a risk, experimentation and transgression that undermines the notion of her retreat to a position of 'safety'. Although Bills suggests Mary abandoned easel painting because she felt her work was a 'pale shadow' (Bills 2011: 16) of what her celebrated husband was producing, she did not give up canvas painting in a defeatist manner (as many Victorian women did on marriage) but with an eagerness to embark on new creative projects. She made a conscious effort to explore and excel in a different domain to her husband not in respectful reverence to him but rather to avoid following in his footsteps, to find a form better suited to the expression of her own ideas and voice, and to develop her own personal style. By working in different fields, they avoided clashes. Unwin's claim that in moving away from fine art, Mary moved 'away from an identification as "artist"' (2004: 239) is disproved by Mary's diary entries which reveal her self-perception and identification as a serious professional decorative artist 'working like a tiger' (1891: 10 February).

In the latest book on Mary Watts, Tromans notes that she was 'a collaborator of genius' who worked with 'friends and neighbours' and 'left few if any masterpieces made entirely by her own hands' (2016: 6–7), alluding to the Watts Chapel and the Compton Potters' Arts Guild. Though it is less widely acknowledged, the Wattses collaborated on several artworks. Just a few months after her husband's death in 1904, Mary painstakingly designed and modelled the 'Flower in the crannied wall' for the hand of the Alfred Lord Tennyson memorial statue created by George, which was hailed a national art treasure and now stands outside Lincoln Cathedral. This 'Little flower' (Tennyson 1987: 693, ll.1, 4), a seemingly minor detail subsequently added to the colossal statue which cannot be fully viewed from the ground, is in fact the focal point of the sculpture of the poet laureate of their time who recognises that an understanding of the simple yet complex flower is crucial to a comprehension of the universe.[2] Together, the Wattses recreated Tennyson's poem in a physical, tangible form that immortalised their close friend in art.[3]

Mary is also said to have painted the prominent basket of roses in George's painting of their adopted daughter or ward, *Lilian* (1904). Lily herself apparently recalled Mary's artistic intervention after George had painted her holding a laurel wreath, which Mary thought 'far too funereal'; she subsequently 'scrubbed out' the wreath and painted in the roses she now holds, and she 'pastiched his style so beautifully that one must acknowledge . . . her talent as well' (Jefferies qtd. in Gould 1993: 13–14). While flower painting in dainty watercolours was perceived in the Victorian period as a typically feminine accomplishment and traditionally female genre, Mary's creation of a wrought iron flower for a large-scale public memorial statue of a famous male literary figure – as well as her painting of the flowers in the centre-foreground of an oil painting by a famous male artist – reflects an artistic ambition and ability that conflicted with Victorian norms of femininity. George not only supported her 'masculine' artistic practice and ambition, but also discouraged her from wasting time on frivolous, typically feminine activities: Mary records in her diary how, on a sunny day, she went into the garden and was

> tempted . . . to spend the morning picking & arranging flowers . . . but [George] thought it wrong I had not managed an hours [sic] drawing – He said gently, though he liked my appreciating the sun & flowers, 'I never think it right to break a principle'. (1887: 3 December)

There are many parallels and points of dialogue between the works of the Wattses who shared an allegorical iconographic vocabulary despite (predominantly) working in different media. The focus on, and inextricable link between, women and death (specifically, maternal angels and female personifications of death) pervades the *oeuvres* of Mary and George, who both lost their mothers at a young age. Mary's *Aldourie Triptych* (1886–1903) (Fig. 1.1) recreates in relief three of George's compositions – *The Messenger* (1884–5), *Love and Death* (1885–7) and *Death Crowning Innocence* (1886–7) – which she modelled in clay and had cast in bronze for the entrance to her family cemetery in Scotland. Mary's panels parallel George's paintings, and the couple may have modelled figures for this triptych together (Gould 2004a: 258). Mary's design of the Marchioness of Waterford's memorial cross at Ford in 1891 was a joint project with George who sent a design for the kneeling angels (M. Watts 1891: 22 October).

The large central triptych panel showing the Angel of Death crowning Innocence was originally designed by George as a memorial to Mary's infant nephew who died in a riding accident, sketched in chalk after receiving her heartbroken letters, and George intended his design to be 'lovingly worked into a monument' ([1886] qtd. in Chapman 1945: 122) by Mary, which she did after their marriage.

Figure 1.1 *Aldourie Triptych*, Mary Watts, 1886–1903 (photograph by John Hammond) © Aldourie Castle Collection.

George later painted *Death Crowning Innocence* and Mary produced a small terracotta copy of it.[4] She also recreated George's Angel of Death in *The Messenger* and the *Recording Angel* in sculpture for his memorial in the cloisters near Watts Chapel. This suggests the personal significance of these images to the Wattses, which were nonetheless designed to have universal appeal, and they can be seen to reflect the social and symbolic importance of women and particularly the mother. The unconventional representation of the mother as 'death-bringer' complicates the traditional, one-dimensional, essentialist perceptions of the mother as merely 'life-giver', merges the 'natural' connotations of the maternal body with the supernatural, and disrupts the ideologically dominant Victorian image or ideal of the mother as an 'Angel in the House' by re-presenting her as an 'Angel of Death'. The couple's powerful life-giving and death-bringing mother figures stand out from the ubiquitous representations of dead or dying female figures and passive corpses in Victorian visual culture, and are imbued with feminist significance in their radical subversion of patriarchal notions of femininity conflated with passivity.

The *Aldourie Triptych* is Mary's deliberate selection and recreation of the most powerful female figures in George's *oeuvre*. While it can be seen as a kind of collaboration, Mary's re-presentation and adaptation of George's paintings – through which she reclaims and reappropriates the female body – can be seen as a subversive complication of male authorship or artistry which undermines male supremacy. The *Aldourie Triptych* can thus be re-viewed as an antiphallocentric work by a female artist. Mary does not merely copy her husband's works but rather translates his images into a new context and different medium, placing them together; this redoubles their disturbing impact and draws attention to their feminist significance. The subversive blurring of boundaries embodied by George's figures of Death is enhanced by Mary's panels: she not only emphasises the dark aspect of the powerful female figures by casting them in a deep bronze, but also literally adds new dimensions to George's paintings by recreating them as relief sculptures. In contrast to George's flat canvases presenting shadowy angelic figures, Mary's raised panels render the female bodies more tangible, making them seem more physically present and highlighting their liminal positions. In the peaks and troughs of the bronze that was originally modelled clay, Mary creates the curves of the female body that are not captured so effectively by George's paintings; she brings to life the female figures on the flat surfaces of her husband's canvases, thematically building on while formally diverging from his work.

The symbiotic relationship between the Wattses' works is further exemplified by Mary's symbolic recreation of George's three paintings *Love and Life* (*c*.1884–5), *Love and Death* (1885–7) and *Love Triumphant* (1893–8) in terracotta panels on a studio fireplace at Limnerslease. These works not only stand testimony to Mary's 'eclectic expression of Wattsian themes' (Gould 1998: 43) but also show her ability to translate paintings into patterns, or transform art into craft, in stylised Art Nouveau and Celtic-style reinterpretations and adaptations of George's works. Her works often re-present his female figures and place them in different contexts, shifting or subverting their original connotations and creating new, feminist significations. On one fireplace panel, Mary transforms George's famous painting *Love and Life* – in which the strong, winged male figure of Love guides the fragile female nude figure of Life up a rocky path – into a winged mother pelican with a scrolled neck pecking its own flesh to feed its chicks, bordered by interlacing umbilical-like Celtic cord. In a more obvious feminist reappropriation of George's *Love and Life*, a 1928 *Punch* cartoon shows the winged figure of playwright George Bernard Shaw – who admired the Wattses' work – leading a young woman dressed in suffragette colours up a mountain labelled 'Equal Incomes'.[5]

Mary's recurring pelican motif represents the mother and specifically her 'succouring, self-sacrificing love'. She explains its significance in her book *The Word in the Pattern*, which she wrote as a guide to her symbolic decoration: 'The bird of Love is the pelican of the legend, who draws blood from her own breast to feed her brood' (1905: 21), and this act of vulning signifies its 'savage maternal instincts'.[6] Mary's pelican embodying both Love and Life (two separate figures in George's painting) can be seen as a symbol of female strength, savagery and self-sufficiency or independence (since there is no male figure in her version), which subverts the patriarchal perception of woman as passive, weak and dependent on man. Mary thus re-creates without copying George's design, transforming a conventional or classic male representation of femininity into a symbol of female power.

While the pelican was adopted by the early Christians as a 'beautiful and expressive figure of Christ' who 'set forth our redemption through His blood, which was willingly shed for us, His children' (W. and G. Audsley [1865] qtd. in Bills 2010: 51), it is clear from Mary's use of the gender-specific pronoun 'her' that she intended the pelican to represent the mother rather than to figure Christ in relation to the Father of Classical Theism. Mary thus reappropriates this patriarchal symbol of the Middle Ages and imbues it with feminist significance, seeking a new feminine artistic language and value system centred on uniquely female characteristics and experiences such as maternity or motherhood. Mary's pelican designs can be seen to dialogise with those of more famous suffrage artists who recognised the bird's feminist significance: the symbol of a pelican piercing its breast to feed its young was depicted by Ernestine Mills on a dish (Cockroft 2005: 17) and by Sylvia Pankhurst on a Women's Social and Political Union (WSPU) banner she designed for the 1908 Women's Day procession (Tickner 1989: 261).[7]

In another example of how Mary reconceived her husband's work, George's most famous painting *Hope* (1886) (Fig. 1.2) shows a solitary blindfolded female figure seated on a globe plucking the last remaining string of her lyre, whereas the stately peacock is the symbolic bird of Hope on Mary's terracotta 'Spirit of Hope' frieze on the Watts Chapel exterior (Fig. 1.3). The downward-facing angels above circular globe-like symbols surrounding Mary's peacock designs are reminiscent of George's *Hope* as well as the androgynous, angelic faces pervading Dante Gabriel Rossetti's and Edward Burne-Jones's art of the 1860s

Figure 1.2 *Hope*, George Watts, 1885–6, Private Collection.

Figure 1.3 *Peacock on 'Spirit of Hope' frieze, Watts Chapel exterior*, Mary Watts, begun 1896, Watts Gallery Trust.

and 70s, suggesting the Wattsian and Pre-Raphaelite influence on Mary's work.[8] Yet Mary also developed her own idiosyncratic iconography in her symbolic decoration of the chapel, producing unconventional images of familiar concepts: the peacock is a symbol of hope for renewed life whose 'wonderful . . . eyes surrounded by rays shining with the colour of light, were cast every year and renewed again, and yet again' (M. Watts 1905: 18). George's 'bowed and stricken' figure of Hope 'cowering in the twilight over a broken lyre with only one remaining twisted string' ready to snap is desperate and fragile, and his 'dim canvas' (Ahlquist 2008: 10) creates a sense of impending doom. Contrastingly, Mary's highly stylised, dignified, majestic peacock stands proudly with its abundant feathers on display, representing infinite renewal in a celebration of eternal life.

Mary's design seems a more optimistic emblem of hope to mourners entering the Watts Cemetery Chapel than George's painting is to viewers. His world-renowned image gave hope to at least one destitute, suicidal woman – supposedly a prostitute – who later told him in a letter that seeing the picture in a shop window had saved her life (Revd James Burns [1908] qtd. in Tromans 2011: 60–1). Yet the bleakness and desolation of George's work led critic G. K. Chesterton to comment that it might just as easily have been entitled *Despair* (Ahlquist 2008: 10). The flamboyance and exuberance of Mary's designs in rich terracotta red contrasts with the comparative simplicity and quietude of George's painting in muted tones. On the chapel as in Limnerslease, Mary replaces George's images of female fragility with symbolic birds of Love and Hope imbued with strength and power. These birds seem to draw on the popular avian association of women in Victorian art while subverting the more typical parallel between women and cage birds. Indeed, the peacock and its feather feature in several works by Mary and the De Morgans as well as other prominent suffrage artists like Ernestine Mills.[9] The peacock was not merely an emblem of Aestheticism or symbol of beauty, but also a favourite Arts and Crafts symbol which became a significant feature of women's art. The blue peacock became a favourite subject for silver pendants, enamelled inserts on boxes, mirrors and bookends designed and crafted by New Dawn Women (produced by the Rowley Gallery) not only because it was a bird, traditionally symbolic of freedom, but also because blue and silver were the campaign colours adopted by the ASL. Mary's and Evelyn's prominent use of the peacock or its feather suggests their deliberate allusion to and employment of early feminist iconography.

While George 'painted poetic ideas on canvas', Mary became an 'extraordinary modeller of ideas', and while his paintings 'were undecorated in order to appeal to all nations, she extended the principle with decorative imagery relating to worldwide civilisations' (Gould 1998: 17, 65). Like George, Mary intended her art to have universal appeal, but whereas he painted a clear message undiluted by decoration, she modelled intricate pantheistic imagery combining primitive Celtic and modern Art Nouveau forms with ancient religious iconography in which a simple symbol conveyed multiple meanings. Pattern for Mary, like paint for George, was a powerful discourse through which to communicate complex ideas about spirituality and universality as well as gender. Mary was no slavish copyist to her husband and never simply imitated or replicated his works. Rather, she translated them into what she called her 'language of symbols' (M. Watts 1905: 17) in her designs and decorations through which she not only expressed their shared ideas and ideals, but also developed her own distinctive voice. The Wattses had a mutual respect and admiration for each other's work, each perceiving the other as the finest in their field. For Mary, George was 'the painter of painters' (qtd. in Gould 1998: 21), and George wrote that Mary had a 'genius for symbolic decoration' (qtd. in Gould 2004a: 295) at a time when the term 'genius' was more typically attributed to him, and to men in general, since it was widely believed that women lacked the capacity for genius on the basis of their sex. This highlights the progressiveness of the Wattses' creative partnership and of Mary's position as a master in her craft in the context of the nineteenth century. Women's supposedly inferior capacities, lack of education and economic dependence formed the basis of anti-suffrage arguments, which were refuted by successful professional women artists like Mary and Evelyn.

Progressive Wife; More Radical Widow

The Wattses established solid reputations in intellectual, artistic, literary and suffragist circles. They formed close friendships with women's suffrage supporters and social reformers – including the De Morgans, George Meredith, Walter Crane, Josephine Butler and Gertrude Jekyll – and they fostered a feminist network in their studio-home. As the partner of Britain's premier portrait painter, Mary had access to the leading writers, artists and women's rights supporters of her day, conversing with creative and forward-thinking people who came to have their portrait painted by George; she took advantage of the opportunity to engage in serious discussions with them about art and society, and became widely respected in her own right. George was pleased that he could give Mary 'something really good', telling her, 'many delightful & great people have been very kind to me & I have made them my friends & now can make them yours' (qtd. in M. Watts 1887: 6 October). Mary's formation and continuation of friendships with women's rights activists and social reformers, as well as her professional training, creative practices and entrance into partnership with George, can be seen as suffragist strategies through which she achieved and supported greater female liberation.

Testifying to the prevailing prejudice against women taking an active role outside the home, and the pressure on famous or public figures to oppose women's suffrage, in 1889 artist and President of the Royal Academy Sir Frederic Leighton wrote to request Mary's signatory support for his sister's appeal against the extension of suffrage to women in *The Nineteenth Century* magazine. He invited her to join 'many well-known women', including his sister, in the anti-suffrage movement which '*opposes* itself to the attempt to obtain the *suffrage* for women – thereby drawing [women] out of the natural sphere in which they exercise such enormous and beneficial influence' ([1889, original emphasis] qtd. in Gould 1998: 33). Yet Mary declined. Influential art critic John Ruskin had previously claimed that woman's 'power is not for rule . . . and her intellect is not for invention or creation, but for sweet orderings' of domesticity ([1865] qtd. in Gilbert and Gubar 1979: 24). Yet the Wattses' unconventional conjugal creative partnership, representing greater gender equality, was consistent with their liberal and progressive socio-political positions. Mary writes in her biography of her husband,

> In talking the matter [of women's suffrage] over with Signor – I think seriously for the first time – I found that we were agreed, and that he believed that feminine influence in politics would have a good effect, especially upon social questions. He recognised the justice of the demand, and regarded it as a natural development consequent on the progress of education. (1912: 2.145–6)

This reveals their like-mindedness and united position as women's suffrage supporters who believed the vote was key to greater social reform. This was in accordance with the (non-militant and non-party) NUWSS (formed 1897), which waged a war not against men but one in which men and women fought together against gender-based injustice and inequality. Mary recalls George saying, 'I rather pride myself on being a real Liberal; that is to say, being liberal enough to see and understand that there are and must be many conditions and many opinions' ([1875] M. Watts 1912: 1.5). The Wattses' recognised the danger of 'automatic thought' – that is, 'so few thinking for themselves – holding tenaciously to [their ancestors'] ideas that they have never thought out' – and George tells Mary, 'I think your liberality of mind is its great characteristic' (qtd. in M. Watts 1891: 20 June).

The Wattses influenced each other's interest in and support of women's suffrage, reminding us that men as well as women actively supported female emancipation and empowerment in the nineteenth century. George's motto 'Forward & Fear Not' (M. Watts 1887: 1 January), for which Mary made a design of ships in full sail, suggests his progressive stance and would have befitted a suffragette slogan and symbol.[10] The importance of George's support for – and influence on – Mary's progressive stance from the beginning of their marriage should not be underestimated. Mary excitedly writes in her diary, 'I see he thinks women given the franchise would entirely alter their habit of thought in two or 3 generations!' (1887: 27 January). Later that year, she writes,

> Woke to speak of Politics. Signor asked me if I had always been so liberal. I said I had been liberal but not so much as I had now become . . . I told him [my sister] Christina used to delight in my <u>advance</u> under him, laugh & say 'Watts is making [Mary] a radical'. (1887: 12 October)

While this remark was seemingly said in jest and George was no radical, it highlights an important development: while Mary was always liberal, she assumed an increasingly progressive socio-political position during her partnership with George. This was facilitated not only by his (mostly tacit) support and her status as his wife, but also the public platform she acquired as an increasingly successful professional artist in her own right. While her liberal position as a 'Victorian Progressive' (Greenhow 2016a) has been fleetingly referred to in previous scholarship, her diaries reveal a more radical private self. This previously unseen vision of Mary is reinforced by a re-view of the work she embarked on – and the causes she became involved in – during and after her marriage.

Mary was an ardent suffragist who believed in evolution rather than revolution; she was liberal and progressive rather than radical and avant-garde, and believed in the 'force of the mind' over the 'force of the fist' (M. Watts 1891: 13 August). She admired the 'great liberality of the non-conformist mind' and people who desired 'to know everything that is good & great & large – dissatisfied with all that is merely conventional orthodox & narrow' (M. Watts 1893: 28 June, 30 May). She was feminist as well as suffragist in the sense that she actively supported the vote as well as the emancipation of women in other fields such as arts and education. Given the Wattses' wide interests and strong sympathies on a number of subjects, Mary may have resisted dedication to the 'single-issue political campaign' (Crawford 1999: ix) for women's suffrage in the same way that she resisted dedication to one religion and one creative medium in favour of embracing multiplicity, diversity and universality. However, she became increasingly active in the women's suffrage campaign after her husband's death and in her later life, about which little is known; the remainder of this section aims to go some way rectifying this gap in her biography.

The large age difference (over thirty years) and intergenerational divide between the couple partly contributed to the differences in their views, voices and interests, and their degrees of dedication to the women's suffrage campaign, highlighting shifts in attitude across the decades of the nineteenth century. George was of a slightly older era, evident in his more cautious and private if genuine support of women's suffrage, the fight for which escalated dramatically after his death. Mary, ever-energetic and optimistic, records her frail husband's heavy dependency on her in his illness and old age; he was unwilling to (let Mary or himself) 'run risks' – 'the only point on which [Mary felt] him to be much older' (M. Watts 1891: 8 January) – and political violence distressed him. She notes in her diary, 'came home to read our Pall Mall . . . Signor begged me not to read [about 'Bloody Sunday'] nor anything political' (1887: 23 November). Although George watched the course of public affairs and discussed politics with friends, he was too nervous and sensitive for any direct political activism. In an interview of 1895 George admits, 'I have only strength enough for my work, and for nothing besides; therefore, I have determinedly kept aloof from politics' (Friederichs 1895: 78). Nonetheless, he was an independent thinker in social, religious and aesthetic matters, and 'found in himself no tendency to become less liberal . . . with years' (M. Watts 1912: 2.145). Speaking of artistic technicalities (while suggesting a wider belief in innovation and rejection of convention), he told an interviewer, 'Rules are good, but make them; don't take them' (qtd. in Friederichs 1895: 80). This was echoed by suffragists' and suffragettes' determination to be law-makers through enfranchisement.

The countless newspaper articles mentioning Mary throughout her lifetime testify to the public and even national interest she generated both during and after her marriage; they reveal her increasingly active social, political and cultural role in a post-Victorian world. Mary became President of the Godalming and District Women's Suffrage Society, affiliated to the NUWSS, in 1909.[11] During this year, various suffrage leagues, associations, unions and federations were founded; suffrage deputations to Parliament resulted in the arrest of Lady Constance Lytton; and prison authorities began forcibly feeding hunger-striking suffragettes. *The Times* reported that William Chance (later a Vice-President of the Godalming and District Women's Suffrage Society) addressed a meeting in support of women's suffrage at Godalming in February 1909, where he read out a letter from 'Mrs. G. F. Watts expressing her sympathy with the movement, and stating that if a branch were formed she would be glad to become a member'; she was appointed President in November that year.[12] Newspaper advertisements and letters

promoting the large Suffragist Demonstration of 1910 – organised
by the Surrey, Sussex and Hants Federation in connection with the
NUWSS, in support of the Conciliation Bill – state that the meeting and resolution would be supported by Mrs G. F. Watts and
Gertrude Jekyll among 'many other well-known Surrey people'
('Meetings and Entertainments: NUWSS', *Dorking and Leather-
head Advertiser* 22 October 1910: 4). Naming local celebrities and
representatives from suffrage societies like Mary was a recruitment
strategy, encouraging 'all who believe in the justice of the women's
cause [to] make a great effort to come to the demonstration ...
walk in the procession or act as banner-bearers' ('The Conciliation
Bill', *Surrey Mirror* 21 October 1910: 8). Mary was part of a much
wider women's movement – in print and procession.

A newspaper leaflet reporting the 'Guildford Division Liberals'
Successful Bazaar' of 1913 features a large photograph in which
Mary occupies a prominent, front-row position on the platform at
the opening ceremony (supplement issued with the *Surrey Times* 24
May 1913). Alongside her sit Iona Davey, local activist, President
of the Women's Liberal Association and secretary of the Women's
Local Government Society; her husband Arthur Jex Davey, a Liberal
politician, President of the Godalming and District Liberal Club and
later Mayor of Godalming (1914–16); Mrs Stopford Brooke and
her husband, a British politician and Liberal MP (1906–10); Liberal
MP Joseph King who, along with his wife Maude, played a key
role in the Peasant Arts movement in Haslemere; and Mrs Charles
T. Bateman and her husband, who wrote a book on George Watts
highlighting the Wattses' humanitarian enterprises (Bateman 1901).
Although husbands' views of their wives' participation in the Surrey
suffrage campaign differed dramatically, this photo, showcasing
several married couples united in their support of women's suffrage
and culture, illustrates how suffragists in conjugal partnerships were
integral to the success of the movement.

Mary and the Daveys were prominent participants in a hundred-
strong, banner-bearing procession in Godalming that was part of the
Great Suffragist Pilgrimage of July 1913.[13] Gertrude Jekyll's large
embroidered banners for the Godalming and Guildford branches of
the NUWSS were paraded through the high streets (Fig. 1.4). This
giant ambulatory advertisement that drew attention to the campaign and to the NUWSS 'excited a good deal of interest' as well
as 'tension', and Mary's name features in a local newspaper report.
Activity was generally peaceful in Godalming but became 'rowdy' in
Guildford, where thousands assembled and speakers were 'rushed',

Figure 1.4 *Godalming Banner*, designed by Gertrude Jekyll, Godalming Museum Archive.

necessitating police intervention. In Godalming, at a meeting where Mary would almost certainly have been present, Sir William Chance presided over the principal meeting held in Godalming Borough Hall (admitting a restricted crowd to avoid the rumoured 'organised opposition') and expressed militant sympathies ('there was method behind their madness') before a resolution was carried: 'calling upon the Government to introduce a Bill to give the vote to women' ('The Pilgrims' Progress: Women Suffragist March Through Surrey', *Surrey Advertiser and County Times* 26 July 1913).

   Yet the fact that 'voting appeared to be about equal' when this resolution was put to the meeting, and 'there were cries of dissent' at its being carried, shows the progressiveness of Mary's position in Surrey at the time. This highlights the importance of her role in reaching people in towns and villages, making the campaign heard by audiences and pockets of society that were not entirely sympathetic. Newspaper articles of the time report sizeable local anti-suffrage meetings intended as a 'counterblast' to the visit of the Pilgrim Suffragists and the rise of 'masculine women and feminine men'; one popular hostess urged her guests to sign an anti-suffrage petition, reassuring them that 'all the best people in Guildford are signing' ('Archives: Tension Mounts as Votes for Women Escalates with March Through Town', *Surrey Advertiser* 26 July 2013). This is the attitude Mary faced when working in Surrey for the suffrage campaign. While the Pilgrimage aimed to demonstrate the growth of peaceful, law-abiding suffragists to show 'there was a constitutional wing to the movement commanding greater support than the WSPU' and the majority of women asking for the vote were opposed to violence, pilgrims were 'accused of not being truly "anti-militant"' (Tickner 1989: 142, 144); participants and leaders risked verbal and physical abuse. Scorn and ridicule were directed at suffragists as well as suffragettes, and since there were 'enough hostile incidents to demand of the suffragists on all routes the courage of their convictions' (Tickner 1989: 147), Mary's bravery in her dedication to the women's cause – in public, in the face of danger, in older age – should not be underestimated. Moreover, there was a 'sensationalism attached to the activist woman in the street' (Green 1997: 11) that shows how, far from becoming a retiring widow, Mary embraced the spectacle of suffrage.

Mary lent her husband's works to exhibitions after his death, and offered his allegorical painting *Faith* (1896) to be reproduced on the cover of NUWSS journal *The Common Cause* in 1913, showing her support for women's suffrage organisations (Cockroft 2005: 47). *Faith*, showing a female warrior soaking her weary feet in the stream of Truth, would have been fitting for the cover of a feminist journal reporting the Great Suffragist Pilgrimage. Mary also supported women's art organisations: she sent a design to be made by the Guild of Women Binders as a cover for George's exhibition catalogues in 1898 (a bound volume of which was presented as a gift to Mary after George's death); and she was appointed Honorary Chair of the WGA at its establishment in 1907, before becoming Honorary President in 1914. The WGA included pioneering suffrage artists and New Dawn Women of the Arts and Crafts movement, providing a new network of women with whom Mary interacted. Such details build up to a picture of Mary's active participation in women's groups and support of feminist politics, as well as showing her growing personal interest in forging new feminist alliances – male and female. Evelyn De Morgan's name features alongside Mary's on the WGA roll, and both women later supported the controversial idea that men should be invited to join the Guild – rejecting separatist ideologies in favour of communication, collaboration and commitment to equality.[14] For these women, feminism meant both supporting women's culture and sharing what was formerly a man's world.

Although Surrey was 'rather slow to make its mark on the suffrage campaign' (Crawford 2006: 186), significant suffrage artists and leading suffragettes resided in the Surrey Hills (especially Peaslake) where they also sourced flints for their window-smashing campaign. Peaslake was home to important campaigners including the Brackenbury sisters, artists who painted Emmeline Pankhurst's portrait and led the pantechnicon raid on Parliament in 1908; Inverness-born Slade-trained artist and militant suffragette Marion Wallace Dunlop, first of the hunger-strikers (1909); and Emmeline and Frederick Pethick-Lawrence (Overton and Mant 1998). Mary, a figurehead of non-militant feminism in her community, convened at least two suffrage meetings in Compton: her friend, fellow craftswoman and suffragist Gertrude Jekyll (Vice-President of the Godalming Women's Suffrage Society) attended a suffrage meeting held by Mary at 'Compton Picture Gallery' (Festing 1991: 210); and a newspaper article of 1913 reports a large suffrage meeting and supper held at Limnerslease by Mary's invitation ('Women and the Vote: Last Night's Meeting', *Surrey Advertiser* 29 November 1913). She thus drew political as well as artistic activity into the domestic sphere, transforming her studio-home into a suffragist meeting ground. Her presidential address on the position and potential of women is recorded:

> Mrs. Watts said that with respect to the movement their common-sense side asked what are women going to get by the vote? Their higher side asked what are women going to give for the vote? The qualities which mankind had agreed to describe as feminine were love, faith, purity, and tenderness. A vote meant a voice, a voice to be heard by the State, whether in the making of new laws or in the reforming of old laws, and the millions of British women in asking for the vote were asking the State to allow them to bring to its counsel, their contribution of those higher [feminine] qualities. In answer to the question which many people were putting as to whether women would be strong enough to do this she quoted the following verse:
>
> > So nigh to grandeur is our dust,
> > So nigh to God is man,
> > When duty whispers lo! thou must,
> > The soul replies, I can.

Mary's affirmative answer (in verse) to the earnest question of whether women were strong enough to be law-makers marks her role as a confident and respected suffragist leader and visionary. Her authoritative educational and presidential positions, as well as her attendance at rousing lectures by influential women in Surrey in 1891 (see Chapter 4), made her fit for this role. While Mary advocates the utilisation of 'feminine qualities' in the campaign and insists the state needs women's virtuous influence (in accordance with the NUWSS), her concluding allusion to the famous final lines from Ralph Waldo Emerson's military-themed poem 'Voluntaries' (1863) – which pays tribute to male volunteers prepared to sacrifice their lives in another fight for freedom – seems more suited to a speech addressed to militant suffragettes than to moderate suffragists. This call to arms couched in poetry suggests her more radical suffragist stance and sympathy with aspects of – perhaps even inclination towards – militancy in later life.

Mary's stance at this time may have been influenced by suffragettes' adoption of more militant tactics in their struggle for enfranchisement, strengthened by the recent death of suffragette Emily Wilding Davison (nearby in Epsom, Surrey, where the Wattses married), and driven by the ongoing imprisonment and forcible feeding of suffrage campaigners; the 'Cat and Mouse Act' was also passed in 1913. Although the NUWSS publicly disavowed militant methods the year before Mary became President of the Godalming branch, by 1913 she may have been inspired by the renewed energy, excitement and force of early twentieth-century feminism as well as the increasingly radical discourse of the NUWSS in the *Common Cause* of November that year, which included war and military metaphors (Tickner 1989: 211–12). She was perhaps losing patience with peaceful and orderly suffragism in the face of women's sustained political oppression, and starting to see milder militancy as a necessary stimulant (perhaps a moral and political duty) after decades of effort devoted to a cause she had supported for a quarter of a century. In light of George's view that 'all rebellion, though its extremes may shock us, is a movement, a struggle towards reform' (1887: 29 April), Mary may well have shared the growing suffrage 'spirit of rebellion when it springs from intolerable injustice' and 'brutality of the government to women' (*Votes for Women* 28 November 1913: 122).

Indeed, Wingerden recognises the differences between suffragists and suffragettes, but also that 'it would be a mistake to draw too firm a line between the WSPU and the NUWSS's ideologies', as 'the two perspectives tended to seep over into each other's territories' (1999: 104–5). Ticker also explains, heroism and sanctified suffering were not to be conceded as the exclusive province of the WSPU. The NUWSS had a greater stake in 'womanliness' than the militants, but they could not afford to seem feeble or servile as they struggled to maintain their identification with the campaign in the face of WSPU notoriety. (Tickner 1989: 212)

These views assist an understanding of Mary's (written and spoken) words, which suggest she was both a virtuous suffragist and militant sympathiser, a progressive wife and more radical widow. In a much-quoted speech at the Albert Hall in October 1912, Emmeline Pankhurst urged suffragettes to 'be militant in [their] own way', and WSPU circulars referred to 'degrees of militancy' (Cowman 2009: 304). This sheds light on Mary's (and other early feminists') seemingly contradictory stance: she merged elements of suffragist and suffragette ideology and discourse to various degrees over her lifetime in response to the political climate. In the absence of Mary's diary material beyond 1908, contemporary newspapers reflect her more radical later views, her active professional role in public life and her status as a key Surrey suffragist.

Mary's strong feminist spirit and powerful urge to sacrifice comfortable married life in order to dedicate herself to women-centred social reform is also implied in her existing diaries. She writes, 'when I think of [the social evil and injustice of prostitution] I feel as if I must get up & go – leave Signor everything!' (1893: 30 January). She cryptically refers to female self-sacrifice and her inner 'animal', writing, 'I might be driven to break Signor's heart, & do something I could never go back upon. So, perhaps a woman may slay her better self' (1893: 20 August). These entries register a conflict between her and her husband's interests, and perhaps also between marriage and suffrage. It is no coincidence that Mary's political activism and public engagement increased significantly after George's death. Mary was, from the beginning of their marriage, acutely conscious of his closer proximity to death; she diligently prepared for it and naturally considered the direction of her own life after it. When George is gravely ill she writes, 'what is to become of my life when [he dies] – to help others is what I want to see before me, that only written in letters of light, in all surrounding night' (1891: 20 May); this she did in her subsequent philanthropic work and support of women's rights. In her final entry for the year of his death, when she still has many years ahead of her, she writes, 'I have followed, worked, loved as you did beloved . . . now for me it must be all looking forward' (1904: 31 December). She

embraced independence, subsequently dedicating herself more seriously to the fight for women's suffrage.

As a respected figure in various (artistic, literary, suffragist) circles,
and due to her public profile, Mary was invited to play central roles
in societies, associations, committees, local events and openings long
after her husband's death.[15] This evidences the high respect she commanded in Edwardian Britain and beyond. She was President of the
Ladies' Watts Rifle Club in Compton (from 1910), which she started
for women; an annual general meeting (AGM) was held in the drawing room at Limnerslease in 1912. She opened the seventh exhibition
of the Art and Aid Association at Godalming in 1909, and opened
the Guildford Technical Institute (surrounded by men) in 1910. Most
notable is Mary's role at the grand opening of the Phillips Memorial
Cloister in 1914.[16] Mary, Iona Davey, Gertrude Jekyll, sculptor Julia
Chance and painter Margery Horne – all members of the NUWSS
and some suffragist pilgrims – were the five women on the Godalming
Town Council Committee for the design and commission of the Cloister (Sullivan 2012: 19). This commemorated 'hero' Jack Phillips, who
sacrificed his life to save others by transmitting SOS calls in Morse
code as the Titanic sank (along with famous passenger W. T. Stead,
who influenced the Wattses' works). The memorial attracted much
attention and support, and Mary – with her personal preoccupation
with erecting memorials (Watts Chapel and Postman's Park) – was an
esteemed contributor. This high-profile project, uniting Mary's interests in art, craft, suffrage and community, propelled her further into
the public sphere.

According to newspaper articles of 1917, a party of Canadian
soldiers from the Godalming YMCA were guests at Mary's home.
She gave them a tour of the art gallery, studio at Limnerslease and
Watts Chapel – where she 'gave a full description of the design and
various symbols' ('Compton: Canadians Visit the Watts Gallery',
Surrey Advertiser 21 July 1917: 5), evidently proud of her own as
well as her husband's work and keen to communicate its messages.
This is another example of Mary drawing the public sphere into the
physical geography of her own domestic space. She recognised the
growing fascination with artists as celebrities – and their personal
lives, studio-homes and work – during her lifetime, and made her
private sphere of public interest. She also delivered her first-ever formal illustrated lecture on 'The Art of G. F. Watts' to Canadians at the
YMCA, where she spoke of the 'resonance that [art] awakens in our
minds' and the 'individual power of will', conveying the 'deep and
noble thoughts' embodied by her husband's art ('A Great Painter and

His Art: Mrs G. F. Watts' Lecture to Canadians', *Surrey Advertiser* 24 November 1917: 6).[17] This is typical of Mary's work after her husband's death: preserving his memory while developing her own public image and professional identity. In 1918 the WGA arranged a public exhibition of soldiers' work, and the involvement of high-profile members including Mary was proudly stated ('Arrangements for Today: Women's Guild of Arts Exhibition', *The Times* 11 May 1918: 9). A 1919 newspaper reports (alongside a segment on votes for women) that 'Mrs. G. F. Watts . . . is busy teaching ex-service men to design and model in clay' ('This Morning's Gossip', *Leeds Mercury* 30 October 1919: 5). This reveals her continued confidence in her authoritative educational role – even presiding over men – after women had partly won the vote and been encouraged to enter employment, useful work or philanthropic schemes during the war.

As a distinguished expert in handicrafts and enterprising founder of a successful handicrafts industry, Mary was an adjudicator at numerous newspaper-worthy exhibitions and prize giving events, where she awarded eponymous prizes (the 'Watts Art Prize' in 1922 and the 'Mrs. G. F. Watts prize' in 1938) to young women.[18] She gave the opening speech at a handicrafts exhibition organised by the Girls' Friendly Society in the Sheffield diocese, where the artistic and literary exhibits were 'largely feminine products' ('Mrs. G. F. Watts on Handicrafts: Interesting Exhibition at Sheffield', *Yorkshire Post and Leeds Intelligencer* 13 April 1923).[19] In 1898 the Wattses had supported the fundraising exhibition for the new premises of the co-educational Powell Corderoy School in Dorking, formerly the British School established in 1816 as a school for girls only – which was extremely unusual for the time. The Wattses loaned the school George's painting of a brave armoured youth, *Aspiration* (1887), and correspondence shows that of all the school's fundraisers, the Wattses, and particularly Mary, were the most kind.[20] Her personal interest in women's education and her encouragement of women's participation in the arts is evident; she clearly recognised and demonstrated that this was key to greater gender equality and female empowerment.

The Wattses' Art and Women's Suffrage

Although Mary does not seem to have designed any 'distinctively suffrage ware' (Cockroft 2005: 13), strong female figures and symbols of freedom pervade her work. Like Ernestine Mills's enamelled series of 'feisty female saints' and martyrs with whom 'suffragists might identify' (Cockroft 2005: 25), Mary's Compton Pottery modelled terracotta figures of St Joan of Arc, St Catherine of Alexandria, St Cecilia and St Hildegard. Joan of Arc was the patron saint of the suffragettes, and featured prominently in their iconography – on suffrage banners and posters, and in WSPU processions.[21] George obsessively depicted Joan of Arc in 1891, 'when her cult intensified' (Tickner 1989: 211), in order to '[do] justice to greatness wherever it is found'; for the Wattses, she embodied 'the lesson of the power of the ideal' (M. Watts 1891: 9 March). The couple's fascination with the heroic quality of Joan of Arc overlapped with that of the WSPU; suffragettes similarly admired her 'simplicity, purity, courage and militancy . . . associations of Justice and Liberty' (Tickner 1989: 211).

Mary was commissioned to design decorative embroidered silk banners as State gifts to Canada in 1906 and 1907.[22] The former, 'Our Lady of the Snows', was presented to Royal Victoria College for Women (McGill University). Mary's banners were part of a series of banners commissioned by Lord Grey while Governor General of Canada, intended to be presented to educational institutions in Canada and to represent a St George theme. Yet while the other banners make clear references to St George, Mary's atypical banners depicting winged female figures are less direct and diverge from the original mandate, seeming instead to represent her own socio-political ideas. Mary records designing and making them in her diary:

> I am beginning my banner – this new banner to be given by the Queen to the children of Canada, I want to put everything into it, that can possibly be thought out – A full rounded aspiration . . . 'The spirit of the years to come' may be the legend written below. (1906: 29 July)

This is comparable with the 'noble sentiment[s]' on other suffrage banners (Cherry 2000: 212). Mary created them at a time when banners had become an acknowledged art form appropriated by female artists flying the flag for women's suffrage, including Sylvia Pankhurst, Gertrude Jekyll and Mary Lowndes – a leading suffrage artist who founded the ASL in 1907 and created huge 'heroine' banners for the 1908 suffragist procession, commemorating great women writers, artists, professionals, activists and visionaries, some of whom were known to the Wattses.

Banners 'radically changed the visual spectacle of women's campaigns for the vote', and became 'central to suffrage spectacle in the years 1907 to 1914'; they were 'formative of the campaign's visual display' and argument at public meetings, demonstrations and marches throughout Britain (Cherry 1993: 207, 211). The prominent banners which decorated halls holding women's suffrage meetings were 'textual with woven, painted, stencilled or appliquéd' mottoes such as 'Women claim equal justice with men', 'calling for the vote, proclaiming key beliefs and advocating action' (Cherry 2000: 210–11, 214). Like Mary Lowndes's embroidered, hand-painted textile suffrage banners combining word and symbol, Mary's embroidered silk banners combine textiles and text, inspirational words and images of liberation; they can be seen as types of text that draw on, and engage with, the early feminist discourse of her day. Female figures, hearts, wings, birds, suns and waves are characteristic elements of both Mary's banner designs and suffrage banner designs; Mary used symbols and images that came to form part of a progressive visual culture, entering into a politically charged iconographic vocabulary.[23]

Mary's banner titled *The Spirit of the Flowers of the Nations* (made *c.*1908, designed 1907 – the year Mary was appointed Honorary President of the WGA – and hung in Government House, Ottawa) (Fig. 1.5) features a large angel-like winged woman rising above the words 'unity', 'justice', 'liberty' and 'strength', with the

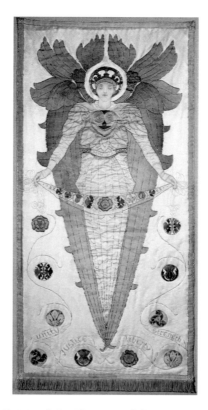

Figure 1.5 *Spirit of the Flowers of the Nations*, Mary Watts, *c.*1908, © Victoria and Albert Museum, London.

word 'strength' also sewn on a banner-like belt across her waist in a kind of writing on and around the female body. These specific terms appear in both Mary's feminist (spoken and written) discourse and in her interior decoration of the Watts Chapel: the circular 'symbols of truths' surrounding the large, red, winged seraphs display the words 'justice', 'unity', 'power', 'hope', 'inspiration', 'aspiration', 'progress' and 'courage'. The chapel's exterior friezes also feature circular designs entwined with the same or similar terms, including 'aim', 'courage', 'liberty', 'unity' and 'justice'. These terms can be seen to have secular, socio-political as well as spiritual significance, and can be seen to dialogise with early feminist discourse privileging these concepts and qualities. For example, the cover image of liberal-feminist newspaper *Shafts* (3 November 1892) showing a female figure drawing an arrow that emits the words 'wisdom', 'justice' and 'truth' has parallels with Mary's banner, the dominant colours of which are the green, white and gold of the Women's Freedom League.

As a 'wielding force in the Arts and Crafts Movement' (Jefferies qtd. in Gould 1998: 8), Mary not only demonstrated women's creative capability but was part of a movement that was 'a deciding factor' in women's campaign for equal citizenship. Along with other pioneering women artists and craftswomen, Mary elevated the developing Arts and Crafts movement – which helped to promote the nineteenth-century women's movement – to 'mainstream history' (Cockroft 2005: 6). Mary was one of the first women to be recognised and represented by the prestigious company Liberty of London for her ceramic designs, and was considered a leading artist in her craft. The Liberty's catalogue published Mary's name while internationally famed men (such as Archibald Knox and Christopher Dresser) whose works featured alongside hers went unacknowledged; it was not company practice to acknowledge the source of their designs but an exception was made for Mary. This not only reflects her status as the wife of a famous artist but also shows how she used it commercially to market her products (while ostensibly maintaining a secondary position to her husband). Her decision to produce garden ornaments was savvy given the 'present fashion for gardening and garden decoration' (M. Watts, letter to Nichol, 17 December 1900, WG), especially among women, for whom gardening was a creative outlet.[24] Mary is championed in the introduction to Liberty's 'Book of Garden Ornaments' (1904), where her work featured prominently, and which highlights and promotes her groundbreaking work:

Never before, in this country at least, has the Garden Pot been treated as an item, *per se*, of decorative skill . . . the present exhibitors have struck out into untrodden paths, and, in this instance largely aided and advised by Mrs G F Watts, the talented wife of our greatest living artist, have shown us what notable results can be achieved by simple forms treated with bold designs. (C. J. Ffoulkes qtd. in Gould 1998: 13)

True to the Arts and Crafts ethos, Mary transformed everyday objects into works of art. That these were predominantly objects associated with the home (pots, rugs, fireplaces, bedsteads and bookends) further illuminates Mary's reconciliation of domestic and artistic, private and public realms in her creative practice through which she negotiated patriarchal binaries. That the catalogue acknowledges Mary as George's 'talented wife' is testament not only to his reputation (whose name she worked under as 'Mrs G. F. Watts') but also to her originality and style which achieved wide recognition. 'Mrs. G. F. Watts' Village Industry' was advertised prominently in newspapers (in business columns and exhibition announcements) after her husband's death, and her award-winning terracotta garden ornaments (pots, sundials, bird-baths etc.) produced by her Potters' Arts Guild were praised in newspapers and 'in demand everywhere' (Jefferies qtd. in Gould 1998: 8).[25] It was in this craft – distinct from her husband's profession – that Mary developed an independent creative identity, 'felt supremely confident and could excel on the national stage' (Bills 2011: 16). Newspaper articles refer to the 'world-wide reputation [. . .of] the famous terracotta potteries established by Mrs. G. F. Watts' ('Watts Art Gallery in Jeopardy: Famous Pottery Works Ablaze', *Yorkshire Post* 18 January 1923: 8). She 'struck out into untrodden paths' not only as a pioneering professional artist but also as a suffragist asserting her 'forthright nature and views on the rights of women' (Gould 1998: 51). It was this fusion of her roles as wife, artist and suffragist that contributed to the public interest she generated. As a professional woman artist and businesswoman, she set a precedent for other aspiring Victorian women artists, representing and actively supporting greater female empowerment through participation in the wider creative arts. She was part of a growing network of professional women artists in respected positions who helped to change the way society perceived women and work.

While George can be seen as a patriarchal 'father-figure artist' conflated with Victorian conservatism, his encouragement of women's participation in the arts reveals his progressiveness. He personally supported and raised the respectability of women's artistic careers by funding Mary's artistic enterprises, becoming friends with female artists like Anna Lea Merritt, replacing his own picture with that of aspiring artist Louisa Starr to give her a place in the 1870 Royal Academy exhibition, and mentoring talented female suffragist artists including Evelyn De Morgan and Henrietta Rae – who worked in his studio at Little Holland House and won a seven-year scholarship to the Royal Academy.[26] George was also one of the Founders and benefactors of Roedean Girls School (Brighton), where the Wattses' ward Lily was enrolled, and he was a great influence on its female Head of Department in Art – Sylvia Lawrence – who exhibited at the Royal Academy (Naughton 2011: 2). Artist Phoebe Traquair, who Mary consulted on artistic technique, describes in a letter a cherished memory of a visit to George's studio full of 'great thoughts' (*c.*1897 WG), as does Georgiana Burne-Jones in her husband's biography where she comments on his 'noble work' and 'vision' (Burne-Jones 1906: 186). George recognised the growing number of discontented women fighting to be accepted as equals and artists in a masculinist society, and both suffragists and suffragettes were influenced and inspired by his work.

George's imagery increasingly appealed to, and was reappropriated by, feminist campaigners. Suffragist Helena Dowson's essay collection *Love and Life* (1902) contains 'musings inspired by the paintings of G. F. Watts' (Crawford 1999: 174), and suffragist Olive Schreiner's *Dreams* (2008; first published 1890) – a favourite with imprisoned suffragettes – were 'said to resemble Signor's pictures' (M. Watts 1891: 14 July). WSPU supporter and Slade-trained artist Olive Hockin kept a print of George's *Love and Death* in her Kensington studio along with a 'suffragette arsenal' discovered by police in 1913 (Crawford 1999: 287–8). The strong, forward-walking, unrelenting and androgynous figure of Death may have seemed relevant to Hockin's feminist fight, and the painting was also a favourite of Mary's. The enamelled silver *Angel of Hope* pendant (1909) made by Ernestine Mills, commissioned by the WSPU to celebrate the release of suffragette Louise Eates from imprisonment for suffrage campaigning, depicts a female figure of Hope kneeling outside the prison bars holding a harp, which is strikingly similar to the kneeling female figure holding a lyre in George's painting *Hope*. Attached to a chain with stones in the WSPU colours of purple, white and green, Mills's pendant depicting Hope is a symbol of literal and socio-political emancipation for women. While her inspiration is uncertain, she would undoubtedly have been aware of George's world-famous work, and her design can be seen to allude to or rework his image specifically to promote the women's cause. An apparently almost identical 'coloured enamel pendant "Hope" and a small chain' was found in Mary's large dressing room after her death (Limnerslease Inventory 1938: 12, WG), suggesting her personal appreciation of this feminist interpretation of her husband's work, painted in the year of their marriage.

However, the relationship between George's work and feminism was far from unproblematic, and the tension between the two emerged overtly in 1913 when three of his paintings were attacked at Manchester Art Gallery by militant suffragettes. These included *Prayer* (1867), depicting May Prinsep kneeling piously in prayer, which may have been interpreted as 'female deference to patriarchal religion' (Cockroft 2005: 28).[27] Suffragettes smashed the glass protecting valuable famous paintings by Pre-Raphaelite and late Victorian artists (including Leighton, Rossetti and Millais) in public galleries, highlighting the hypocrisy of a masculinist society that revered women as beautiful aesthetic objects but was indifferent to women's lived experience of brutality and oppression. This attack, combining window smashing with suffragette iconoclasm, was also in protest against the heavy sentencing of Emmeline Pankhurst (in connection with an attack on Lloyd George's Surrey summerhouse) the previous day. It was subsequently 'reported everywhere that [Watts Gallery] [was] closed for fear of an attack upon the collection by the suffragettes', and George's nudes were believed to be under threat; yet this was denied in the Curator's letter to the newspaper editor, reminding readers of 'the great artist['s] . . . generous and untiring devotion to the cause of human progress and enlightenment' (Charles H. Thompson, *Surrey Times and Advertiser* 14 June 1913). Newspapers reported that Mary 'felt compelled, as a precautionary measure' to close her late husband's art collection to the public 'in consequence of the suffragette outrages' and mutilation of art in picture galleries in 1914 (including the slashing of the famous female nude, the *Rokeby Venus*, at the National Gallery), though it is acknowledged that Mary was 'herself an advocate of woman's suffrage' (*Liverpool Echo* 26 May 1914: 8; *Birmingham Mail* 27 May 1914: 4).

In addition to his sympathy with women's suffrage, George's ambiguous attitude to religion is recorded by Mary: while he felt a deep religious reverence, he 'hate[d] theology' (1891: 24 May) and 'reasoned and rebelled against the unreality of ordinary religious teaching' (G. Watts qtd. in M. Watts 1912: 1.15–16) at church. She also records 'his wisdom in not insisting [on] any particular dogma or doctrine' (1887: 13 March), which undermines any rationale for the suffragette attack on *Prayer* specifically. Despite notions of his 'extreme traditionalism', this book aims to show that he did not 'unquestioning [accept. . .] the dominant ideologies of his society' (Gould 2004b: 73). Ultimately, whether in protest or as propaganda, suffragettes used George's famous images of women in their campaign, showing his work's continued relevance to early feminism.

Interestingly, a newspaper article of 1930 titled 'Outrage Outside a Bournemouth Church' ('outrage' implying a suffragette attack) reports the mysterious breaking of Mary's statue of St Francis of Assisi, which stood in front of a recently erected Immanuel Congregational Church; this was a deliberate act of violence investigated by police, following a protest over the choice of figure (*Lancashire Evening Post* 14 October 1930: 2). This reveals the controversy surrounding both Mary's and George's works during a time of socio-political and religious turbulence, and it seems significant in light of the popularity of Mary's chosen figure with early feminists. Militant suffragette Constance Lytton was compared to Francis of Assisi (Betty Balfour [1925] qtd. in Hartman 2003: 38), and he held importance for feminist activists like Emmeline Pethick-Lawrence. As a preacher and 'great spiritual leader' who allegedly received the stigmata, he inspired the 'suffrage spirit' driving the wider movement with its aim 'to turn the world upside down' (*Common Cause* 9 May 1913: 67). The Wattses greatly admired St Francis as 'a true soldier ready to sacrifice himself & give up all that he possesses for the cause he believes to be the right one' (G. Watts qtd. in M. Watts 1893: 7 May).

George's symbolist paintings of (all-)powerful androgynous or 'unfeminine' female figures – such as Death in *The Court of Death* (*c.*1870–1902), an androgynous God in *'The All-Pervading'* (1887–90) and Eve in *She Shall Be Called Woman* (*c.*1875–92) (Fig. 1.6) – can be seen to dialogise with early feminist iconography promoting female empowerment. He rejected overtly Christian iconography in order to present traditionally religious subjects in original ways and imbue them with secular, socio-political as well as spiritual significance, 'appealing to all minds' (M. Watts 1887: 3 September), and often represents women as strong, independent beings. Mary records in the *Annals* that in *She Shall Be Called Woman* (the first in a narrative trilogy), the 'columnar' (rather than fragile or hourglass) figure of the 'newly created Eve' who dominates the large painting was intended by George to 'represent the central figure of the universe' which he wanted 'not so much to stand in light as to emit light' (1912: 2.138–9). Mary proudly records the progression of the 'Created Eve' in her diary: 'she is growing up radiantly, a wreath of clouds & light, of wings, of her own golden hair, is girdling her, the light & colour is becoming superb' (1891: 20 December). George explains to Mary, 'she is, of course the Eve new-born in her first feeling of life & sense of new powers, & then she is besides the newly awakened woman, or <u>mind</u> of modern times' (1891: 3 July): the 'New Woman'. The painting – in which the figures of God, Adam

Figure 1.6 *She shall be called woman*, George Watts, *c.*1875–92, © Tate, London 2017.

and the angels are notably absent – can be seen to represent the awakening consciousness, enlightenment and transformation of woman, as well as the emergence and rise of the feminist movement over the later nineteenth century. The combination of delicacy and drama, ethereal beauty and female strength in the painting perhaps appealed to early feminists. Indeed, suffragette Lettice Floyd provided a print of George's (*She Shall Be Called*) *Woman* to decorate a new WSPU shop in Newcastle (*c.*1910) (Crawford 1999: 225).[28]

Mary was somewhat complicit in her own effacement: she endlessly promoted her husband's profile and dedicated herself to maintaining his legacy by creating and managing Watts Gallery (completed with the Watts Chapel just in time for his death in 1904). She organised exhibitions of his work, catalogued his pictures, varnished and photographed his paintings, and wrote his biography which is still the principal reference source for research on him. Yet an exploration of her marriage and collaborations with her husband – as well as a consideration of her life within a wider network of women (professionals, artists, suffragists and suffragettes) – reveals her role as an active, assertive, imaginative cultural producer who carefully negotiated social and gender boundaries through her creative practice and partnership. She seemingly respectfully relinquished her fine art practice on marriage and yet fervently took up another (arguably more ambitious and successful) creative practice; she apparently reverentially recreated her husband's works while developing her own form of symbolic decoration and iconographic vocabulary; and she publicly maintained a secondary place to her husband yet assumed an increasingly dominant and authoritative role in their marriage and in the studio. By incorporating her artistic activities into the traditional Victorian female role of housewife, working with her husband and within their studio-home or its grounds, she found a way to reconcile her professional creative practice with her persona as 'wife of a great artist' who gradually emerged from his shadow. Mary used the idea of duty to her husband and the preservation of his memory – compatible with her domestic role – as a justification for her entry into the public sphere as an artist, writer, philanthropist and suffragist.

Notes

1. Mary's father Charles Edward Fraser Tytler was a writer of esoteric dissertations; he wrote *New View of the Apocalypse* (1852).
2. These lines are engraved in the base of the statue: 'Flower in the crannied wall, / I pluck you out of the crannies, / I hold you here, root and all, in my hand, / Little flower – but if I could understand / What you are, root and all, and all in all, / I should know what God and man is.'
3. The Wattses greatly admired Tennyson, who featured in several of their works: George painted several portraits of him, and Mary devoted the frontispiece of her decorated photograph album to him, quoting from his proto-feminist epic poem *The Princess* (1847).
4. See Mary Watts after G. F. Watts *Death Crowning Innocence*, terracotta relief (14 x 9.5 cm), WG.
5. Women's Suffrage 'Gradus Ad Millennium: Mr Bernard Shaw as the "Intelligent Woman's Guide" (with apologies to G. F. Watts's "Love and Life")', 1928, original wood-engraving by Bernard Partridgel for *Punch* 13 June 1928. This refers to Shaw's book *The Intelligent Woman's Guide to Socialism and Capitalism* (written 1928). Shaw reviewed Ronald Chapman's biography of Watts, *Observer* 23 December 1945 (qtd. in Pitcher 2013: 15).
6. Mary Watts's journal entry emphasises this dual aspect of the mother: 'beautiful maternal love may become savage maternal instincts' (A14: MSW/3/8, p. 21, WG). Mother pelicans were believed to pluck their own breasts to feed their starving young, sometimes dying in the process.

Mary's pelican motif also features on her chapel exterior, her Limnerslease ceiling panels, and her Liberty's pelican rug (retailed 1903) which made it famous.

7. Mary's pelican motif can be seen to allude to the adoption of the pelican as a symbol of female strength centuries before, when it was used to represent Queen Elizabeth I as the devoted, self-sacrificing mother of her Protestant nation and an independent, courageous woman; it became one of her favourite symbols. Queen Elizabeth was commemorated by a 1908 ASL banner.

8. A related use of globes and angels can be seen in Burne-Jones's *The Days of Creation* (1877), depicting androgynous winged angels with tilted heads bearing spheres representing the earth and universe. Mary bought a photograph (by Frederick Hollyer) of *The Days of Creation* in 1891. Its influence is visible in the androgynous angels carrying circular symbolic medallions on the interior walls of Watts Chapel, painted in rich, Pre-Raphaelite colours.

9. The peacock design can be found on Mary's chapel exterior, on Limnerslease ceiling panels and in her decorated photograph album. The peacock feather features prominently in Evelyn De Morgan's *The Prisoner* as well as in William De Morgan's designs. For further discussion of its feminist significance see Cockroft 2005: 17.

10. See 'Handicapped': the joint winner of the ASL poster competition in 1909, designed by Duncan Grant. The woman only has a pair of sculls in heavy seas, while a young man glides gaily by in a boat, the wind inflating his sail – the vote (Tickner 1989: 51).

11. See Craddock's Godalming Directory (1910–15), Godalming Museum Library; 'County Jottings', *Surrey Mirror*, 2 March 1909: 2. While there is no evidence that Mary signed women's suffrage petitions, it is likely that she signed the NUWSS Voter's Petition (with over 280,000 signatories) for the General Election in December 1909. In 1917, the Guildford and District Women's Suffrage Society joined other NUWSS branches in presenting a 'Memorial' to Parliament, simultaneously with the Representation of the People Bill (1918), urging the necessity of enfranchising women (Godalming and District Suffrage Society letters, Surrey History Centre archives, G173/149/1-4); Mary may also have signed this.

12. 'Dr. A. R. Wallace and Woman Suffrage', *The Times* 11 February 1909. In November 1909 Mary addressed a meeting at which Gertrude Jekyll – who visited Mary on at least nine occasions (*c.*1867–93) – took her place in support on the platform. Sir William Chance was also President of the Women's Local Government Association, and barrister and High Sheriff of Surrey in 1884; his wife Julia Chance had articles printed in *Women's Suffrage and Mortality* and wrote books such as *Words to Working Women on Women's Suffrage* (1912). Jekyll designed the Chances' garden in 1899.

13. The NUWSS Suffragist Pilgrimage of 1913 is well-documented by *The Times*, *Surrey Advertiser* and *Surrey Times*: suffragist marches started from numerous cities and culminated in London. The original appeal of the Pilgrimage to Mary – who read John Bunyan's *The Pilgrim's Progress* (1678) – is clear, as it was intended as an act of devotion to the cause and its originators. Suffragists held meetings en route in Haslemere, Godalming and Guildford, gathered petitions, sold the *Common Cause*, literature and accessories, and enlisted sympathisers (Tickner 1989: 141–7). Newspaper articles report over 8,000 people present in North Street, Guildford, 1913. In the early nineteenth century, Godalming was larger than Guildford, and was connected to London and Portsmouth by railway around the mid-nineteenth century. In 1913 Godalming became a member of the Surrey, Sussex and Hampshire Federation of the NUWSS.

14. Paper copy of the WGA roll (membership list), William Morris Society Hammersmith archives. Also listed are J. C. Chance, Emily Ford, Mary Lowndes, May and Jane Morris, Lisa Stillman and Estella Canziani. See Letters of 1913, WGA Archives. Walter Crane and William De Morgan's business partner Halsey Ricardo gave speeches at the first official meeting of the WGA in London, which Mary chaired (Thomas 2015, 2016).

15. Mary is listed among famous attendees in press reports of weddings, funerals (that of Meredith, Morris and Burne-Jones), lectures and meetings as well as 'hotel arrivals'; and featured in 'gossip' and 'current affairs' newspaper columns.

16. See *Surrey Mirror* 4 June 1909: 8; film clip featuring Mary at the large formal opening of the Phillips Memorial Cloister held at Godalming Museum, 'The Path of Duty was the Path to Glory', 15 April 1914 (Sullivan 2012: 21).

17. Mary also designed a large terracotta memorial to a Canadian officer at Aldershot (1911).

18. Mary was one of three judges at the exhibition of the Royal Drawing Society of Great Britain and Ireland in 1895 (*Yorkshire Gazette*, 27 April 1895: 7), and she awarded prizes at the Royal Drawing Society's annual exhibition at the Guildhall Art Gallery, London (*Bexhill-on-Sea Observer*, 8 April 1922: 2).

19. The products included photographs, short stories, poems and designs. In her applauded speech, Mary praises the 'minor arts' which were 'really the basis of great art'.

20. 'Miscellaneous papers', letters to/from Mary Watts (*c*.1904), Surrey History Centre archives, C/ES/115/6/2. Mary also supported the British School in Godalming, suggesting her interest in the British School movement.

21. For example, a poster advertising the WSPU *Suffragette* newspaper in 1912, designed by Hilda Dallas, shows a suffragette dressed as Joan of

Arc. She was the archetypal militant, continually evoked in the final years of the WSPU campaign, and was made the central emblem of feminist rebellion against the state (Tickner 1989: 209–11). St Joan of Arc identified St Catherine of Alexandria as one of the Saints who counselled her; St Catherine of Siena featured on an ASL suffrage banner. George Watts also painted Ellen Terry as Joan of Arc with an inner vision, dressed in armour: *Watchman, What of the Night?* (*c*.1864).

22. Earl Grey, Governor General of Canada, commissioned Mary to design two silk banners for the Canadian people, as part of a collection of banners gifted to educational institutions in Canada. See his letters of 1945 concerning banners 'by Mrs Watts (or her school)', 'really beautiful works of needlework. One of them . . . very symbolic', Archive of Art and Design, V&A, MA/1/G1790.

23. See Mary Lowndes's Banner of the Oxfordshire, Buckinghamshire and Berkshire Federation of the NUWSS (1908), *Caroline Herschel* and *Katherine Bar-lass* suffrage banner featuring hearts (1908), and Miss Burton's winged heart design for a Women's Freedom League banner (1911), The Women's Library Suffrage Banner Collection. See also the Electrical Trades Union banner: a female angel stood on a globe above a banner with the words 'Light and Liberty'.

24. See Elise Lawton Smith's forthcoming work on the importance of nature and gardening for Mary Watts, both personally and professionally.

25. Mary's architectural and garden ornaments designed for Liberty's were awarded medals from the Royal Botanical and Royal Horticultural Societies. See Gould 1998: 51; *Surrey Mirror*, 6 April 1906: 8; *Dublin Daily Express* 18 April 1907: 4.

26. According to the autobiography of the female artist Estella Canziani (1887–1964), daughter of the painter Louisa Starr, 'Mr Watts took down his own picture, replacing it with my mother's, thereby giving her a place on the line' in the Royal Academy exhibition of 1870 (Cockroft 2005: 10).

27. George Watts's *Paolo and Francesca* (1872–5) and *The Hon J L Motley* (*c*.1861) were also attacked on 3 April 1913 by university graduate Lillian Forrester and governess Evelyn Manesta, and had to be reglazed (see Cowman forthcoming 2018).

28. Emery Walker published a colour reproduction of this painting around 1911, and the painting itself would have been very well known: George sent this picture, independent of the trilogy, for exhibition at the Royal Academy in 1892, and it has been at the Tate in London since its establishment in 1897.

Chapter 2

Evelyn and William De Morgan

Practice and Partnership

In a subversion of the masculinist emphasis of Wilhelmina Stirling's biography titled *William De Morgan and His Wife* (1922) which centres on the male figure, this chapter focuses primarily on the critically neglected female figure in this conjugal creative partnership. It aims to reveal Evelyn's progressive socio-political position as a pioneering professional woman painter, a creative partner to her husband, and an active suffragist whose work dialogised with late nineteenth and early twentieth-century feminist discourse. In its representations of powerful female figures and women embodying tensions between captivity and liberty (as well as a transformation from the former to the latter), Evelyn's art has more overt feminist elements and messages than Mary Watts's.

Sources of information about Evelyn's life and works are extremely scarce, the most major and established being the writings of Stirling, Evelyn's sister. Yet in addition to being 'biased, limited, and sometimes erroneous' (E. L. Smith 2002: 17) as well as incomplete, misleading and hyperbolical according to the only two other books dedicated to Evelyn De Morgan, *Evelyn De Morgan: Oil Paintings* (Gordon 1996) and *Evelyn Pickering De Morgan and the Allegorical Body* (E. L. Smith 2002), Stirling's biography contributes to Evelyn's eclipse and effacement as an artist even as it apparently attempts to preserve her reputation. Stirling introduces Evelyn by reducing her to the nameless, contingent, secondary position of 'Wife' in the title, defining her in relation to the male figure as merely a marital – rather than also a creative – partner. She disguises the unconventionality of their marriage, diminishes Evelyn's role as a talented, independent artist in her own right long before her marriage to William, and only turns to a discussion of her over a hundred pages into the book to 'measure the quality of her influence' on her husband. While Stirling acknowledges Evelyn's significant role in William's life as 'the most prominent factor in the moulding of his later career' (Stirling 1922: 135), her focus on William's works and discussion of Evelyn primarily in relation to him is at the expense of an exploration of Evelyn's art in the depth it deserves.

More recent attempts have been made to compensate for this neglect, most notably the book by Smith and that edited by Gordon. Yet the latter makes no real attempt to examine Evelyn's affiliation with the women's rights movement, and Smith's discussion of Evelyn's art in relation to feminism is overshadowed by her focus on spiritualism. Evelyn is otherwise invariably overlooked or undervalued and remains curiously absent even from texts focusing on women 'excluded from the history of art' (Nunn 1987: 132). There are some entries on Evelyn's work in Jan Marsh's *Pre-Raphaelite Women* but their brevity seems to reflect and perpetuate Evelyn's underappreciated status as a late Pre-Raphaelite artist, and Evelyn is introduced even in this feminist study as the 'wife of the ceramic artist William de Morgan' (Marsh 1987: 132). The lack of critical material on Evelyn is disproportionate to her vast creative output and remarkably successful career – spanning half a century – as a professional female artist who actively exhibited her work in various reputable galleries throughout her lifetime. Yet this lack is consistent with the historical marginalisation of women and women artists by masculinist culture and the male tradition of fine art.

Evelyn was one of the most significant and prolific Victorian women artists and yet, along with Mary Watts, became one of the forgotten female artists of the nineteenth century. This is not only due to the suggested shortcomings of the available biographical information but also the questionable handling of Evelyn's work after her death. Evelyn's paintings might have been better known had Stirling not purchased many of them for a private collection over which she had control, preventing them from being widely exhibited or reproduced. Although Stirling left her collection in trust to the De Morgan Foundation which she established in 1968, there were initially neither resources nor premises available to allow the adequate display of the material (Gordon 1996: 7), so a substantial portion of Evelyn's work languished in storage, unseen for many years. Also, sixteen paintings by Evelyn were destroyed by a warehouse fire in 1991. The limited space for – and loss of – visual material combined with the lack of literary material largely contributed to Evelyn's effacement as an artist. Moreover, her extended winters in Florence distanced her from the London art scene, and she was not driven by desire for fame.

The reception of Evelyn's work was shaped by her relationships with – and perceived indebtedness to – various male figures. She has consistently been defined by and reduced to her relation to men despite her talent and originality. An exhibition booklet on Evelyn's drawings states,

> the art of Evelyn De Morgan will remain overshadowed by the better known ceramic works of her husband, William De Morgan. Even now, those who know her painting tend to regard her art as purely a manner derived from Burne-Jones . . . but the important and early influence was the style and character of her uncle, Roddam Spencer Stanhope. (unknown author 1970: 2)

Some of her works were mistakenly attributed to Burne-Jones, whose influence they show. Yet she was greatly admired by her male contemporaries: Oscar Wilde – to whom Mary Watts 'felt very much drawn' (1891: 6 July) – praised Evelyn's imaginative painting in an 1879 review; and Spencer Stanhope acknowledged that Evelyn 'had achieved a mastery of technique in which [he] failed', telling her, 'you can draw infinitely better than I do . . . I can only envy you!' (qtd. in Stirling 1922: 191).

Evelyn's unusually passionate and persistent dedication to art from a young age coupled with her prosperous upper-middle-class background meant that she was educated and trained in art as a teenager. This provided her with the knowledge and skills to pursue a professional career in fine art at a time when female painters of her status were typically only aspiring or amateur artists. Although her mother Anna Maria Wilhelmina Spencer Stanhope (sister of John Roddam Spencer Stanhope, related to the upper classes) had studied art, she apparently viewed her drawing as no more than a genteel ladylike accomplishment and disapproved of Evelyn's serious commitment to an artistic career. She dismissed her artistic brother as eccentric and believed that paid work for women was 'not only unfeminine but petit bourgeois' (Cherry 1993: 32). She proclaimed, 'I want a daughter, not an artist' (Stirling 1922: 174), reflecting the prevailing view of these roles as mutually exclusive. For a woman to be a professional artist at the social level of Evelyn's family was unconventional, but the fact that her maternal uncle was an artist to some extent legitimised and fostered her career. He bought a villa in Florence, moving there permanently in 1880, which provided a convenient means for Evelyn to travel and study in Italy; the classical and artistic aspects of the city influenced her artwork, and the climate later proved beneficial to William's health. With her family connections and friendship with

Edward Burne-Jones and the Pre-Raphaelite Brotherhood (PRB), Evelyn emerged as a late Pre-Raphaelite painter – a rarity as a woman in a predominantly male movement.

Despite her mother's hostility towards and attempts to obstruct her artistic development (one master was secretly given instructions to tell her she had no artistic talent and another was ordered to restrict her to fruit and flowers [Cherry 1993: 32]), the 1870s was an intensely active and pivotal period in Evelyn's life as an artist. She began tuition with 'Green, the Drawing Master' (Gordon 1996: 9) in April 1871 when she was just fifteen years old, and was training at the South Kensington National Art Training School (with its emphasis on design) in October 1872 by the age of seventeen; Mary Watts also supposedly trained here (Chapman 1945: 115).[1] At the Slade, Evelyn's outstanding artistic ability was acknowledged by a three-year scholarship as well as numerous prestigious prizes she was awarded for drawing, painting and composition, which gave her a reputation as 'the most distinguished of the first batch of "Slade girls"' (Nunn 1987: 54).[2] In the *Magazine of Art*, Evelyn features first in the short list of Slade students who had 'obtained a position of standing among the artists of the present day' (Weeks 1883: 329). Although a carriage and a maid were provided to take her to the Slade, since it was socially unacceptable for an unmarried young lady to be seen in the street unchaperoned, Evelyn dismissed the former and determinedly evaded the latter in pursuit of independence, walking the last few streets to arrive on foot (Stirling 1922: 179).

In 1876 Evelyn exhibited her first painting *St Catherine of Alexandria* (1873–5) at the Dudley Gallery in London, and in 1877 she was invited to exhibit her painting *Ariadne in Naxos* at the opening exhibition of the prestigious Grosvenor Gallery in London, where her work was sold and where she exhibited until 1888. She became a regular exhibitor through the invitation policy of the Grosvenor Gallery, where other suffragist artists (including Emily Ford, Louise Jopling, Emily Mary Osborn and Louisa Starr) exhibited; it 'lent suffrage a certain fashionability' (Cherry 2000: 155). This was set up in opposition to the classical, conservative and masculinist Royal Academy whose jury system and stifling views on the arts were incompatible with forward-looking artists of the day like Evelyn; she continued to exhibit in progressive independent galleries throughout her career. While George Watts exhibited at the Academy because of his friendship with Frederic Leighton, he preferred to exhibit at the Grosvenor, where Evelyn was invited to exhibit her work alongside his as well as that of Burne-Jones and Spencer Stanhope. Her one-woman exhibition at the Bruton Gallery (London) in 1906 signified her success and popularity as a painter; very few other women artists of this period exhibited their works in a solo show. Evelyn demonstrated how women could gain greater social and financial freedom through professional art practice. She represented the increasingly active role of women in fine art over the nineteenth century as well as (the potential for) their integration into this male tradition.

Evelyn was a remarkable rarity for her time not only as a successful professional woman artist breaking new ground in a male-dominated academic art world, but specifically as a female painter. She mastered the male tradition of fine art at a time when there were few – and little serious competition from – other professional women artists, and women were more typically associated with 'feminine' craft. Indeed, Mary Watts was predominantly a craftswoman who positioned herself in the applied arts, distinct from her husband's domain of fine art. While Evelyn's *oeuvre* consists of a vast number of oil paintings, drawings, pastels, watercolours and sculptures, she was primarily an oil painter despite – and in defiance of – the widespread perception in Victorian England that women had 'neither the necessary concentration or stamina for painting' (Walter Sickert qtd. in E. L. Smith 2002: 21) and that oil painting was 'too smelly and dirty for women to practise' (Nunn 1987: 19). Upper-middle-class women were encouraged in the practice of certain prescribed 'feminine' accomplishments that were socially acceptable for ladies, such as flower painting in dainty watercolours or craft hobbies such as 'sand pictures, feather pictures and shell-box making' (Nunn 1987: 19). Contemporary definitions of femininity held that a woman's domestic role and inferior inventive capacity equipped her both mentally and physically for craft and supposedly subordinate artistic genres. Evelyn overtly rejected conventionally feminine activities and 'clearly eschewed traditionally womanly or humble genres such as still life . . . flower and fruit paintings' (Nunn 1987: 125–6), landscape and domestic narrative, moving beyond this traditional female iconography and concentrating instead on ambitious large-scale figure pictures inspired by literary, classical, mythological and historical subjects.

Such 'masculine' traits in a woman – emphasised by Stirling's description of Evelyn's artistic ambition as her 'virility' and of her art as 'virile and strong' (Stirling 1922: 146, 312) – were generally condemned by Victorians. Professional women painters like Evelyn and Henrietta Ward were 'accused of exhibiting inappropriate masculine assertiveness' (E. L. Smith 2002: 19). In 1870, when

Evelyn was fifteen and had just started drawing lessons, the *Saturday Review* criticised women who took up 'the manly professions' such as fine art, and in 1883 Eliza Linton wrote in *The Girl of the Period* that 'passionate ambition, virile energy, the love of strong excitement, self-assertion, fierceness, an undisciplined temper, are all qualities which detract from her ideal of womanliness' (qtd. in E. L. Smith 2002: 19). Evelyn refused to conform to Victorian notions of womanhood and norms of femininity not only in her 'manly' profession but also in her 'unladylike' character as described by Stirling, who portrays Evelyn as the antithesis of Linton's conception of 'womanliness': she was 'a most trying inmate, all fizz . . . and excitement from morning till night' (Stirling qtd. in Gordon 1996: 10–11); she was 'like a thunderstorm . . . she seemed as brilliant, restless and withal frightening . . . she disturbed the Victorian placidity of our home like a flash from an alien world' (Stirling 1924: 26–7). Stirling also records Evelyn's 'lightning rapidity of invention and construction' (Stirling 1924: 237).

The comparison of Evelyn to a 'thunderstorm' and 'lightning' 'flash' has parallels with her painting *The Storm Spirits* (1900) (Fig. 2.1), in which Thundercloud and Lightning are personified as strong winged female figures causing chaos and turbulence in the world

Figure 2.1 *The Storm Spirits*, Evelyn De Morgan, 1900, © De Morgan Collection, courtesy of the De Morgan Foundation.

below. It was exhibited in 1903, 1904 and 1907 at reputable galleries during a time of increasing political unrest as the suffrage movement was escalating. The powerful red-winged figure of Lightning steps forward as she emits bolts from her extended hand, assuming the traditionally male role of the Greek god Zeus and Michelangelo's God in the Sistine Chapel that George Watts so admired. This figure can be seen to some extent as a (psychological or emotional) self-portrait by Evelyn in the absence of any traditional one, and it was prefigured by a childhood poem about the Spirit of the Lightner. Evelyn's irrepressible ebullience and passionate rage convey her frustration with her restricted position as a woman in patriarchal society and reflect her contestation of limits in her struggle for greater liberty.

Evelyn defined 'herself and her role in life largely in opposition . . . to the female models then available to her' (E. L. Smith 2002: 21), including ideals of female practitioners as '"the fair artist", "the gentle painter", "this accomplished lady"' (Nunn 1987: 21). Evelyn's 'unladylike' or 'masculine' behaviour and profession is significant from more recent theoretical perspectives which recognise 'transgression of the existing [gender] conventions as a mode of resistance, and therefore [take] an interest in behaviour traditionally classified as perverse' (Meaney 1993: viii). Gender theorist Judith Halberstam discusses the subversive impact of 'female masculinity' on conventional understandings and classifications of sex, gender and gendered behaviour, arguing that the very existence of such 'masculine' women 'urges us to reconsider our most basic assumptions about the functions, forms, and representations' of gender. Echoing Stirling's and Linton's emphasis on 'virility', and suggesting Evelyn's subversive position as a Victorian 'masculine woman', Halberstam writes,

> Some popular accounts of female masculinity suggest that the appearance of the virile woman is a relatively recent occurrence and that she is herself a product of feminist ideologies. Other accounts situate her as a sign of the relaxation of gender conformity and a harbinger of greater latitude for gender identification. Few popular renditions of female masculinity understand the masculine woman as a historical fixture, a character who has challenged gender systems for at least two centuries. (Halberstam 1998: 45)

Stirling describes Evelyn as 'handsome rather than pretty' in childhood, whereas her younger brother Spencer 'was of a more pronounced beauty' and was 'completely in subjection' to her. While George Watts 'enthusiastically pronounced [Spencer and Evelyn] to be the most beautiful children he had ever seen', he apparently painted only the portrait of cherubic Spencer. Evelyn's 'unfeminine' physical appearance corresponded with her character and conduct, 'for Evelyn was never a cipher or a saint' (Stirling 1922: 147); she was a cultural producer rather than an aesthetic object.

In marriage, Evelyn and William 'teased and chaffed one another as school-boys do' – and this is precisely what brought and kept them together, since their 'temperaments [were] completely in accord' (William Richmond qtd. in Stirling 1922: 11). Revealing her unusual comradeship with men, Stirling recalls, 'when Burne-Jones, my uncle and my sister got together the fun waxed fast and furious' (Stirling 1924: 211). Evelyn apparently recognised that to be a successful woman artist, she needed to work in the company – and join the banter – of men and be seen by them as an equal. While anti-suffrage discourse warned of the masculinisation of women and the loss of feminine identity that would come with gaining the vote, female masculinity was an important part of WSPU militancy and iconography, including propaganda featuring armoured women warriors and celebrating women's physical prowess (Wingerden 1999: 104). Evelyn painted androgynous angels and powerful, warrior-like biblical, classical and mythological female figures including *Medea* (1889), *Cassandra* (1898) and *Helen of Troy* (1898). Like Mary Watts, Evelyn depicted early Christian saints and female martyrs such as *Saint Catherine of Alexandria* (c.1873–5; her first exhibited painting), *The Christian Martyr* (ND) and *St Christina Giving Her Father's Jewels to the Poor* (1904) as well as St Francis (1905). These heroic female figures seem to symbolise not only feminine spiritual freedom and social responsibility but also feminist activism. Recognising the nexus between spiritualism and feminism in the late nineteenth and early twentieth centuries, Evelyn (along with other suffrage artists) sought heroines through which to construct her own images of Victorian–Edwardian womanhood and create narratives of heroic female struggle and triumph.

Through her professional artistic practice, Evelyn demonstrated Judith Butler's theory that the term 'woman' itself is 'a term in process, a becoming, a constructing that cannot rightfully be said to originate or to end . . . open to intervention and resignification' (Butler 2006: 45). Evelyn disrupted the 'myth of a unified femininity', representing the 'multiple significations' (Butler 2006: 4) of the term 'woman' and revealing it to be plurivocal and fluid. She showed sex to be a 'performatively enacted signification (and hence not "to be")' (Butler 2006: 46). According to Butler and de Beauvoir, nobody 'is' a woman, since 'becoming a woman' is a constant cultural process of constructing that is never complete – there is no 'being' behind 'becoming' or 'doing'. Prefiguring feminist and gender theorists' call for a 'politically motivated deconstruction of the term "woman" itself' (Jones 1985: 90), Evelyn demonstrated a deconstruction of patriarchal notions of womanhood and femininity through her professional art practice. That the term, concept and image of woman was radically redefined and re-presented in the Victorian period is attested to by the highly controversial emergence of the New Woman in the nineteenth century, as embodied by Evelyn: 'a young woman from the upper or middle class concerned to reject many of the conventions of femininity and live and work on free and equal terms with the opposite sex', whose distinctive traits were her 'autonomy and her quest for personal freedom' (Cherry 1993: 75). Evelyn was an archetypal New Woman in that she entered into formal education, developed a career, married late and supported women's suffrage. Authors of New Woman novels (including Mona Caird, Sarah Grand and Olive Schreiner) offered fierce critiques of patriarchy and oppressive marriage, as do Evelyn's visual and literary texts.

Stirling records that male students at the Slade, seeing Evelyn's name heading the list of competitors for the Slade Scholarship that she won, assumed she was a male artist, not only because successful painters (especially those exhibiting large oil paintings of classical subjects in reputable galleries) were widely presumed to be men, but because the (then) gender-ambiguous name 'Evelyn' caused some confusion. That she painted under the name 'Evelyn' despite being born 'Mary Evelyn Pickering' suggests her deliberate de-feminisation. She rejected a traditionally feminine name and assumed a more androgynous name just as many nineteenth-century female authors (such as the Brontës) used androgynous pen names to avoid the prejudice and rejection of publishers and the public. William De Morgan's sister Mary De Morgan wrote her only novel under the decidedly male pseudonym William Dodson (her maternal grandfather's family name). Evelyn's (conscious or unconscious) use of a gender-ambiguous name is another example of Victorian women's strategic transgression of traditional gender boundaries and barriers.

The De Morgans met in 1883, were engaged in 1885 and married in 1887 – almost two decades after Evelyn first embarked on formal art training. Stirling recalls that when Evelyn and William first met at a fancy-dress ball through mutual friends, they 'laughed together about art, life and the eccentricities of humanity' and 'found in each other the affinity for which each had been waiting': 'Evelyn, in rose-colour, wrote herself down as "A tube of rose-madder"; [William], asked to name his costume, described it as "madder still"' (Stirling 1922: 193–4). Evelyn entered freely into a marriage that allowed her to continue to develop her artistic career. By the time she married, she had already studied art, exhibited and sold her paintings, developed an independent creative career and achieved notoriety for her work. Like the Wattses, the De Morgans represented a revolutionary approach to marital politics as a creative partnership of husband and wife who enjoyed a harmonious and mutually supportive relationship that facilitated and furthered their artistic endeavours.

Unlike many men of the Victorian period, William was fully supportive of his wife's creativity and shared her passion for art; 'their concern for the continuation of her career as well as his seems to have been a dominant characteristic of the marriage' (E. L. Smith 2002: 26). They bought the lease of a house in Chelsea – where leading suffrage campaigners lived, offering a forum for exchanges of ideas – and built a large studio for Evelyn with the understanding that for a woman to sustain an art practice after marriage, and to produce the kinds of art on which an academic reputation depended, it was essential that she had an allocated workspace or 'room of her own'. A friend of the De Morgans describes the rejuvenating effect Evelyn had on William (comparable with Mary's effect on George): '[i]t was the splendid quality of courage and the never-say-die in Evelyn . . . which revived [William's] spirits' (Barrington *c*.1922: 29). The same friend calls them 'two artists of rare and distinguished characters' who were indifferent to others' opinions or passing fashions, and claims their home (like Limnerslease for the Wattses) had 'an atmosphere of cheery restfulness' but that 'the key-note of this home was work' (Barrington *c*.1922: 71).

Combining his passion for art with his concern for women's rights, William De Morgan – like his friend and contemporary William Morris who employed women as embroiderers in his company – actively supported and facilitated the involvement of women in art and craft production through which they could gain greater creative, social and financial independence. Both William De Morgan's and Mary Watts's commercial potteries offered craft skills and employment to women and the working classes; about six women were employed at any one time to paint and decorate the tiles William designed. True to the Arts and Crafts philosophy, they both wanted to improve the quality of women workers' lives by giving them an 'empowered role in the production process' (Unwin 2004: 238) and enabling them to become trained, professional craftspeople. The highly skilled labour of female outworkers and craftswomen was essential to the Arts and Crafts industry.

Nonetheless, William's work resists association with one influence or movement. While his popular early tile designs featuring simple flowers are reminiscent of the flower patterns produced by William Morris (the influence of which can also be seen in the backgrounds of Mary Watts's 1880s portraits of her sisters), his later designs depicting fantastical animals were drawn from his own imagination; they were also inspired by his detailed knowledge of medieval manuscripts and his drawing sessions with Edward Burne-Jones. Evelyn's sister writes,

> It is difficult not to think of William De Morgan as forming one of the Pre-Raphaelite group and their following; yet although intimate with all the circle, and in a measure an outcome of the movement, with its rarefied mingling of realism, of idealism, and gorgeous, arresting fantasy, he remained a being always apart both in his output and his personality. (Stirling 1924: 224)

He was both part of the Arts and Crafts movement with its political and socialist undertones, and of the Aesthetic movement with its emphasis on beautiful decoration and rich interiors. His decorative tiles are not imbued with the same symbolic language or moral messages found in the Wattses' works, and though there is narrative and humour to be found in them, and much technical thought behind them, they do not share the deeply spiritual and socio-political lexicon that Evelyn uses in her paintings.

The De Morgans' marriage in 1887 – an unconventional wedding for which the bride wore red (Stirling 1922: 195) – legalised a partnership already made with joint exhibitions of their painting and pottery held in William's showroom on Great Marlborough Street during their engagement. Unlike the Wattses, they made no exotic honeymoon plans, but opted for a low-key trip to the Isle of Wight by train. Though the De Morgans' works are visually disparate in style and media, they share sources of inspiration (for example, the Italian Renaissance) and are complementary in their vibrant colours and shared themes or motifs (including the sea, mermaids, floral designs, birds and reptilian creatures). They both explicitly depict female alchemists in William's oil painting *The Alchemist's Daughter* (date unknown) and Evelyn's painting *The Love Potion* (1903) in a rare association of women and science, and they both painted

Tobias and the Angel (a decade apart: William *c*.1865; Evelyn in 1875), which suggests their shared interests. Evelyn and William collaborated, inspired and facilitated each other's visual and literary work in various ways. For example, William invented the complex method that he called 'The Process' by which Evelyn painted two of her paintings,[3] and Evelyn was fundamentally involved in William's creative writing process during his second career as a novelist (see Chapter 5). In a fitting fusion of visual and literary, Evelyn's design for William's headstone depicts two figures (Grief and Joy) and bears an inscription taken from one of the De Morgans' automatic writings, purporting to come from an 'Angel': 'Sorrow is only of earth; the life of the Spirit is Joy' (De Morgan and De Morgan 1909: 24). Both the De Morgans and the Wattses are buried in Surrey (Brookwood Cemetery and Watts Chapel Cemetery respectively) where the couples are united in death as in life.

While the Wattses' partnership represented a more traditional gendering of creative activities (masculine art/feminine craft) in that George was primarily a fine artist and Mary was primarily a decorative artist, the De Morgans' partnership clearly subverted the traditional art/gender binary and its masculinist hierarchical order in that Evelyn was primarily a fine artist and William was primarily a potter. William wished to become an artist and began his career as, in his own words, 'a feeble and discursive dabbler in picture-making' (qtd. in E. L. Smith 2002: 28) – a strikingly feminine description – at an old-fashioned art school in 1855 and then the Royal Academy Schools in 1859. He became disillusioned with the latter and soon realised his talents were better suited to the decorative rather than the fine arts, in which he had failed and in which his wife flourished, and he subsequently turned to stained glass and ceramic design in 1861. Thus the De Morgans' creative partnership involved an even more radical gender-role inversion than that of the Wattses, overtly subverting the traditional power relations between the sexes through professional art practice. Evelyn demonstrated the potential and capability of women to excel in territory previously unexplored by (because denied to) women, and that by transgressing traditionally female domains, women could break out of strictures imposed by patriarchal society.

This more radical gender-role inversion was not only embodied by the De Morgans' creative practices but also their economic positions (which were inextricably linked). Although Mary Watts's professional and commercial activities as a crafts practitioner who established and ran a pottery business (until her death in 1938) gave her some income, she still largely relied on her more famous husband for financial support. Yet while George Watts took portrait commissions to finance his wife's creative projects, it was Evelyn who worked on commission to sustain her husband's ceramic studio and subsidise his pottery. Evelyn contributed substantial emotional and financial support to William's enterprises, funding his struggling pottery business (until its demise in 1907) with her own capital gained partly from her success as a painter; William's firm relied on Evelyn's large cash injections.[4] While William was the foremost ceramic artist of the Arts and Crafts movement in the latter half of the nineteenth century whose work won much artistic acclaim, his ceramic work never provided a large income and he was financially dependent on Evelyn. Not only did she have more capital than him but Sir William Blake Richmond (R. A.) notes that 'she had more [business capacity] than he. His capacity as a business man was probably nil' (qtd. in Stirling 1922: 11). Similarly, George Watts's 'complete inability to manage anything like a professional career (despite his fame and success) tested [Mary's] patience' (Tromans 2016: 7). Just as Joanna Boyce was 'the head of the firm' in her artistic partnership with her husband Henry Tanworth Wells, and Louise Jopling was the 'principal income-generator' in her marriage to Joseph Jopling, so Evelyn was in her marriage to William: the woman artist was the 'mainstay of the business' (Cherry 1993: 36–7) in these atypical marital partnerships, where she appropriated traditionally male privileges. Evelyn was the dominant figure in various ways, challenging prevailing power relations and conjugal dynamics of the period.

Evelyn's financial success and supremacy was extremely unusual for a woman at a time when men had economic power, were widely considered the breadwinners and legally had control over their wives' finances up until the 1870s. Although marriage was widely considered the only means of financial security for most middle-class women in Victorian England, Evelyn was financially successful prior to this union, demonstrating the potential for women to gain financial security independently as well as to maintain it within marriage. Evelyn consciously postponed marriage and refused to conform to the customs of the Victorian marriage market; even during her relatively long engagement to William, she declined an engagement ring (Barrington *c*.1922: 34), wrote to her uncle, 'we are only engaged . . . we should not dream of getting married for at least fifteen years', and wanted 'a run-away wedding' to avoid 'a fuss' (Stirling 1922: 195).

Mary Watts arguably inhabited the 'borderlands' (Unwin 2004: 237, 245)[5] that accommodated women who acted outside the traditional private, domestic sphere to some extent but still avoided drawing adverse attention to themselves, blurring the boundaries between art and craft and public and private in a careful negotiation of social propriety. Evelyn's lifelong dedication to the (traditionally male) profession of fine art – and entrance into the public, commercial sphere of art education and exhibition – represented a bolder, clearer or more overt transgression of traditional female spaces and feminine norms. While Mary's projects (for example, her decorative domestic features and creation of a community chapel) were mainly private, not for profit and inextricably linked to the home, Evelyn painted professionally for profit – often depicting women's transgression of domestic spaces or protesting against women's domestic captivity in her artwork – and her 'relatively lucrative series of sales' (E. L. Smith 2002: 13) was in itself a remarkable achievement for a Victorian woman artist. Thus, in professional creative practice, economic position and feminist iconography, Evelyn can be seen to represent an even less conventional or more radical position than Mary.

Politics: from Captivity to Liberty

The unconventionality of the De Morgans' partnership was paralleled and reinforced by their progressive socio-political views. The De Morgans were early feminists as well as spiritualists who, as a couple, embodied more radical socio-political positions than the Wattses in their more active, public and explicit support and promotion of the women's suffrage movement. Evelyn was a supporter of the movement for women's rights and a signatory for the Declaration in Favour of Women's Suffrage in 1889 (alongside artists Emily Osborn and Louise Jopling, writers Olive Schreiner and Augusta Webster, and philanthropist Josephine Butler) – in reply to the same appeal against women's suffrage that Mary refused to sign. Evelyn later added her name to a similar petition sponsored in 1897 by the Central Committee of the National Society for Women's Suffrage.

Unlike his father, who refused to 'join political agitations, or associations for procuring changes in the political machine' ([1867 letter to J. S. Mill] qtd. in S. De Morgan 1882: 370), William served as Vice-President of the Men's League for Women's Suffrage (founded 1907) in 1913, overtly supporting the campaign. A newspaper reports the League's passionately worded 'Men's Memorial' sent to the Prime Minister, signed by William among others including the Earl of Lytton and Israel Zangwill – whose work was read by the Wattses (*Yorkshire Post and Leeds Intelligencer* 15 July 1913). Another newspaper article on 'Women and the Vote' lists William along with George Meredith and George Bernard Shaw among the 'literary men . . . coming forward to help women in their arduous fight for justice . . . who have determined that woman shall have all the help they can give towards gaining their freedom' (*Berwickshire News and General Advertiser* 21 March 1911). This reveals William's high profile as a male suffragist writer at this time. Stirling not only claims that William was 'in favour of the feminine vote' but also that 'some of his royalties found their way into the coffers of the W. S. P. U.' (1922: 334). William's interest in experimental artistic techniques and scientific innovations evidently extended to his support of progressive socio-political movements; he embraced constructive change.

William's mother Sophia (in addition to being a clairvoyant medium) was a social activist, abolitionist, friend of George Eliot, and an early supporter of women's education and suffrage, dedicated to improving the conditions of workhouses, asylums and prisons.[6] William's father Augustus was friends with John Stuart Mill, and he signed a women's suffrage petition, though he refused Mill's invitation to join the committee of the National Society for Women's Suffrage in 1867 (S. De Morgan 1882: 370). William's sister Mary was a suffragist, acquainted with those in the Garrett Fawcett circle. William's parents held progressive views on various issues, and likewise, Evelyn and William's interests were invariably on the side of progress and reform in accordance with the humanist tradition, which emphasised the value and agency of human beings (individually and collectively) over established doctrine, custom or faith. Similar to the way in which George made Mary more of 'a radical' in their early years of marriage, William's progressive and liberal upbringing undoubtedly influenced Evelyn in their early years of marriage; this highlights the crucial role of husbands in their influence (igniting and stoking or else dampening and extinguishing) on their wives' socio-political stances. Evelyn not only championed progressive causes such as the education of the working classes (a task taken on personally by Mary Watts) but also expressed her social concerns about constraints on women, and portrayed her distinctly feminist vision of new freedom for women, in her art.

Around the time that William published his novel *An Affair of Dishonour* (1910) he was asked to pronounce an opinion on what he called 'another "Affair of Dishonour"' – the 'exclusion of women from the franchise', 'a flagrant injustice, due to the exclusion of women from the electorate' – at a time when 'the question was rending the social and political world with a rancour' (Stirling 1922: 334–5). William entered into a public discourse contesting double standards and female oppression. He expressed his opinions in the press, and wrote to Member of Parliament and suffrage campaigner George Lansbury in a letter of 1913 (the same year that Mary Watts held a suffrage meeting at Limnerslease) on the 'amendments for the inclusion of women in the Franchise Bill'. Like Mary, William's words suggest his sympathy with militancy. In his letter, William recognises the 'broad merits of the question' (suffragettes had previously been arrested merely for asking it in the House of Commons) and argues that Prime Minister Mr Asquith's refusal to hear a 'peaceful deputation of ladies . . . brought "militancy" into existence'. He urges Lansbury (who publically denounced Asquith for the cruel treatment of imprisoned suffragettes) to focus on the subject and 'forget those pillar letter-boxes' famously damaged by suffragettes. His passionate anti-patriarchal view on the controversial subject is evident in his rhetoric:

> Above all it is true now, as heretofore and always, that a large proportion of males are unfitted by the inspirations of their own carnal impulses for legislating for the feminine half of Creation; and nevertheless, half brute half imbecile as they are in all that relates to women, have a voice in the decision of crucial questions that affect the well-being of maids wives and mothers – and of posterity! . . . At least let the wives and mothers of the proposed corpses in the next War have a voice in the National decisions that relate to it! Let them have their say in a system which bids fair. (W. De Morgan 1913: 12 January)

William's letter, echoing contemporary WSPU literature, may have influenced Lansbury's subsequent conduct: he publically supported violent militant action at a WSPU rally around three months later (26 April 1913), for which he was sentenced to three months' imprisonment, during which he went on hunger strike in solidarity with suffragettes. William was not one of the 'Chelsea men artists, always conservative, [who] were not in general supporters of the women's suffrage movement' (Crawford 1999: 131), and his stance was much more radical than George Watts's comparatively conservative claim to being a 'real liberal'. Despite his pacifist principles, William's letters show a surprising bloodthirstiness induced by war: 'I am sorry to say that I am barbarous by nature and catch myself gloating over slaughter – slaughter of Germans, of course!' ([October 1914 to Phelps] Phelps 1917: 441). He became preoccupied with devising ways to increase enemy casualties to the extent that his literary activity decreased ([December 1915 to Phelps] Phelps 1917: 441).

A greater radicalism can also be detected in Evelyn's work when compared to Mary's. Evelyn developed a more overtly feminist iconographic vocabulary, which dialogised more distinctly with the suffrage discourse of her time. Her recognition of the politics of culturally constructed categories serving to sustain separate spheres and sexual difference is evident in her politically charged paintings of women straining for liberty in domestic spaces. Female captivity is a strikingly explicit, persistent and pervasive theme in Evelyn's literary and visual work, with which she was preoccupied throughout her life and career. Her plethora of paintings depicting the confinement of women – most notably *Hope in the Prison of Despair* (*c*.1887) (Fig. 2.2), *The Captives* (*c*.1888), *The Prisoner* (1907–8) (Fig. 2.3) and *The Gilded Cage* (*c*.1919) (Fig. 2.4) have been previously perceived by critics as a series of spiritualist allegories of the 'soul's imprisonment' (E. L. Smith 2002: 115) or the 'bondage of the spirit' (Yates 1996: 62). Yet they can be re-read as feminist statements about the

Figure 2.2 *Hope in the Prison of Despair*, Evelyn De Morgan, *c*.1887, Getty Images.

Figure 2.3 *The Prisoner*, Evelyn De Morgan, 1907–8, © De Morgan Collection, courtesy of the De Morgan Foundation.

Figure 2.4 *The Gilded Cage*, Evelyn De Morgan, *c*.1919, © De Morgan Collection, courtesy of the De Morgan Foundation.

bondage of specifically female rather than 'non-gendered' human embodiment. These paintings represent women incarcerated within feminised bodies and/or traditionally female (domestic or private) spaces, and Evelyn consistently represents prisoners as female protagonists. Evelyn, like the Wattses and other suffrage artists, produced allegorical female figures and drew on personifications of concepts and 'cardinal virtues' which had been 'symbolised from time immemorial by a woman's form' (Tickner 1989: 51) in order to engage with women's issues.

Hope in the Prison of Despair, one of Evelyn's earliest allegories of female imprisonment, portrays the emancipation of woman by woman: a liberated female figure brings light to an imprisoned female figure and guides her to freedom. This image is strikingly similar to the 'Votes for Women Fellowship' suffragette badge which shows a woman holding a lantern aloft, surrounded by the words 'To Spread the Light'. Evelyn's painting is reminiscent of her early verse, including the lines 'Hope is upward striving, / Seeking realms of light' in 'Death' (*c*.1869–70), and an untitled poem of 1868:

> Slowly the iron gates unclosed
> And a vision of joy and light
> Burst through the bars all darkness dispelling
> And death and its horrors all vanished from sight.

The De Morgans' automatic writing publication also contains a message purporting to be from an 'Angel' named 'Hope' who is 'bright, strong, free' (1909: 37, 44, 50). The allegorical personification of Hope as a woman in Evelyn's painting parallels and was perhaps inspired by George Watts's *Hope* painted around a year before. Yet Evelyn's Hope does not sit blindfolded and vulnerable but stands upright, strong and protective behind the female prisoner hunched in despair, lighting her way to liberation after having apparently unchained her. Thus female passivity is replaced by female agency, and Evelyn's is a 'hope' specifically for female liberation. While George's Hope is a solitary figure in a desolate setting, Evelyn's Hope offers the possibility of redemption and liberation through female interaction and companionship. The newly liberated woman occupies a liminal space as she approaches the daylight streaming through the window but 'resides for this brief, fixed moment in a [physical and] psychological state caught between light and shadow, freedom and confinement' (E. L. Smith 2002: 111); she can be seen to represent the shifting socio-political position of nineteenth-century women and the progression of the women's rights movement.

A conviction in the transformative power or potential of the female figure pervades Evelyn's paintings, which envision a liberated future for women.

In both *The Prisoner* and *The Gilded Cage*, painted during the feminist agitation of the early twentieth century, the tension between captivity and liberty corresponds to interior (closed, artificial) and exterior (open, natural) spaces: the woman looks longingly out of the barred window at a wide world beyond the claustrophobic confines of the room in which she stands. This visual imagery is prefigured by an untitled 1869 poem by Evelyn: 'To pine in a dungeon is now my fate, . . . And in vain I seek through the iron grate / To sooth my straining wearied eye . . . With a glimpse of the ocean, the earth, or sky.' In both paintings, the woman gazes towards the distant peaks or hilly horizon representative of freedom; the woman with clasped hands in the former painting seems to be praying for liberty, while the woman in the latter painting reaches up towards the sky.

The avian imagery in *The Gilded Cage* is more overtly imbued with feminist significance than in Mary Watts's work featuring symbolic birds. In Evelyn's painting, the wild bird soaring freely in the sky, symbolising liberty, is juxtaposed with the caged pet bird symbolic of woman's domestic captivity. The visual parallel between the confined woman and the caged bird is emphasised by their lifted necks and open mouths, which suggest the woman trapped in this suffocating space and relationship is gasping for air. Like the pet bird, she is a 'kept woman' dressed in finery and living in luxury that is nevertheless stifling and lifeless in contrast to the freedom of the wild bird. This painting can be seen to represent the entrapment of Victorian women in domesticity, and women's struggle for liberation from such oppression. It alludes to the avian association or identification of women in much nineteenth-century art and literature, such as Walter Deverell's paintings *A Pet* (exhibited 1853) and *The Grey Parrot* (1852–3), Charlotte Brontë's proto-feminist novel *Jane Eyre* (1847), and Henrik Ibsen's proto-feminist play *A Doll's House* (1879), where it signifies either woman's obedience and captivity or resistance and liberty. Entering into the same metaphorical discourse in her diary, Mary Watts suggests the liberatory power of inner strength: 'no doubt the bird within does lift the cage' (1891: 10 June).

The Gilded Cage not only portrays the 'cushioned confinement of middle-class domestication' (E. L. Smith 2002: 117) but also seems to be a specifically conjugal bondage – a 'wedlock' in which woman is traditionally perceived as man's property, possession or pet. As the public debate around women's rights escalated, writers and critics of the institution of marriage described women's position within it as one of captivity or slavery: John Stuart Mill attacks marriage laws which enslave women in his essay 'The Subjection of Women' (1869) and early feminist Mona Caird draws parallels between Victorian women and slaves in *The Morality of Marriage and Other Essays on the Status and Destiny of Woman* (1897). Through her painting, Evelyn participated in the public expression of concerns in visual and literary texts about the relations between the sexes, particularly in marriage, over the late nineteenth and early twentieth centuries. Her motifs of chains, manacles, bars and ropes in her various images of imprisoned women serve a radically different function from the 'thinly disguised erotic bondage depicted in so many late nineteenth-century images by male artists of nude slaves' (E. L. Smith 2002: 120). Rather than conforming to and continuing this male tradition of painting titillating, eroticised images of bound or incarcerated women, Evelyn's images of female confinement such as *The Prisoner* and *The Gilded Cage* can be seen to serve a feminist function to expose and condemn the oppression and objectification of women.

This is more overtly visualised in *The Prisoner*, in which the woman's thick cuff-like gold bracelet on one wrist is linked by a chain to an iron circlet on her other wrist to form a manacle. The links of the chain morph from gold into black in a more literal representation of her imprisonment, exemplifying Evelyn's striking, conspicuous symbolism. This is reinforced by the gold chain across her chest, the silk headscarf tied around her head and the pearl-studded hairnet. The luxurious clothing and jewellery of Evelyn's female figures signifies their bondage, both in the sense that Victorian women were incarcerated by restrictive feminine fashions – the woman's dress in *The Prisoner* is in 'the height of Aesthetic fashion' (E. L. Smith 2002: 113) – and in terms of the bondage of materialism (or material wealth).

In *The Gilded Cage*, the man who is apparently the young woman's much older husband is also a 'father figure' representative of the patriarchy that forces women to conform to restrictive norms or social conventions and male ideals of femininity. Yet Evelyn's own remarkably unrestrictive marriage, despite being to a considerably older man, was a radical departure from traditional power relations between the sexes. William himself addresses 'that curious subject, Matrimony . . . marriage considered as harness' which 'determines the relations of the two sexes, or upsets them' in his novel *The Old Man's Youth*, completed by Evelyn (De Morgan and De Morgan

1920: 402, 170). To read *The Gilded Cage* as autobiographical – as a kind of double portrait – would be to misread the De Morgans' relationship, though it reflects Evelyn's own early resistance to marriage according to Stirling (1922: 181) as well as her empathy for, and sense of community with, other women of her time for whom conjugal bondage was a reality. *The Gilded Cage* does not reflect Evelyn's personal life but rather her social concerns and political views, engaging with contemporary discourses and debates about marriage and gender.

Numerous paintings by Evelyn focus on women at moments of existential crisis. The female figures in *The Gilded Cage* and *The Prisoner* are not as passive and submissive as Victorian women were widely expected to be: their restless, expressive hand gestures in addition to their intense, longing gazes out of the window suggest their agitation, discontent and ardent desires for liberation. In *The Gilded Cage*, broken jewellery (used to adorn women in Rossetti's Aesthetic works) and a discarded book lie at the feet of the woman who has apparently thrown them to the floor in a rage and now stands in dishevelled dress at the window, looking out and reaching up, desperate for freedom. She is turned away from the male gaze, suggesting both protagonist's and painter's rejection of oppressive ornamentation and feminisation. Despite her confinement, her nonconformist attitude and desire to break away from patriarchal norms is evident. This is something Jan Marsh apparently overlooks in her argument that 'the enclosed rooms in which these ladies live, looking out on inviting sunlit landscapes . . . are surely metaphors of woman's condition, signifying the docile, passive . . . domestic role that dominated Victorian ideas of femininity' (Marsh 1987: 152). On the contrary, Evelyn's female figures can be seen to embody the increasing social unrest in Victorian–Edwardian England induced by women's growing demand for social and political liberation. Indeed, the WSPU's smashing of windows and motto 'Deeds not Words' seems symbolised by the smashed jewellery and discarded open book at the woman's feet in *The Gilded Cage*. The female figure does not fall into the Victorian categories of womanhood laid out by Marsh as 'woman as desirable, woman as chaste, woman as dutiful, woman as witch' (Marsh 1987: 9). Rather, Evelyn depicts a new type of woman in response to the shifting socio-political climate: woman as rebellious, resistant, resilient. She makes the 'feminist body visible' (Green 1997: 5).

Disturbance and conflict, present in Evelyn's works as sites of female struggle, were central to the suffragettes' campaign. After famously being arrested and charged with disorderly behaviour for unfurling 'Votes for Women' banners at an election meeting where Winston Churchill was speaking, leading WSPU member Christabel Pankhurst stated in 1905, 'we must be disorderly. There is no other way whereby we can put forward our claims to political justice' (qtd. in Housego and Storey 2012: 15–16). In *The Gilded Cage*, the disorderly, defiant woman is the active force standing with raised arms in an 'energized diagonal' (E. L. Smith 2002: 119) while the man sits passively, and her angled position disrupts the division of the space by the barred window into two halves or spheres. She turns away from the traditionally female domain of 'stagnant domesticity' towards the 'positive energies of creative expression' (E. L. Smith 2002: 121) symbolised by the wild bird and dancing gypsies. Far from being 'docile' (Marsh 1987: 152) or 'droop[ing] in resignation' (E. L. Smith 2002: 13), she seems desperate and determined to break out of domestic captivity and break away from restrictive social norms and gender roles. This representation of woman as actively striving for liberty is a striking contrast to the passivity or 'permanent collapse' of many 'late Victorian languid women reclining in cushioned comfort' (E. L. Smith 2002: 126) in paintings by Dante Gabriel Rossetti and Frederic Leighton, apparently unaware of – or content to remain in – their confinement. Evelyn's work can be seen to dialogise with the early feminist discourse of the late Victorian period concerning 'a woman's search for autonomy and for the physical and psychic space needed for independent action' (E. L. Smith 2002: 109).

Evelyn alludes to the male Pre-Raphaelite tradition of dressing up women in rich dresses and jewellery to become aesthetic objects; these muses, models and mistresses are prisoners of Pre-Raphaelite style and perception, trapped in the 'gilded cage of the Pre-Raphaelite picture frame' (Marsh 1987: 152). Evelyn to some extent worked within the late Pre-Raphaelite and Aesthetic movements in which her work is historically placed. Her combination of precise brushwork, polished surface, vibrant palette and detailed drapery is similar to that of Burne-Jones and Rossetti, showing how she drew on the work of her predecessors in technique and style. Yet she developed her own idiosyncratic iconography, and the substance and symbolism of her art makes it more comparable with George Watts's allegorical work as well as early feminist imagery. Her employment of excessive accessories, elaborate costume, synthetic fabrics and gaudy golds in *The Prisoner* and *The Gilded Cage* can be seen to satirise or criticise the abundant use of these motifs by the PRB in their paintings of idealised, eroticised women. Evelyn seems to allude to these in order to critique and challenge ideological (patri-archal) assumptions behind such portrayals. Evelyn worked within the Pre-Raphaelite tradition but to different ends, since her art had a feminist function, combining an Aesthetic style with images pro-moting female emancipation. She consistently re-presents women as embodied subjects striving for liberty.

While Rossetti sexualised the female body with his voluptuous, provocative 'stunners', George Watts – whom Evelyn greatly admired – intended his allegorical female figures to symbolise ideas for social edification and female liberation rather than salacious-ness or eroticism. George's painting *The Wife of Plutus* (c.1877–86), which depicts a woman grasping pearls and jewels amidst rich silks as she writhes on a pillow with her face twisted away from the viewer, was intended to convey the 'sickness and lack of fulfilment wealth might bring' in a condemnation of the 'growing materialism of the Victorian age'. 'Compositionally' George's picture is related to his *Study with the Peacock's Feathers* (c.1862–5) and associ-ated in its rich colouring, decorative elements, luxuriant setting and sensuous reclining model with Rossetti's Aesthetic pictures of the 1860s. Yet 'programmatically' (A. Smith 2001: 141) it is aligned with his own meaningful allegorical paintings critiquing wealth, which influenced Evelyn.

The tension between monetary and spiritual wealth, or Mam-monism and spiritualism, plutocracy and democracy, is explored by both George's and Evelyn's art. Evelyn's painting *The Worship of Mammon* (1909) (Fig. 2.5), which recalls George's earlier painting *Mammon* (1884–5), criticises materialism and wealth without moral responsibility, and the moral message has a feminist function in both works. That both George and Evelyn personify Mammon as a pow-erful male giant or monster holding moneybags, with a powerless woman at his feet, can be seen to represent and indict a masculinist society in which monetary wealth was a male privilege. There were comparatively very few job opportunities for Victorian women, who were widely perceived and treated as domestic, aesthetic or sexual objects that could be owned, bought and sold. George's and Evelyn's paintings can be seen to depict the oppression of women in a patri-archal Victorian society, reflecting the artists' similar stances; such works by Evelyn are more symbolist than Pre-Raphaelite or Aes-thetic, and more akin to George's work than Rossetti's.

Nonetheless, the dynamic pose and upturned face of the woman clutching at the legs of a giant muscular male statue in Evelyn's *The Worship of Mammon* seems less defeatist and hopeless than

Figure 2.5 *The Worship of Mammon*, Evelyn De Morgan, 1909,
© De Morgan Collection, courtesy of the De Morgan Foundation.

the lifeless naked woman slumped face down under the more grotesque Mammon's paw-like hand in George's work (which focuses
on male monstrosity). While Evelyn's painting has been seen to
represent the replacement of the love of money with the love of
Mammon himself, the female Mammon-worshipper (the focus of
the painting) is presented sympathetically. The starred blue sky
over mountainous terrain signifies hope and redemption in contrast to the landscape of fire and destruction revealed behind the
curtain in George's painting (reinforced by the red and gold palette
and the skulls decorating Mammon's throne). This perhaps reflects
Evelyn's greater optimism, hope or desire for female liberation and
her stronger feminist position. Her work, at first glance, looks like
Aesthetic movement painting and yet she is left out of most scholarship on 'art for art's sake' because her feminism – as revealed
though an analysis of her female-dominated allegorical imagery
and the overtly feminist elements of her iconography – complicates
any straightforward association of her with it.

There is an evident tension and implied transition between the states of captivity and liberty in Evelyn's works, representing the shifting socio-political position of women. Both women in *The Gilded Cage* and *The Prisoner* stand in a liminal space (between two places or spaces and states of being) at the window. This serves as a 'transitional device' – an opening in the wall of the symbolic or literal prison connecting inside and outside, representing the potential for liberation – which 'confirms that we are witnessing in that painting the very moment of rupture' (E. L. Smith 2002: 115–16). While this contrast between interior and exterior, glimpsed through the apertures, 'carried an ideological separation of the spaces of masculinity and femininity' (Cherry 1993: 190), these women are depicted on the threshold of the liberation they actively desire or attempt to experience. The window, door, border or threshold – that 'peculiarly Victorian image of barrier, of lines crossed and partition established, determined space' (Armstrong 1993: 356) – is a recurring image in Evelyn's and Mary's works, and was an incipient feature of suffrage iconography featuring women locked outside doors (political exclusion) or locked inside gates (political oppression). Evelyn's art in particular offers a consistently vivid expression to the sense of female exclusion and oppression that formed an essential part of feminist discourse at the *fin de siècle*, a sense that her works more than any of her contemporaries embodied, functioning themselves as windows into Victorian women's experience.

In the political context of the period in which they were produced, Evelyn's paintings of female imprisonment foregrounding the tension between captivity and liberty can be seen to protest against the political bondage of womanhood and promote the women's suffrage campaign. They seem to allude to militant suffragettes who smashed windows and chained themselves to railings in protest against the legal position of women and willingly went to prison for their actions – an incarceration that was crucial to their fight for political liberation. While the suffragists of the NUWSS maintained their peaceful pressure for women's suffrage, the disorderly behaviour of the suffragettes of the WSPU – which broke away from the NUWSS in 1903 to undertake more militant action – led to many arrests which attracted unprecedented media interest (even national news coverage), public attention and sympathy for the women's suffrage movement. Imprisonment became a means of protest against and resistance to patriarchal society, a martyrdom to be celebrated, a powerful campaign advertisement and an important feminist strategy for female emancipation. Evelyn's paintings of female prisoners are comparable with the likes of suffragette Sylvia Pankhurst's and Katie Gliddon's sketches of women and Holloway Prison cells, and Laurence Housman's famous 'From Prison to Citizenship' WSPU banner (depicting a symbolic woman in front of prison bars with a broken chain in her hands) carried at a large Prisoners' Pageant of 1911.[7] They are comparable with the numerous representations of women as victims used in the suffrage campaign's 'most militant imagery', which 'depict what made the Militant Woman militant' (Tickner 1989: 212).

Suffragette artists used prison-related symbolic imagery to promote their campaign, and suffragettes often wore pieces of chain to represent their oppression (as pendants, pins or brooches, commissioned by the WSPU as fundraising and promotional items around 1909). The chains, bars and handcuffs used in Evelyn's symbolist lexicon to reference captivity and liberty can be seen to draw on, dialogise with and contribute to this early feminist iconographic vocabulary. A badge designed by Sylvia Pankhurst (1909–10) for the suffrage campaign depicts a woman breaking free, stepping through a gate with iron bars, over heavy chains, carrying a 'Votes for Women' streamer and surrounded by birds flying from captivity into the open space symbolic of liberty. This can be seen to parallel elements of Evelyn's *Hope in the Prison of Despair* and *The Gilded Cage*. The Holloway Prison Brooch also designed by Sylvia Pankhurst (*c*.1909) comprises a portcullis symbol of the House of Commons superimposed with a broad arrow (typical of those marked on prison clothing) which was presented to suffragette ex-prisoners and proudly worn by them. Elements of this are prefigured by Evelyn's *Hope in the Prison of Despair* and *The Prisoner* in which the handcuffed woman stands within the stone walls of a castle looking through a grid of iron bars. Dolls dressed as suffragette prisoners were made and sold by supporters to raise funds for the campaign, and a special WSPU medal was made as a mark of recognition for those who served prison sentences for militancy; the first of these medals were presented in 1909, soon after Evelyn's painting *The Prisoner* was completed. In this context, Evelyn's paintings of female captivity can in fact be seen to signify women's brave fight for liberty, and engage with debates surrounding the status of suffragettes as political prisoners.

Evelyn's paintings – the vast majority of which depict female protagonists in pivotal positions, transitional states or liminal spaces – can be seen to make an important Victorian–Edwardian statement about the evolving roles and shifting socio-political positions of women from domestic to artistic, passive to active, feminine to feminist. Evelyn was part of the world of the British avant-garde, but did not just produce art for art's sake; her paintings have psychological depth, offering insight into the interiority and individual struggles of her female figures. Evelyn employed the female body not only as an allegorical signifier, as George Watts did, but also as a model for socio-political transformation from incarceration to liberation. Evelyn's images of imprisoned women who 'struggle against the boundaries of a restrictive society' are juxtaposed with her images of women freed from such constraints who 'operate as powerful and assertive agents . . . actively in control of their destinies' (E. L. Smith 2002: 13) such as *The Storm Spirits* and *Daughters of the Mist*. Her art can be seen to reflect a tension between female captivity and liberty as well as to trace a (not unproblematic) movement from the former to the latter. Where previous critics have categorised her work into spiritualist allegories, depictions of sacred heroines, war paintings and history paintings, this book aims to explore the more unique, unusual and understudied feminist elements of her literary and visual discourse in depth and isolation for the first time, show-ing how it can be understood as part of the early feminist discourse that developed over the late nineteenth and early twentieth centuries. Evelyn's art combined aspects of late Pre-Raphaelitism, symbolism, Aestheticism, Victorian classicism and, significantly, feminism.

These two chapters have shown how the Wattses and the De Morgans facilitated and advanced each other's professional cre-ative practices, and actively supported and promoted greater gender equality and female emancipation, reclaiming Mary and Evelyn as influential creative partners, cultural producers and early feminists.

Notes

1. However, this is unverified as there is no documentary evidence and no list of pupils for the time when Mary supposedly attended.
2. In 1874 Evelyn was awarded a scholarship at the Slade, and she received significant awards for her work from the antique, drawing and paint-ing from life, and composition (Gordon 1996: 9).
3. 'The Process': the colours were ground in glycerine and spirit and when the painting was finished the glycerine was sucked out by a sort of poultice on the back of the picture, and the picture was finished with transparent oil-colour. Evelyn's painting *The Soul's Prison House* (1888) was produced using this method.
4. The establishment of the business partnership between William and Halsey Ralph Ricardo in 1888 involved the additional capital of £8,000 provided by equal contributions from Evelyn and Ricardo (Gordon 1996: 11).

5. These 'borderlands' (originally Anne Digby's term), formed at the site of overlapping spheres, accommodated nineteenth-century women who pushed the boundaries of the traditionally female domestic sphere – acting both within it and to some extent outside it – without drawing adverse attention to themselves.

6. Sophia De Morgan's interests and aims thus overlapped with those of prison and social reformer Elizabeth Fry, and prefigured the campaign of militant suffragette Lady Constance Lytton.

7. See also Mary Lowndes's design for Elizabeth Fry Banner, Women's Library Suffrage Banners Collection, 234124.2 (details including prison bars, ball and chain, sunrays); Cicely Hamilton's *Beware! A Warning to Suffragists* ('rhyme book', ASL, 1909); Laurence Housman's Suffrage Banner postcard (*c.*1910) (featuring a woman walking out of prison gates, broad arrows and the words 'bring the prisoner out of captivity'); A. L. F. Leop's postcard *Votes For Women Means Their Emancipation From These Shackles* (1907–22), Women's Library Suffrage Collection; and 'For All the Prisoners and Captives', *Votes for Women*, 28 November 1913: 126.

Chapter 3

Self/Portraits

This chapter explores the Wattses' and the De Morgans' self-portraits and portraits of each other as well as of their famous contemporaries in order to examine the construction of artistic identities, gender-role inversion within creative partnerships, and the self-fashioning of suffragists. It explores public and private self/portraits (that is, self-portraits and/or portraits) in the form of neglected paintings, sketches and photographs in which images and perceptions of these figures as individuals and as couples are built. It also compares the Wattses' and the De Morgans' self/portraits with those of their contemporaries, placing them in a wider context to reveal their standpoints and focuses. It explores the gender politics of portraiture and shows how their self/portraits fit into the tradition of Victorian portraiture. A consideration of these figures' relationships to self-image and self-promotion offers a more nuanced understanding not only of their characters and identities but also of the various extents to which they supported the women's suffrage movement (actively or tacitly, publicly or privately, visibly or invisibly). Central to this chapter is the argument that Mary and Evelyn subverted the hierarchical male artist/female muse dynamic more typical of their time through their portraits of their husbands, and de/re-constructed Victorian notions of gender through their self/portraits. Both women 'seize the narrative of the traditional relationship between artist and model by asserting the right of her gaze' (Mancoff 2012: 14). Both life writing (see Chapter 4) and the painting of self-portraits by these women, and Victorian women more broadly, can be seen as assertions of identity and political acts which challenged dominant ideologies and the patriarchal presupposition that the only life worth recording or representing was that of a 'great man'.

The Wattses' Self/Portraits

Portraiture played a larger part in the Wattses' than the De Morgans' *oeuvres*. This reflects the Wattses' greater interest in the practice of portrait painting (Mary in her early years, when she planned to pursue a career in portraiture) and their deep concern with the immortalisation of influential visionaries, thinkers and creators in art for posterity and social edification. This is embodied by George's portrait collection of his famous contemporaries, the 'Hall of Fame' (bequeathed to the National Portrait Gallery for posterity in 1895), featuring artists, writers and women's rights supporters. Self/portraiture helped to shape the Wattses' own artistic identities and public images as well as those of their contemporaries, promoting figures and causes they personally supported. I aim to show how self/portraiture held personal and political significance for the Wattses by exploring their self-portraits and portraits of each other, which paint pictures of them as individuals and as a couple, before focusing on the feminist function of George's portraiture.

The Wattses had a somewhat problematic relationship with publicity and self-image. An interviewer describes George as 'timid, nervous, shy to excess' with journalists: 'talking . . . to the public, is the last thing he desires to do, unless it be by his paintings'; George refuses to provide the interviewer with the 'abomination' of an autograph, and Mary would 'not allow' the interviewer to write about her own role in the HAIA (Friederichs 1895: 76, 81, 78). Yet while Mary records George saying, 'I wish I could just work on quietly & never show anything' (1891: 21 April), the numerous self-portraits he produced show his interest in – and even preoccupation with – self-image. George was considered one of the finest portraitists of the Victorian era, producing a plethora of portraits during his lifetime; he founded a successful career on portrait commissions (by aristocratic and public figures) and society connections.

Mary claimed not to 'care for celebrities' when asked by George Meredith: 'No – I said simply & felt a little hurt – I have not much temptation not being brilliant myself'. Yet she admits relishing the company of her husband's celebrated friends, writing, 'to be with them is to gain a step in the climb towards fuller & larger life' (M. Watts 1893: 5 April). Mary's purported lack of brilliance seems disingenuous, since her diaries elsewhere display her creative ambition and self-assertion despite her public reverence to her husband and other famous male figures, and she had already achieved a great deal as an artist by this time.

Though she avoided appearing fame-hungry and was careful to maintain public modesty, her diaries document her keen integration into George's social circle. Before her marriage, Mary painted self-portraits as well as numerous portraits of female relatives – for personal interest rather than exhibition, although at least one was commissioned (McMahon 2013: 33). She also posed for photographs with and without her husband, developing an interest in photographic portraiture, and worked almost obsessively to preserve her husband's memory in various media, producing monuments to them both. An oil portrait of Mary by C. H. Thompson (1887), her own portrait painting, and the book *Portraits of Men and Women* (Granby 1900) were found in her bedroom and dressing room at Limnerslease after her death. The Wattses took themselves seriously as artists whose work had meaningful messages and an important social role; they used self/portraits, which helped shape their public personas, as strategies to indirectly promote their own ideas and campaigns.

The Wattses' unconventional creative partnership is manifest in their portraits of each other, which provide a unique insight into their perceptions of one another, and reinforce the portrayal of the couple in Mary's diaries (where her entries provide character sketches). Though the majority of Mary's surviving portraits were produced in the years before her marriage, her portraits of her husband – and her diary entries detailing the progression of his portraits – show her continued interest in portraiture. Mary's representations of George include her pen and ink caricature of him as *An Epsom Beggar, Drawn from Life by the Beggar's Wife* (30 May 1895) (Fig. 3.1), and her two small watercolour profile portraits of *G. F. Watts in Bed* (24 and 25 October 1894) (Fig. 3.2) – one of which she kept in her bedroom until her death, indicating its personal value.[1] These two watercolour portraits, dated on two immediately successive days, are almost identical except for the added figure of herself in one of them, which is framed by a painted border. She painted herself into it to create a unique, intimate double portrait of the Wattses, reflecting her dual role as a loving wife and a devoted artist. Viewed together, the two scenarios create a narrative imagined by Mary: George nursed by her in sickness; and George in solitary sickness or death. The Wattses' awareness of the inevitable pain of parting in death is evident in Mary's diaries, as is her awareness of her vital role in George's later life, and these watercolours further show that this preoccupied her thought.

Mary's portraits dared to parody and subvert George's powerful public image as Britain's premier portrait painter. This is an image George perpetuated in his regal self-portrait of 1903–4 where he has 'the air of a Renaissance master' (Gould 1998: 17), and his

Figure 3.1 *An Epsom Beggar*, Mary Watts, 1895, Watts Gallery Trust.

Figure 3.2 *G. F. Watts in Bed*, Mary Watts, 1894, Private Collection: Iain Cameron.

self-portrait of 1864 in which his black hat – held out upturned for change in *An Epsom Beggar* – is firmly on his head as he sits staring sternly back at the viewer. Mary's *An Epsom Beggar* had a serious purpose in showing her husband begging for money for the HAIA, specifically promoting and raising funds for her own project and supporting a wider Home Arts Movement involving women at all levels. She drew and sent the portrait to their wealthy friend Archibald Primrose, Earl of Rosebery and (at the time) Liberal Prime Minister, at his Epsom house The Durdans (where he entertained political colleagues and royalty) on the same day that the Compton Parish Council discussed her letters offering 'on behalf of Mr Watts' to build a chapel on the land bought for a new cemetery.[2] By August 1895 Mary had made a model of the chapel, while the first clay modelling class at Limnerslease (November 1895) produced symbolic tiles she designed for the chapel. George painted portraits on commission to support her chapel project. Mary's remarkably lifelike sketch reveals her largely unacknowledged drawing skills (showcased in her sketchbooks and illustrations) and confidence in her ability to depict her husband even after noting that it was 'impossible for those who know Signor well to make anything like' (1891: 1 October). It shows her shrewd wit and her canny, tactical use of her famous husband's widely recognised image as a powerful tool to further and fulfil her own artistic ambitions. She used her husband's high profile, and the respect he commanded as an artist, to her advantage. While her self-definition as 'Mrs. Watts, Wife of G. F. Watts, O.M.R.A.' in the carving on the altar of the completed chapel suggests her deference, her allusion to her famous husband, whose name she worked under long after his death, could be seen as a self-advertising strategy rather than a self-effacing tribute. It facilitated her entrance into the public sphere of business and politics, and benefitted her social prestige, whilst reinforcing her respectable image as a doting wife.

Mary's caricature depicting George as a beggar embodies an ironic, irreverent gender-role inversion in which the powerful male artist is rendered powerless by his wife who assumes the (traditionally male) position of artist–creator. This in itself can be seen as a powerful comment in its demonstration of female artistic agency and ability. This bold sketch undermines a perception of Mary as a self-sacrificing wife who simply worshipped her husband, and of him as a grand monarchical figure. Mary's caricature is comparable with William De Morgan's cartoons and those in *Punch* (which the Wattses read); it also prefigures covers of NUWSS journal the *Common Cause* featuring caricatures of anti-suffrage men (3 February 1910:

Vol. 1, No. 43) and suffrage propaganda produced by the ASL – with which Mary would have been familiar, and where her talent would undoubtedly have been valued. The use of humour in the promotion of a cause is present in Mary's sketch as in suffrage art, though Mary's is not satirical; rather, her caricature illustrates the comradeship of the Wattses in their conjugal creative partnership and support of the same schemes.

A gender-role inversion is also registered in Mary's small, detailed watercolour study of George in a state of absolute passivity as an ill, elderly man, bed-bound and propped up on pillows, and especially in the version where she is present. Her figure which rises up over him, with her face positioned directly above his, highlights through contrast his powerless position. In its subversion of patriarchal binaries (male/female, active/passive, powerful/powerless), this double portrait represents their unconventional relationship. On the one hand, this painting ostensibly presents the couple in conformist gender terms: George is foregrounded while Mary stands behind him; the relative size of the figures gives precedence to George; the use of light and dark relegates Mary, in dark dress, to the shadows while George lays in light linens; the style or focus means Mary's features are blurred while George's are clearer; and, in terms of the dynamics of the gaze, Mary looks dotingly at him – tending to him in sickness and watching over him like a guardian angel – while he seems oblivious to her. The small piece of paper in the foreground left-hand corner of the painting on the table next to George is possibly one of the many scraps on which he jotted down philosophical thoughts on art and life, which Mary then pasted into books and published in the *Annals*, suggesting his position as creator and her subservient, secretarial role.

However, Mary – who stands (alert, active) while George lays (asleep, passive) – places herself in a position of power as a central figure towering up over George through the middle of the picture, looking down on her weak husband in a subversion of the traditional dynamics of the gaze (male/female, spectator/spectacle, subject/object). This image contrasts with Mary's awestruck first impression of a younger, brown-haired George as a knight-like embodiment and epitome of male greatness, strength and 'chivalry'; she writes that she would not have been surprised if, on another visit, she had 'found him all clad in shining armour' (M. Watts 1912: 1.288–9). In the painting, Mary is a spectral, maternal figure reminiscent of George's numerous paintings of powerful female 'angels of death', especially *The Messenger*. Mary is a shadowy figure hovering over George in dark clothes; one side of her face and body sinks into the darkness of the background, and her blurred features suggest her non-materiality. She blurs the boundaries or borders of the body as well as those between life and death, corporeal and spiritual, mortal and immortal, concrete and abstract, self and other – on the threshold but paradoxically seeming to embody both sides of these dichotomies. While women have traditionally been seen as the 'non-human half of the living structure', Mary seems to both acknowledge and challenge her 'fate' as 'relegation to the shadow thrown on [her] by patriarchy' (Foster 1990: 66). The neutral tones of George's crumpled clothes make him merge into the white sheets enshrouding him, and highlight through contrast his wife's curiously regal purple robes (anomalous in the otherwise monochromatic palette). While George is foregrounded in the picture, the viewer's eye is distracted by the dark figure hovering over him, disturbing what could otherwise be seen as a straightforward portrait of her husband reflecting her reverence.

In a photograph of the couple at Little Holland House (*c*.1890), Mary stands with her head bowed behind the foreground figure of George, who is seated in a throne-like chair reading a paper, surrounded by his paintings, while she fades into the background next to a vase of flowers as though part of the furniture. Critics have claimed that this photograph 'revealingly capture[s] a sense of their relationship' (Wilson 2004: 177), and it has been reproduced to illustrate and reinforce such claims, sustaining the popular image of Mary as the servant or shadow of her husband. Yet a recently discovered photograph of the Wattses, reproduced here for the first time (*c*.1900) (Fig. 3.3), shows Mary sitting tall and upright beside her comparatively small and withered older husband; she appears to be in the act of reading to him as he sits passively, gazing into the distance, unanimated and seemingly disengaged. A photograph of the Wattses reclining in the 'niche' at Limnerslease (*c*.1894–5) also shows Mary engaged in the act of reading and turning pages while George lays listening; this can be seen as a portrait of Mary's literary and intellectual agency rather than her submission to wifely reading duties. While the more familiar photograph of the Wattses at Little Holland House may capture something of their early marital relationship, the recently discovered photograph paints a portrait of their relationship in later life, when George, in his illness, deafness and old age, became increasingly dependent on Mary in a subversion of traditional power relations between the sexes. This is comparable with Ford Madox Brown's intimate double portrait of prominent suffragist couple Henry Fawcett and Millicent Garrett Fawcett (1872) – later President of the NUWSS (1897) – which shows Millicent sitting

Figure 3.3 *The Wattses*, *c*.1900, Watts Gallery Trust.

in a higher position beside her blind husband, holding a quill and paper that he cannot see. In subject, composition and gender-role inversion, these portraits showing suffragist wives in dominant positions (over less able-bodied husbands) are strikingly similar.

While Mary's portraits of George present him as weak and powerless, George's portraits of Mary (like her self-portraits) present a confident and somewhat severe woman, challenging the longstanding public perception of her as a meek and mild wife or model of submissive femininity. Contrastingly, George's painting of his first wife Ellen Terry – a teenage actress thirty years his junior – as *Ophelia* (1875–80) presents her as a fragile and somewhat infantile feminine figure. Ellen posed for his paintings in typically feminine settings and positions (for example, surrounded by flowers in *Choosing* [1864]), 'happy because [her] face was the type which the great artist who married [her] loved to paint' (Terry qtd. in W. Blunt 1989: 110). Although Ellen developed a remarkably successful acting career independent from George and later joined the Actresses' Franchise League, he married her in an attempt to protect her from a controversial life on the stage, and

Figure 3.4 *Mary Seton Watts (three-quarter profile portrait)*,
George Watts, 1887, Watts Gallery Trust.

she was more of a muse and ward to him during their brief marriage. George's 1887 three-quarter profile portrait of Mary (Fig. 3.4)
presents her as dignified, serious and somewhat haughty, with her
eyebrows slightly raised; her sharp features such as her pointed chin
and straight nose give her a strong and striking appearance. George's
portraits of Mary capture something of her character as well as his
perception of – and respect for – her: she is presented in a formal
manner, in her dark dress and collar, as an intellectual companion and
conjugal creative partner.

George's portrait of Mary in relatively plain dress with her hair
fastened back is comparable with Mary's remarkable yet little-known
watercolour self-portrait of 1882 (Fig. 3.5), painted before her marriage. Here, her modest dress consisting of a thick, high-necked,
buttoned-up green shirt with minimum adornment beneath a grey
jacket is notably more masculine than the frilly white dress she wears
in her oil self-portrait of 1881. In the earlier and more typically feminine self-portrait, her flushed cheeks and rosy lips are complemented
by the predominantly pink background decorated with flowers, and

Figure 3.5 *Self-Portrait*, Mary Seton Fraser Tytler, 1882, Watts Gallery Trust.

the light chiffon-like material she wears is very feminine, alluding to fashionable Victorian dress (although here, too, she looks comfortable and would not have been corseted, given her views on the subject). Unlike George's three-quarter, lost profile and back-view 'honeymoon' portraits of Mary (and her own profile portraits of her sisters), Mary paints herself staring straight back at the viewer in her 1882 self-portrait, in which she dominates the canvas. She represents herself as a confident, composed and unapologetically 'unfeminine' woman assuming a traditionally male artistic role. Mary's choice to present herself unsmiling, with her hair simply tied back, in plain, practical clothes without the decorative ruffles, lace, flowers and jewellery that were common accessories in portraits of women in this period (such as those by Rossetti) suggests a deliberate defeminisation. It signifies her rejection of, or resistance to, the beautification, idealisation and objectification of women in art as in society. This self-portrait reflects her refusal to conform to Victorian norms of feminine beauty and her desire to be taken seriously – and to establish a respectable reputation – as a professional woman artist.

During the second half of the nineteenth century, portraiture became increasingly important to the women's movement as it gained momentum; the self/image of woman was a topic politicised by early feminism. Portraits gave visible identity to women who were voicing demands for women's education and employment before feminism was organised as a movement. Women artists painted portraits of fellow suffrage supporters for exhibition (Emily Osborn painted portraits of Barbara Bodichon [1884] and Jane Cobden Unwin [1889]), and later in the century portraits of suffragists were commissioned by women's institutions. In the early twentieth century, suffrage artists drew on the Victorian obsession with images of figureheads as portraits or miniatures in order to promote their campaign. Leaders were pictured on suffragette propaganda such as badges, posters and postcards (portraits of Emmeline Pankhurst were common and widely distributed), and banners were emblazoned with famous women writers' and artists' names along with symbols of their professional identities. Mary's self-portraits were thus produced within – and can be seen to dialogise with – suffrage debates on the spectacle of woman.[3]

Parallels between the well-known 1886 portrait of pioneering feminist Lydia Becker (who graced an ASL banner) by suffragette artist Susan Isabel Dacre, and Mary's 1882 self-portrait, are highlighted by Deborah Cherry's description of the former work. Mary's appearance and self-representation was perhaps influenced by leading early feminists like Becker, with her distinctive public image, in a similar suffragist self-fashioning: 'she cultivated a severe expression and unadorned style of dress, probably considering like many suffragists that [plain and] dark dresses, particularly in black and not necessarily high fashion, were the hallmark of respectability'. In Mary's 1882 self-portrait (as in George's three-quarter profile portrait), she rejects the current codes of fashionable feminine styling, supine pose, hourglass figure and lavishly trimmed gown. Her facial features are not 'moulded into a blank mask of beauty' and her gaze is not coy, charming, dreamy or demurely averted but rather activated and direct. She is 'plain and hard-looking', and her severity of manner 'connote[s] a refusal and reworking of hegemonic definitions of womanhood . . . declining the visual protocols which transformed women into a visual icon of masculine desire' (Cherry 1993: 209). Further illuminating the subversiveness of Mary's self-portraiture, Mancoff states that 'women artists who chose to gaze upon and depict the female form – including their own – released the female body from its function as a personification of ideal beauty, recognizing its . . . expressive potential' (2012: 14).

Photographs further evidence Mary's decision to dress smartly and soberly rather than ostentatiously, typically in dark garb after her husband's death, which helped her to construct a professional self-image and blend in among men at public events. A large formal photograph of Mary in the Watts Gallery archive (possibly by Hollyer, who photographed George and Mary individually, much to her delight) is very like her later self-portrait: in a confident pose and dark, modest yet elegant dress with a high collar, and with her hair pinned back, she looks seriously and even sternly back at the photographer, meeting the male gaze.[4] Such visual (painted and photographic) representations aid an understanding of her self-fashioning as a 'brutal taskmaster' working 'like a tiger' in her diaries. Mary's life writing and self/portraiture, when read in conjunction, strongly convey her unequivocal sense of professional identity.

Although Mary's self-portraits were apparently not publicly exhibited during her lifetime, her earlier self-portrait stands centrally in the photograph of her busy Sanquhar studio (*c.*1881) in an elaborate gilt frame, surrounded by other portraits in progress, suggesting her confidence in her own ability and her pride in her work and self-image. Her self-portraits both symbolised and helped to shape her artistic identity. Just as Cixous urges women to 'write themselves' (Cixous 1976: 880), Mary painted herself, asserting her artistic agency and inscribing her identity by signing her decorative monogram (the intertwined letters of her maiden initials) prominently (one is in bright blood-red paint) on the front of both self-portraits. While historically women haven't been viewers but have been looked at as (art) objects, as the subject of her portrait she allows herself to view and re-view, to paint as well as to be painted; in her self-portraits, we see Mary through her own eyes (as opposed to her husband's). By 'crafting her own image, she presents herself as she wishes to be seen' – a strong, determined, aspiring professional woman artist – and 'subverts the traditional power of the male artist to determine the public perception of the female subject' (Mancoff 2012: 129). She is in control and command of her own self-image, and this has wider socio-political significance in the context of nineteenth-century debates about the rights, roles and representation of women.

Mary's little-known lifelong interest in photography and particularly photographic portraiture shows her constructing or 'seizing the narrative' (Mancoff 2012: 85) through this medium. She thus traces the development of her artistic identity, documents her unconventional marriage and family life, and renegotiates her place in relation to the world. Mary's decorated photograph album (*c.*1865–7), her earliest surviving work produced when she was between the ages of fifteen and eighteen, signifies the importance of portraiture to her even as a teenager, when she discovered the creative potential of photography. This is a masterpiece of photocollage uniting family photographs and collected *cartes-de-visite* of notable figures, including Tennyson and Queen Victoria, surrounded by colourful, detailed drawings and elaborate hand-drawn frames. Her early artistic skill is visible in her use of architectural features, interesting perspectives and witty, imaginative watercolour settings. Her images of birds, butterflies, peacocks and women at windows anticipate central elements of her own as well as wider feminist iconography. Mary was later given photography lessons by leading Brighton-based photographer Thomas Donovan (around 1888–9) at a time when photography was growing as a profession for women.[5] Mary's diaries show her keen interest in this relatively new technology. As an amateur photographer, most of her output featuring close family members was for personal use or as a way of recording completed artwork.

A close investigation of the unattributed, informal or intimate family photographs in the Watts Gallery archive (distinguishable from the work of an accomplished professional photographer) suggest that Mary took photos of George and their ward Lily at their residences in Scotland, Brighton and Surrey, providing valuable insights into the Wattses' personal and professional relationship, working practices and family life.[6] It is likely that she took the photograph of George's *Lady Godiva* (1880–90) – a painting of feminist significance – surrounded by her decoration in the Watts Chapel in a photographic portrait of their creative partnership.[7] She may have taken the photos of Lily in front of George's portrait *Lilian* (c.1904) and of George holding the basket used in this painting (demonstrating his intended composition) – in which she supposedly painted the flowers. Mary would have taken these photographs with an awareness of her husband's fame, and her own by association; by recording his life and work, she could showcase her own skills, experiment creatively and secure her own legacy while maintaining a respectful role. Many photographs – some of which were almost certainly her own work – were found in Mary's bedroom and dressing room after her death.

Mary's portraits of family members can also be seen to some extent as self-portraits. Mary's oil portrait *Mrs Edward Liddell* (Christina Catherine Fraser Tytler) (1870) shows her elder sister absorbed in papers, the roughly finished hand suggesting her engagement in the active process of writing. Christina had recently published her first short story collection *Sweet Violet and Other Stories* (Fraser Tytler 1869) – featuring an 'old-maid's chronicle' (62) and commentary on mercenary marriage (253) – for which Mary provided six full-page illustrations. Intended as a gift-book for girls, it was well-received and praised for its characterisation and power of portrait painting. Mary's portrait of her sister with a pile of (seemingly illustrated) pages alludes to her own work and to their little-known creative partnership, to Christina's emergent professional identity as a woman writer (of short stories, poetry collections and novels) and to her own largely unrecognised role as an illustrator. This further reveals how, for Mary as for other women professionals, self/portraiture was a means of self-promotion, or else the promotion of their careers, views and projects. Although Mary remained somewhat anonymous on the title page of Christina's book which states only her initials 'M. F-T.', this was her 'first opportunity to produce [monogrammed] artwork for the public eye' (McMahon 2013: 17), and she went on to produce illustrations for the improving periodical *Good Words for the Young* (from the early 1870s) and for Richard von Volkmann's book *Fantastic Stories* (1874) in which she is credited as 'M. Fraser-Tytler'. This suggests Mary's growing confidence and reputation in illustration, where she could create portraits of literary characters. Her illustrations for these texts feature portraits of women and scenes of adventure or emotion, and foreground specifically female experiences: motherhood, female companionship, a ballroom scene and women standing in transitional spaces at open windows and doorways.

Portraits of Feminist Friendships: the 'Hall of Fame'

George's portraiture, including his 'Hall of Fame', exhibits his support for women and women's culture, as well as the unexpected elements of agreement between the apparently rival agendas of such 'father-figure artists' (Cockroft 2005: 10) and mid-Victorian feminists. George painted the portraits of several notable nineteenth-century women who were professionals, social reformers, and/or (related to) early feminists, including: British feminist Josephine Butler (1895), commemorated by an ASL banner (1908); social reformer Florence Nightingale (1868), also commemorated by an ASL banner (1908), whom George championed as 'the greatest woman in England' (M. Watts 1887: 5 October); actress Ellen Terry as Joan of Arc (*c.*1864); Edith Villiers (Countess of Lytton)

(1862) and Edward Robert Bulwer-Lytton (1st Earl of Lytton) (*c*.1884), parents of suffragette Lady Constance Lytton; and Jane Nassau Senior (Jane Elizabeth Hughes) (1859), philanthropist and Britain's first female civil servant, who worked with impoverished children in Surrey. George also planned to paint the portrait of poet Christina Rossetti (W. Rossetti 1911: lviii), who – despite signing the anti-suffrage petition of 1889 – privately believed that female voters and even female MPs were 'only right and reasonable' (C. Rossetti [*c*.1878–9] qtd. in Marsh 1994: 418–19). Josephine Butler and Christina Rossetti feature alongside Elizabeth Barrett Browning, Elizabeth Fry and Queen Victoria in the 'Noble Women' portrait windows of Liverpool Cathedral (1910), commemorating women who made significant contributions to society in a similar way to George's 'Hall of Fame'.

George painted pioneering female photographer Julia Margaret Cameron (*c*.1850), who photographed him (*c*.1865–9) as well as Mary and her sisters for the group tableaux *The Rosebud Garden of Girls* (1868); this was inspired by Tennyson's *Maud* (1855) and was produced as a *carte-de-visite*. While Virginia Woolf's farce (and only play) *Freshwater* (written 1923, performed 1935, published 1976) ridicules George during his first marriage, he encouraged and influenced Woolf's great-aunt Julia Margaret Cameron throughout her career as a photographer; she compiled an album for him, and he became her artistic mentor and muse. Inspired by George's 'Hall of Fame', Cameron created photographic portraits of distinguished men and 'approached photography in the manner of an allegorical painter' (Mancoff 2012: 41). George also actively supported women in the traditionally male field of fine art portraiture: he personally put lesser-known portrait artist Ida Verner forward for the Society of Portrait Painters, where prominent suffragist portrait artist Louise Jopling campaigned for equal rights of women members.

George painted male feminists George Meredith (1893), Walter Crane (1891) and John Stuart Mill (1873) – who presented the first suffrage petition to Parliament in 1866. NUWSS leader Millicent Fawcett 'saw that the portrait encapsulated Mill's refined, delicate look' (Gould 2004a: 111). George also painted Russell Gurney, a Conservative MP involved in the Married Woman's Property Act of 1870 (women could be legal owners of money they earned and they could inherit property) and the UK Medical Act of 1876 (women could be licensed as doctors). George's numerous portraits of progressive public figures reflect his recognition of the importance of their work. Indeed, Cherry points out that a feminist politics often

informed the painter's choice of sitter, and although she only cites
women's paintings of women (1993: 208), George's progressive
socio-political views apparently informed his selection of (female
and male) social reformers and women's rights supporters or activists
for his portraits and 'Hall of Fame'. This, in turn, helped shape their
public identities and create a visible feminist community to promote
the women's cause.

Dominated by a plethora of male portraits, George's 'Hall of
Fame' might seem to support the popular perception of him as a
patriarchal artist with a masculinist focus. Yet the fact that the one
woman he chose to include in his 'Hall of Fame' was the pioneering British feminist Josephine Butler (1895) (Fig. 3.6) subverts ini-
tial perceptions. Butler was a pioneering women's rights worker
of the period who was active in early feminist campaigns, and was
particularly concerned with the welfare of prostitutes and women's
higher education.[8] She has been seen as 'the most complete and . . .
advanced Victorian feminist' (Caine 1992: 151) and was championed

Figure 3.6 *Josephine Elizabeth Butler*, George Watts, 1895,
© National Portrait Gallery, London.

by Millicent Fawcett. The Wattses recognised her beneficial political role as a women's rights worker and moral and social reformer, since they believed 'that feminine influence in politics would have a good effect, especially upon social questions' (M. Watts 1912: 2.146). As fellow philanthropists and proponents of women's rights, the Wattses believed in women's education as a natural progression of educational reform, and shared Butler's 'great sympathy with the poor and working people' (Butler [1895] qtd. in Ormond and Ormond 2012: 82) – especially 'fallen women'. This is evidenced by the Wattses' work and particularly George's late 1840s social-realist paintings depicting female exploitation, poverty and suicide (see Chapter 6). Revealing George's and Butler's poignant and somewhat unusual friendship, Mary writes in her diary that her husband gave Butler a copy of his painting *Love Triumphant* (1896: 27 August), and Butler praised George's 'bold drawings' in a letter (Butler [1895] qtd. in Ormond and Ormond 2012: 82). Their mutual respect for each other's work stands testimony to George's largely unrecognised support for and affiliation with the early feminism of the nineteenth century.

George admired Butler's spirit, achievement and life's work, which he felt to be superior to his own, even to the point of 'self-reproach'. He confided to her that he was troubled by not having been 'wakened up to try to do good to unhappy people till he was seventy'. Butler recalls their conversation in a letter:

> he said 'what would I not give to be able to look back upon such a life as yours!' . . . I said I did not take it up willingly, I was *driven* into it by anger against injustice. He replied, 'O yes, I know you were driven into it. You were destined for it. But some people refuse to be driven; and you did not refuse.' (Butler [1895] qtd. in Ormond and Ormond 2012: 82 [original emphasis])

George's immense respect and admiration for Butler – as a women's right's worker and early feminist standing up to, and standing out in, a patriarchal society – seems symbolised in his 'Hall of Fame' where she stands out in a sea of male figures, and stares out from amongst a multitude of male gazes. Speaking of the portrait, Butler recognised that her deep-sunken eyes have 'no brightness' in them and seem to be 'looking into Eternity, looking at something no one else sees' (Butler [1895] qtd. in Ormond and Ormond 2012: 82). George wanted to present her as a visionary leader, looking sad yet purposeful, staring beyond the picture plane towards a space that is not visually accessible to the viewer. Mary similarly recognises 'a beauty in the very loss of beauty that is very attractive' in portraits of women, and notes that 'some sadness . . . shows how she looks into the graver side of living; not her own sorrows, but those of the world' (1891: 9 September).

George's portrait of Butler suggests their close friendship based on their socio-political ideas, rather than the hierarchical active male artist/passive female muse dynamic more typical of the time. Significantly, George's portrait of Butler is, in her own words, 'not at all pretty' (Butler [1895] qtd. in Ormond and Ormond 2012: 82). In this sense it is a stark contrast to the watercolour portraits of her by J. H. Mole (1845) and E. H. Odell (pre-1974); the smooth-skinned and shiny-haired drawing of her by George Richmond (1851); and Alexander Munro's marble bust of a much younger Butler (1855) aged about twenty-six, which is a beautiful and even eroticised presentation prefiguring Rossetti's paintings of the 1860s. George's portrait of Butler is more comparable with the 1903 profile portrait drawing of Butler by Slade-trained suffragist artist Emily Ford, showing her grey hair and 'old face . . . with all its thinness and wrinkles' – which Butler thought 'really artistic' and 'much better than what [George] Watts did'.[9] The Wattses received visits and long letters from Emily Ford (who was also friends with Evelyn De Morgan); Mary notes, 'she writes in intense earnestness . . . afraid lest we should not sympathise' (1891: 28 July) with her beliefs and work – namely, her painted panels in All Souls Church, Leeds.

George's 'Hall of Fame' is consistent in focusing on the head and face of the sitter, rather than on figure, dress or accessories, selecting subjects noted for their intellectual power and moral vision. 'Each is an individual study; not only a face, but a mind, a heart, a soul' (Friederichs 1895: 82), and his portraits for posterity contrast with Rossetti's 'art for art's sake'. His approach to painting portraits was that 'he would never undertake a likeness until he knew a person thoroughly' (Greenhow 2016a: 11). George's portrait of Butler was designed to convey to the nation the admirable hardship of moral reform, social work and philanthropy rather than to gratify the male gaze. It eschewed prevailing, aesthetically pleasing male ideals of feminine beauty perpetuated by many of his contemporaries (such as Rossetti and Leighton, also included in the 'Hall of Fame') in its focus on Butler's aging, 'strong and gaunt' (Butler [1895] qtd. in Ormond and Ormond 2012: 82) facial features: the emphasised lines of the nose, jaw and eye sockets. Her plain black dress is a stark contrast to the luxurious fabrics draped seductively around the beautiful, bejewelled female figures in many of Rossetti's paintings, such as *Monna Vanna* (1866). George's portrait of Butler is more comparable (in dress, demeanour and setting) with his 1887 three-quarter profile portrait of Mary. It is concerned with portraying the serious struggle rather than the superficial beauty of woman, and conveys his support for her social work rather than any interest in beautifying or idealising her physical appearance.

Butler's social struggle and fight for women's rights is inscribed in George's portrait of her which, by her own admission, 'bears the marks of storms and conflicts and sorrows so strongly', tracing her 'hard life work'. Butler told George that when she first saw the portrait she 'felt inclined to burst into tears': 'Your power has brought up . . . the record of a conflict . . . It is written in the eyes and whole face' (Butler [1895] qtd. in Ormond and Ormond 2012: 82). Butler's use of the term 'written' here in relation to art and the female body is significant from a Cixousian perspective. In this light, George's painting (a kind of inscription, a visual text) can be seen as a rare, antiphallocentric male 'writing of the female body', which conveys specifically female experiences and emotions as well as a feminist struggle, revealing the ways in which woman has been 'marked' by patriarchal society. That George painted Butler with such sensitivity suggests his sympathy with her suffering and his support for her women's work, demonstrating his own progressive position in relation to the early feminism of his day.

George's portrait of Butler helped to shape a 'public identity for a woman leader' just as Susan Isabel Dacre's portrait of Lydia Becker had when exhibited in 1886 at the Manchester Academy of Fine Arts alongside 'portraits of the city's worthies' (Cherry 1993: 209). His portrait undoubtedly increased her prominence and helped to promote her campaigns by giving her a visible identity and national profile. Earlier in 1872, the London organisation for suffrage split over the question of whether to openly support Butler's anti-Contagious Diseases Acts; in 1889 the Women's Franchise League, including Butler and Emmeline Pankhurst, was formed. While Butler's contentious campaigns made her unpopular with many, George's portrait of her as a dignified, stoic, resilient crusader afforded respectability and eminence to her and her work with prostitutes; it can thus be seen to have a feminist function.

The friendship between Butler and Mary was seemingly no less affectionate. Mary's 1896 diary paints a picture of an intimate relationship between them. Butler writes to Mary saying, 'Your expressions of affection are to me very precious', and Mary proudly documents a conversation with her husband in which he tells her, '[Butler] has I think taken very much to you' (1896: 26 August). Mary painstakingly recounts their exchanges of words and letters in detail, and directly quotes Butler from memory, indicating the strong and lasting impression she made on her. She writes, 'there is no woman worker to whom I can feel such reverence' (1896: 27 August). In another entry devoted entirely to Butler, Mary notes, 'In our evening we begin [reading] Mrs. Josephine Butlers [*sic*] life – a record of a great crusade – a wonderful Joan of Arc! What has she not accomplished – She too so delicate, so pretty, so sensitive' (1896: 20 October). While both George and Mary greatly admired and respected Butler's social work and moral reform, Butler's fight for women's rights perhaps particularly resonated with Mary as a fellow woman, philanthropist and suffrage supporter. Mary writes,

> [Butler] tells us that after her long life & conflict, in the last ten years, feeble as she is & alone – her sense of hope is constantly growing – she said first to me 'I never dare allow a single pessimistic thought for a moment.' (1896: 27 August)

Butler represented a 'growing hope' specifically for women – for the attainment of women's rights and greater empowerment – and the Wattses' close connection to her reveals this hope to be one they all shared. Butler may have indirectly influenced Mary's art: her 'Spirit of Hope' chapel frieze was begun in 1896. A reading of Mary's neglected diaries, in light of her own and her husband's artistic projects, offers a unique insight into the couple's response to and support for early feminists and feminisms.

The De Morgans' Self/Portraits

The De Morgans' interest in portraiture is evidenced by Evelyn's portraits of her model Jane Hales and Mary De Morgan's niece (*c.*1887), and William's portrait of his niece Millicent De Morgan (undated), as well as their representations of each other. Yet, in contrast to the Wattses, the De Morgans became increasingly opposed to self-advertising and Evelyn increasingly felt that 'all celebrity was hateful' (Stirling 1922: 12). This is confirmed by the De Morgans themselves in the Preface to *The Result of An Experiment*, published anonymously by the couple, which alludes to their 'quiet retired life', and states that 'the writers . . . were unwilling that any particulars should be given that would lead to their identification' and wished to 'remain incognito' (1909: xii, xiii, xiv).[10] A visitor offers a vivid image of the couple in later life as cultural producers who were serious about their creative practices without being self-promoting: 'he writing, she painting glorious pictures. The novels don't get published and the pictures don't get exhibited; but both author and artist seem supremely happy!' ([*c.*1905] qtd. in Stirling 1922: 237). The De Morgans were more modest than the Wattses, whose names were attached to their high-profile visual and literary works through which they gained fame (George's 'Hall of Fame'; the Watts Chapel; Mary's biography of George).

When publisher William Heinemann proposed to include frontis-piece portraits of William by Evelyn in the two volumes of his novel *It Can Never Happen Again*, the De Morgans declined. William hum-bly replied in a letter, 'two portraits in one work savours a little of egotism, and will make a poor bloke (when he's me) feel ridiculous'. He continues, '[t]he portraits are not my property, but my wife's. My personal identity (as far as I retain the copyright) is at [her] disposal' (W. De Morgan qtd. in Stirling 1922: 317). He gave Evelyn full con-trol over his image and identity, and she ultimately refused the pub-lisher permission to reproduce the 1909 portrait (Fig. 3.7):

> Both my husband and myself agree that what with the volumes in the background, and the pot in the foreground, to say nothing of inkpots, etc, it is far too bumptious a thing to be tolerated and too self-advertising to be allowed outside the family circle; so the idea must be given up. (E. De Morgan qtd. in Stirling 1922: 317)

Evelyn's use of the term 'bumptious' and William's use of 'ridiculous' in response to the publisher's request to use both portraits evinces their aversion to self-promotion. As a result only the earlier portrait was reproduced, while the later portrait featuring William's creative outputs was first exhibited in the year of Evelyn's death. However, the fact that she bequeathed the latter portrait to the National Por-trait Gallery in her will, and the ceramic pot – foregrounded in the hands of William in her painting – to the V&A museum, suggests her awareness of his as well as her own reputation, and that she cared about their creative legacy.[11] A full-page article on 'The Romance of the De Morgans' in *The Graphic* reports that while William 'was much too fine a gentleman, and much too old a bird, to have his head turned by his success as a novelist', he nonetheless 'liked it, enjoyed it, and so did his wife' (Milne 1922: 808) – whose own literary ambi-tion is revealed by her juvenilia (see Chapter 5). Despite their humble posture, it seems that the De Morgans, like the Wattses, were acutely aware of their role in, and contribution to, Victorian culture.

Evelyn painted two oil portraits of William (1893; 1909) out of respect rather than reverence, suggesting her admiration of – and close bond with – him as a fellow artist, suffragist and spiritualist. Although

Figure 3.7 *William De Morgan*, Evelyn De Morgan, 1909,
© National Portrait Gallery, London.

Evelyn thought these portraits were too self-promoting to be publically exhibited, they have shaped the public perception and reputation of William, and offer insight into the couple's creative partnership
and practices. While the detailed brushwork and colour palette of
the 1909 portrait evoke Pre-Raphaelitism and Aestheticism, Evelyn
produced 'a faithful likeness' of her husband with 'uncompromising
accuracy' (Stirling 1922: 316–17) – with a greying beard and signs of
ageing etched on his face. She paints him surrounded by his literary
and ceramic works, shortly before his fourth novel was published, in
a tribute to his talents. He holds one of his own lustreware jars, and
another large lustreware plate can be seen mounted on the wall behind
his right shoulder, while his first three novels *Joseph Vance* (1906),
Alice-for-Short (1907) and *Somehow Good* (1908) along with manuscripts and a quill and ink are clearly visible on the bookshelf behind
his left shoulder.

The painting's compositional divide represents William's dual creative identity as potter and writer, and perhaps his transition between
the two professions, as by this time his pottery business had deterio-
rated (it closed in 1907) and his literary career was developing. The

ceramic work he clutches was one of his last, and the manuscript sheets on the shelf signify another novel in progress. These objects not only reflect his creative interests and professional status but also Evelyn's, since she was the driving force behind the production of his novels. In this sense, the painting is a portrait of the De Morgans' creative partnership that conjoins the work of the two. The intricate detail on William's carefully painted works implies Evelyn's private pride in his skills and success. While correspondence reveals her pride in his lustreware, she was perhaps especially proud of his later literary success not only due to her role in it but also because it gave her the freedom to paint without exhibition and sales. This seems reflected in her depiction of William dressed rather smartly in a jacket, shirt and tie, surrounded by objects and detail, which contrasts with her earlier portrait of William in his blue artists' robes against a tiled wall, which is comparatively bare, plain and lacking in personality. In the later portrait, William clasps the iridescent rotund jar in both hands like a crystal ball, which seems to illuminate at the touch of his lower finger-tips; he stares directly back at the viewer not with a look of 'profound boredom' (Stirling 1922: 316–17) but with a wise or knowing gaze. This suggests the couple's interest in spiritualism and clairvoyancy. He is imbued with a captivating mystical power more convention-ally associated with female figures or femmes fatales in Victorian art, for example, Edward Burne-Jones's *Astrologia* (1865), John William Waterhouse's *The Crystal Ball* (1902), and Evelyn's own paint-ings *Medea* (1889) and *The Love Potion* (1903). In both portraits, William becomes the model or muse seen from Evelyn's perspective in an inversion of traditional gender roles in art.

The couple's composite monogram designed by William, which combines his own and Evelyn's initials to create a smiling stick figure, and his cartoon 'une demande en mariage' depicting his proposal to Evelyn, can be seen as types of double portrait. The monogram serves not only as a 'visual sign of the union of marriage' or a 'kind of marital portrait or modern-day coat-of-arms' (E. L. Smith 2002: 26) but also as a symbol of their creative partnership. The cartoon, though a simple humorous pencil sketch, reveals something of their characters and relationship: Evelyn stands hiding her face with her hand in apparent embarrassment or disbelief, while William smiles as he gazes up at her from a kneeling position. Significantly, it contains no obvious signifier of gender or sexual difference, and Evelyn's columnar, hairless figure suggests both her rejection of con-ventional femininity and William's perception of her as an equal. The photograph of the De Morgans seated in a gondola in Venice with their luggage, leaving Italy for the last time (1914), is another double portrait of contented togetherness and equality much like that of the Wattses standing outside Limnerslease.

Given George's high praise of Evelyn as 'the first woman artist of the day', and his awareness of her work, it seems curious that he did not paint her portrait for his 'Hall of Fame'. In light of Evelyn's view of fame, she perhaps declined an invitation to sit for portraits in a feminist rejection of spectacle, the role of muse and the male gaze. Given her personal aversion to self-display, it is unsurprising that she posed for few photographs and portraits, and never created any traditional or identifiable self-portrait. Nonetheless, photographs of her, and her paintings of female figures, offer valuable insight into her character and preoccupations. The three-quarter profile photographic portrait of Evelyn (Fig. 3.8), in which she sits gazing downward in an artist's smock with her hair tied loosely up in a bun, shows a creative, practical, modest, serious woman. Yet she is self-consciously posed holding an object that is evidently of significance to her due to its prominent position. Despite speculation that this is a studio prop or tool, it is most likely a versatile silver nutmeg grater

Figure 3.8 *Three-quarter Profile Photographic Portrait of Evelyn De Morgan*, date unknown, © De Morgan Collection, courtesy of the De Morgan Foundation.

(with a wire-style handgrip and edges perforated with small rasped holes) repurposed to perform clairvoyancy; it is strummed using the thumb protector she wears to summon spirits, which purportedly speak in her automatic writing. Evelyn's reclamation and innovative repurposing of a domestic household implement to facilitate her spiritualist practice is comparable with her own use of the insides of household box lids to draw on as a teenager, with William's use of the household 'washing-book' and 'torn envelopes' (Stirling 1922: 233) to write his novel *Joseph Vance*, and Mary Watts's 'Recipe Book' which was one of creative concoctions rather than culinary ingredients. This illustrates how traditionally women-enslaving domestic objects became creative, experimental and/or political tools of suffragists and suffragettes – who used housewives' toffee hammers in their window-breaking campaign.

George Watts's portrait of Josephine Butler can be compared with Evelyn De Morgan's chalk *Study of Jane Morris* (*c*.1904) (Fig. 3.9), created almost a decade later. Both artists depict well-known women in later life, focus on faces rather than figures, and create realistic likenesses and character studies rather than decorative objects. Despite their links with the PRB, their portraits reject Aestheticism

Figure 3.9 *Study of Jane Morris*, Evelyn De Morgan, *c*.1904, © De Morgan Collection, courtesy of the De Morgan Foundation.

and reflect their feminist perspectives. Jane Morris – best-known as the wife of Arts and Crafts designer and social activist William Morris, and favourite muse of Dante Gabriel Rossetti – was a close friend of the De Morgan family as well as other suffragist artists (including Barbara Bodichon). William sent Jane his novels, and she replied urging him to 'please write a great many more' (15 July 1907, DMF). Jane shared the De Morgans' and the Wattses' socio-political beliefs to some extent: her letters reveal that while she disapproved of militant suffragettes, she believed in equal rights, and that women should have the vote and access to education (Sharp and Marsh 2012).

Though Jane's distinctive face is ubiquitous in Rossetti's later work, she is almost unrecognisable in Evelyn's depiction of her in widowhood, old age and poor health. This portrait of her with a head of grey hair propped up against a pillow, a worn face and a weary indirect gaze is a stark contrast to the radiant, raven-haired, brooding beauty pervading Rossetti's works. While Evelyn's sketch was intended as a preparatory work for her allegorical painting *The Hour Glass* (1904–5; Fig. 3.10), where Jane is transformed into an anonymous queenly figure contemplating the passing of time, it alone eschews the highly idealised and eroticised representations

Figure 3.10 *The Hour Glass*, Evelyn De Morgan, 1904–5, © De Morgan Collection, courtesy of the De Morgan Foundation.

of Jane by Rossetti. Evelyn's sketch re-presents her (in the final words of Christina Rossetti's poem 'In an Artist's Studio'), 'as she is' rather than 'as she fills his dream' (1856: l.14), recasting her as an individual and subject. Discussing this painting, 'one of the more opaque of [Evelyn's] canvases dealing with Victorian sexuality', Van Valkenburgh notes the contrast between the unrealistic breasts of the carved figure supporting the table and those of the former queen femme fatale, recalling her prior function as a sexual object (1992: 10). Viewed together, Evelyn's sketch and painting of Jane can be seen to comment on the brevity of life and superficiality of beauty, as well as to critique the shallow or narrow focus on female beauty in the Aesthetic work of her male contemporaries. This is made all the more pointed by Evelyn's choice of an iconic figure, who embodied the Pre-Raphaelite ideal of female beauty, to convey her message. Evelyn's painting can be seen to condemn the treatment of women as passive aesthetic objects in art as in society even as it depicts it; the painting 'disrupts what it appears to value' (Van Valkenburgh 1992: 10).

In *The Hour Glass*, the faded beauty's whitening hair is just visible beneath her heavy headdress (linking it back to the sketch), and the rose that might adorn her hair in another Pre-Raphaelite painting (such as Rossetti's *Blanzifiore* (Snowdrops) [1873]) lies dying on the floor. The theme of time and the hourglass symbol (on which the female gaze and touch is fixed in the painting) was of personal significance to Evelyn, as shown by her strong aversion to timewasting expressed in her diary, and especially wasting time on feminine frivolities such as changing dress instead of producing meaningful art. While the medievalised interior and enthroned figure in rich draperies may seem removed from the socio-political issues of Victorian society, the painting can also be seen as a portrait of a privileged Victorian woman's sorrowful enforced passivity in domestic captivity, which Evelyn experienced in her youth and depicted throughout her life. Continuing Evelyn's iconographic vocabulary foregrounding the tension between female captivity and liberty, the former is juxtaposed with the open doorway leading to the winged, piping figure of life and a sunlit world of jubilant liberty. While this composition can be seen to symbolise immortal life after death, it can also be seen to highlight the burden of Victorian feminine beauty conflated with passivity and dreary domesticity, and the potential for freedom from it through creative activity. Indeed, the tapestries behind the model allude to Jane Morris's embroidery, reflecting an aspect of her creative identity whilst simultaneously testifying to Evelyn's. Painted soon after the formation of the WSPU in 1903 and exhibited in 1907 and 1908 when the women's suffrage movement was gaining momentum, *The Hour Glass* can be seen to represent a long, tiresome wait for women's rights and the imminent end of a patient, peaceful fight for sexual equality; a brighter future for women is envisioned beyond the threshold of the door.[12]

This chapter has shown how self/portraiture held personal and socio-political significance for the Wattses and De Morgans, tracing their formulation of self-image and (individual or conjugal) identity. While their self/portraits reflect their curiosity or fascination – and the wider Victorian obsession – with self-image, they challenge traditional views of themselves and their spouses as well as their famous female contemporaries. The gender-role inversions and subversions in their visual works reinforce their departure from Victorian gender norms and their support of gender equality. In addition to the portraits of Butler and Morris, an examination of the couples' neglected or previously unseen self-portraits, double portraits and portraits of each other builds up pictures of these under-researched suffragist artists as individuals and in partnerships, giving faces to neglected nineteenth-century figures and early feminists. This is crucial to an understanding of their self-perceptions and perceptions of each other, and of how they used self/portraiture to challenge patriarchal perceptions and power relations in the Victorian–Edwardian period.

Notes

1. 'A small water colour drawing, a profile portrait of G.F. Watts, Esq. by Mrs G.F. Watts' is listed in the Limnerslease inventory 1938: 10, WG.
2. See WG Adlib notes (Ann Laver). George Watts painted the portraits of Rosebery and his wife.
3. See Tickner 1989, Cherry 1993: 209, Green 1997 and Mulvey 1999 for further discussions on suffrage spectacle and the spectacle of woman.
4. See large formal photographic portrait of Mary Watts with 'H' on the reverse, currently unattributed, possibly by Hollyer (see also Mary Watts 1887: 21 September), WG: B49.
5. See Amy Levy's novel *The Romance of a Shop* (1888); 'Mr. Thomas Donovan, Artist and Photographer, The St James's Portrait Studio, St. James's Street', in W. T. Pike & Co.'s booklet *Views and Reviews: Brighton & Hove*, c.1897.
6. WG: COMWG2010.1: 69, 84, 111, 64, 36, 77, 11, 19.

7. 'Not best' is written on the glass plate negative, WG. *Lady Godiva* alludes to the legend of the British noblewoman who rode naked on a horse through the streets in protest against her husband's oppressive taxation system; George's painting depicts her not in the act of riding naked but in the moment when, her task fulfilled, she falls into the arms of waiting women who wrap her in robes. It focuses on Godiva's martyr-like suffering and sacrifice undertaken to redeem the people.

8. Butler came to prominence in her campaign to repeal the Contagious Diseases Acts (1864–9), which penalised female prostitutes by forcing them to undergo medical examination and treatment with no such penalties for men. She used her influence in support of numerous social and philanthropic causes for women.

9. Josephine Butler, letter to Stanley, 2 March 1903, University of Liverpool Library, JB 2/1/9, available at <http://www.liverpool.ac.uk/library/sca/highlights/h1006NobleWomenwindows.pdf> (last accessed 20 April 2017).

   Emily Ford was a member of the Ladies' National Association for the Repeal of the Contagious Diseases Acts and family friend of Josephine Butler. She became Vice-Chairman of the ASL and a member of the Society for Psychical Research. Ford's work was influenced by the Pre-Raphaelite movement, particularly Burne-Jones. Much like the Wattses' studio-home, Emily's London studio was 'a meeting-ground for artists, suffragists, people who *did* things' (Crawford 1999: 226).

10. Possibly, they also withheld their identities for fear of backlash against their controversial spiritualist practice.

11. This jar (1888–98) was bequeathed to the V&A museum by Evelyn. It has achieved iconic status due to its placement in Evelyn's painting, which was probably a joint decision by the couple.

12. Mary Watts shared Evelyn's interest in the image of Jane Morris: 'A sketch, "La Donna Della Fiamma" [The Lady of the Flame, 1870] after D. G. Rossetti', a painting of feminist significance featuring Morris, was found in Mary's dressing room at Limnerslease after her death.

Part II
Artists' Writings:
Private and Published

Chapter 4

Women Artists' Diaries

This chapter studies the neglected diaries of Mary Watts and Evelyn De Morgan in conjunction for the first time. Excerpts from Mary's eight extant diaries (1887, 1891, 1893, 1896, 1898, 1902, 1904 and 1906–8) were recently published (Greenhow 2016b) on the completion of a collaborative transcription process, over a century after they were written. Yet the majority of Mary's diary writing remains unpublished, as does Evelyn's one extant diary (1872).[1] This chapter includes an analysis of my own transcriptions of Mary's diaries and of Evelyn's diary, bringing to light previously unseen archival material in order to assist the recovery and revival of women's marginalised life writing. Despite the disparity in volume and the production of them during different stages of life (Mary's in married middle age; Evelyn's in unmarried adolescence), their similarity as Victorian women artists' diaries – recording interests in interdisciplinary creative practices and tracing the evolution of professional as well as feminist identities – calls for a comparison. A reading of Mary's multiple, detailed diaries informs a reading of Evelyn's relatively short, single diary, and the significance of the latter is highlighted through comparison with the former. I aim to show how these women artists' narratives, views and voices relate to each other and to other women's diaries and life writing of the period, challenging traditional assumptions about these women as well as ideological assumptions about Victorian women writers.

Mary's and Evelyn's diaries register their private resistance to Victorian feminine norms, document their professionalisation as woman artists, and trace the emergence of their distinctly feminist voices. They are sites of artistic inception, and each can be read in its entirety as a fragmented or truncated Victorian *künstlerroman* (that is, a narrative about an artist's growth to maturity). Combining word and design, Mary's diary narrative logs her first experiments with gesso and photography in 1887, and the creation of her ceiling panels and reading alcove at Limnerslease in 1891, tracing the formation of her artworks. Evelyn's diary logs her early training at the South Kensington National Art Training School in 1872 (then aged 16–17) before joining the Slade; her last diary entry marks her 'last day at Kensington' (1872: 20 December). Mary's first diary of 1887, an example of a Victorian honeymoon diary and of women's travel writing, and Evelyn's only diary of 1872, an example of Victorian juvenilia and narrative of adolescent girlhood, record critical stages in their personal lives and careers during a time of significant sociopolitical and cultural change. Their diaries are crucial to an understanding of both their professional self-development and their lived female experience, and are valuable to a broader study of women's roles in Victorian Britain and in the Victorian art world, as well as the role of the diary in the life of a Victorian woman artist. This chapter reclaims Mary and Evelyn as culturally important diarists for the first time, contributing studies of suffragist artists' narratives to the growing field of Victorian women's life writing.

Both Mary and Evelyn meticulously record their artistic activity as well as their frustration with the feminine norms and domestic duties that obstruct it. Their diaries reveal their serious, self-critical professional artistic identities as well as their acute awareness of their social or domestic roles as women: Mary's role as the respectable middle-class wife of a world-famous artist; Evelyn's role as an unmarried upper-middle-class lady. Central to this chapter is the argument that while domestic and artistic concerns are inextricably linked in both Mary's and Evelyn's diaries, they are generally more compatible in the former, whereas they are in conflict throughout the latter. While Mary's domestic routine in her marital studio-home is ordered around artistic activity (and she generally records positive experiences), Evelyn's artistic activity is ordered around the domestic routine in her parental home (and she generally records negative experiences). Although 'artist' and 'wife' were not mutually exclusive for Mary, 'artist' and 'lady' were for Evelyn. A conscious preoccupation with the restricting demands of femininity pervades Evelyn's adolescent writing, conveying her chronic agitation with gender conventions that limited her artistic productivity. Therein lies her feminist voice, whilst Mary's emerges in her recorded interactions with her husband. The difference between their diaries partly reflects their difference in circumstances (age; marital status; class), yet they both inscribe struggles to reconcile feminine conventions with professional careers, and trace journeys to greater freedom and self-expression.

Mary's Diaries: Sex, Studio, Suffrage

In addition to publishing her husband's biography, *The Annals of An Artist's Life* (1912), and a memoir of her friend Jessie Godwin-Austen co-written with Gertrude Jekyll (1913), Mary kept her own notebooks, journals and diaries. Her eight daily-written annual diaries – generally updated first thing in the morning, sometimes in bed or at a writing table on the landing – cover the Wattses' marital years and a few years after George's death (1886–1908), bridging Victorian and Edwardian periods. Mary affectionately named each of her diaries 'Fatima' and talked to them as though they were living female confidants rather than domestic household records. This is intriguing in light of the painting *Fatima* (1862) by the Wattses' close friend Edward Burne-Jones, depicting a woman unlocking her husband's secret closet with a key.[2] Mary's diaries offer an unprecedented insight into her professional as well as personal relationship with her husband, revealing their marital dynamic and Mary's own character to be far more multifaceted than critics have previously perceived. Challenging traditional perceptions of Mary as George's secretary, biographer and amanuensis – his 'acolyte and servant' (Bills 2011: 16) who 'worshipped him blindly' (W. Blunt 1989: x) – this chapter reveals Mary's complex role and creative agency as devoted wife, creative partner and self-proclaimed 'brutal taskmaster' (1893: 27 February). Her diaries explore a broad range of contemporary topics (including aestheticism, socialism, philanthropy, religion, marriage, education, temperance and science), commenting on the politics and personalities of the nineteenth century, and revealing the strength of her support for early feminism.

According to Linda Peterson, women's ways of conceiving and representing the self are 'relational' or 'contextual' – that is, they focus on relationships with another person or group – whereas the basic masculine sense of self is separate or individual (Peterson 1999: 4, 22, 39). In this light, Mary's self-conception and self-representation in her diaries assumes a specifically female form. Her diary writing can be seen to exemplify the 'relational mode of women's self-writing, which ... grounds identity "through relation to the chosen other"' (Mary Mason qtd. in Peterson 1999: 39): her husband. It foregrounds gender-relevant familial matters and domestic details – themes of marriage, the home and the family – in accordance with the highly feminised genre of the domestic memoir. Peterson argues that 'the memoir – domestic in its focus, relational in its mode of self-construction – allowed women to write as mothers, daughters, and wives' (1999: 20). Mary records events and experiences from the specifically female perspective of wife as well as mother to the Wattses' ward Lily, and recalls most of her experiences relationally. Her diaries are primarily records of the Wattses' togetherness: their daily life, artistic collaborations, joint reading practices, shared spaces and beliefs. Mary writes, 'What a record of happiness this Fatima is: so seldom apart for an hour, a constant interchange of thought, no book read but together, what a sublime life it is for me' (1887: 20 November). She concludes her first diary with, 'I asked [George] how I should end my Fatima for 1887 he said "Say that nothing could make us more to each other than we are"' (1887: 31 December).

However, the non-gendered, traditionally male account of a professional artist's career punctuates Mary's ostensibly conventional wifely narrative. Her diaries document her approach to her own creative practice, and commemorate her own artistic achievements, as well as her husband's. They provided her with imaginative and intellectual spaces, life writing opportunities and forms of self-representation, which Victorian women were ideologically denied; Evelyn's diaries, too, allowed her to express 'masculine' artistic ambition which could not be articulated in polite society. Domestic and artistic, familial and professional, highly gendered and non-gendered interests and narratives are inextricably linked in Mary's diaries, combining two ostensibly 'contradictory autobiographical modes' (Peterson 1999: 32). Mary's diary writing presents an atypical example of a Victorian woman whose sense of self is defined in relation to her familial status (as wife) as well as to her occupational status (as artist); she demonstrated how these two apparently mutually exclusive identities could successfully coexist. This dual aspect of Mary's identity registered in her diaries challenges traditional assumptions about Victorian women and women's writing, disrupting patriarchal binary structures and ideologies of the period.

Mary's diaries may be compared with those of her predecessors Dorothy Wordsworth and Edith Simcox in the way they are 'characterised by their tendency to consistently foreground another person' (Millim 2010: 982). Mary's own self-effacing three-volume biography or hagiography of George gives a detailed account of their married life revolving around George's work and health. Yet unlike Edith Simcox's '"tribute"-diary to George Eliot' and Dorothy Wordsworth's diary which 'left out the self' (Millim 2010: 982) in its focus on William Wordsworth, Mary's diaries reveal her self-perception as a serious professional artist and record her largely unrecognised influence on her husband's work. Although Dorothy Wordsworth's journals show her creative partnership with William, she never presents herself explicitly as an influence; Mary shows no such reticence. While Mary mentions or quotes George in almost every entry, some record her defiance rather than deference, and several critique his artwork; she confidently asserts herself and expresses aesthetic views distinct from his. This chapter reveals both the joys and tensions of togetherness, exploring moments of power play and gender-role inversion in the Wattses' partnership, showing how Mary's diaries can be seen as sites of struggle and subversion rather than submission. Its reading of Mary's diaries as a record of her anti-patriarchal conjugal creative partnership offers a contribution to the feminist life writing and auto/biography scholarship that has attempted to recover neglected nineteenth-century women writers and re-read forgotten women's texts.

On one occasion, George 'take[s] up the little pen' and writes in Mary's 1887 diary on the subject of the 'harmony' of 'the human form' (9 January). From the beginning, then, Mary troubles the conventional privacy of the diary by allowing her husband access to it. The presence of both Mary's and George's handwriting on the (typically private) page – a unique example of the Wattses' double diary-writing – suggests the intimacy between the newly married couple while travelling on their exotic six-month honeymoon (to Egypt, Greece, Italy and France). Mary's 1887 diary can be seen as a culturally important 'Professional/Intellectual' Victorian honeymoon journal or artists' travel journal popular in the 1870s, though it is omitted from Michie's study of over sixty honeymooning couples during 1830–98 (Michie 2006: 44–5). In a chapter on women's diary writing in a book on Victorian marital partnerships, the (non-)act of sex in Mary's honeymoon diary cannot be ignored. While there are no explicit references to sex (beyond the social issue of prostitution or 'fallen women') in Mary's diaries, the sexual subtext of certain recorded experiences and episodes can be investigated. One night in Egypt, after the couple read parts of her diary together (itself an intimate act), Mary writes,

I kissed him tonight through his mosquito curtains & said 'The kiss through the veil' – 'Ah there is no veil between us', he said 'Nor ever can be now' – There is nothing for me to fear – I have only to be myself no need for me to feel in what was called 'a very difficult position.' (1887: 3 April)

This is Mary's most explicit record of physical intimacy between them: a kiss through a mosquito net. Yet the couple's entrance into a discourse of 'veils' and the suggestion of the metaphorical bridal veil being lifted or penetrated – 'his hand coming through the limitation of mosquito curtains to [hers]' (1887: 10 April) as she kneels at his bedside – seems sexually charged. Indeed, this is the kind of euphemistic, indirect or 'veiled' language that a Victorian middle-class woman like Mary is likely to have used to refer to sexual activity; one must be attentive to language choices and delivery, to uneasy verbal constructions and the unsaid. Michie notes that 'the honeymoon puts pressure on language' (2006: 31), and feminist critics have analysed Victorian women's use of 'veiled' (as opposed to open, direct or explicit) comments on controversial issues (Armstrong 1993: 372–3; Marsh 1994: xxvii). The De Morgans' use of the phrase 'veil of flesh' in their automatic writing (1909: 14, 42) apparently refers to the binary of spirit/flesh but also suggests the fleshly connotations of 'veil' in Mary's diary. When Mary sees her sister on the morning after her return from honeymoon, she writes, '[she] would not tell me that I was changed which I said was disappointing! I ought to be – I <u>am</u> in many ways' (1887: 6 June). This, too, may be a veiled reference to sexual initiation or consummation among other eye-opening experiences on her travels, acknowledging the 'transformative elements of the honeymoon' abroad with its 'carnal knowledge/s' and 'ritual of firsts' (Michie 2006: xv, xiii). Indeed, 'signs of positive change, readable upon the body, were expected outcomes of the honeymoon' (Michie 2006: 4) that affected how women were seen by relatives on their return.

A few months later Mary writes, 'we seemed to be nearer to each other through the lifting of the curtain', although she references only how they are 'bound in spirit and mind' (1887: 18 September) – 'body' being conspicuously omitted. Nonetheless, she regularly rubs his legs with lanoline to prevent cramps, and they are in close enough proximity to talk when he undresses and bathes; she knows the 'intricacies of [his] scrubbing process . . . ending in an air bath' (1891: 30 January). This offers answers to questions about 'issues of space, body, and privacy' – intricately connected to issues of sexuality – posed in Michie's study of Victorian honeymooners: 'how were these men and women to negotiate dressing for dinner . . . sharing a . . . room . . . bathing . . . or resting with someone at newly close proximity?' (2006: xii).

Michie's discussion of euphemism in the letters of Maud Sambourne Messel, daughter of a respected *Punch* cartoonist, sheds light on Mary's entries in her honeymoon diary. Like Mary, Maud writes from bed: she emphasises the fact that she has not slept well, details her (always carefully asexual) physical contact with her husband, and adheres decorously to the language of illness – which Michie reads as remarkable for its 'flirtation with the topic of the sexual'. She argues that sex and care are linked in the telling and the doing, 'using a code that substitutes physical care for sex' (2006: 144). In this light, Mary's well-known role as her husband's nurse and carer is far more complex that it seems. The link between illness and sexuality, Michie argues, is most acutely expressed in Maud's 1898 letters by her references to feeling 'seedy' or 'not quite well', which is a euphemism for 'menstruating' (2006: 124). Using the same lexis, Mary describes how feeling 'seedy' (mentioned five times in her 1887 diary) prevents her from 'giv[ing] [her husband] what he needs' (1887: 3 August), apparently aware of cultural expectations and her duty as a wife. Michie discusses a spectrum of intimacy during the '"alone together" of conjugality' (2006: 143) that includes a variety of expressions of physical affection. In Mary's diaries this includes the couple talking during the night when they are in restless semi-dream states, and laying in bed talking on cold early mornings. Michie argues further that 'what can be read as euphemism or substitution . . . can equally well be read as metonymy' (2006: 144), suggesting that the rubbing of Maud's temples by her husband is an erotic act. Mary's rubbing of George's legs during the night, then, is also perhaps metonymic, and her many euphoric or ecstatic descriptions of their married bliss may be linked to sexual pleasure – which was perhaps one of the freedoms Mary enjoyed as a New Woman.

Mary's private self-reassurance and cryptic reference to 'a very difficult position' in her diary can be read in relation to the earlier diary of honeymooner Eliza Dickinson (Mrs Francis Wemyss), which registers her sexual fear and identifies the honeymoon as 'the most unpleasant in a girl's life' ([1838] qtd. in Michie 2006: 9). As Michie's study illustrates, this is 'representative of the way many Victorian women . . . thought about sex' (Michie 2006: 117). Yet unlike Eliza Wemyss's diary, Mary's expresses no such sexual apprehension, uneasiness or displeasure on her honeymoon, though she does allude to past 'fears' and acknowledges her need for 'much reassurance' that she and George 'suit each other' during their late-night 'little talk[s]' (1887: 9 September). It is generally assumed that the Wattses' marriage was unconsummated due to George's older age, ill health, disciplined dedication to art, and desire 'to get as far away from the animal as possible' (M. Watts 1891: 23 August), shunning all things base or indulgent. In an interview he paradoxically claims that 'every artist ought to take a vow of celibacy' – but only 'for a dozen years . . . temporarily' (qtd. in Friederichs 1895: 81). Discussing eminent Victorian men's habitation of a 'Glass Case Age', Lytton Strachey famously said, 'they were enclosed in glass. . . . Have you noticed, too, that they were nearly all physically impotent? – . . . Arnold, Jowett, Leighton, Ruskin, Watts' (qtd. in Regan 1986: 118–19). Whether or not their marriage was consummated, Mary's diaries document a depth of emotional, intellectual and sometimes physical intimacy, reflecting their closeness and contentment. For Mary, the majority of her sexual energy was perhaps sublimated into creative energy and artistic activity. Ultimately, Mary's euphemistic terms, tantalising blanks and mysterious missing pages render futile further interrogation into this aspect of her private life.

That George highly valued Mary's opinion as a creative partner is conveyed by her diary of 1893, in which she records how he frequently requested her opinion, and how she was not afraid to speak her mind:

> 'Are you there' he calls up to my studio sometimes, & then he asks me to come & look at something he has done – Once, today, it was to see the [painting of the] little boy 'Promises'. What do you think of it? I said 'You have made the wings too real, & have lost the dignity of the work – It is more sweet but less noble' – I dare to say what I think, I must! as he is too much in earnest not to wish me to do so – he has lost colour and quality in the wings and the picture is much damaged by it . . . An hour afterwards, & he had much restored the quality. (1893: 16 January)

George earnestly asks Mary for advice and hastily amends his painting *Promises* (1892–3) to meet her approval in an inversion and subversion of the male tutor/female student dynamic typical of the earlier nineteenth century (and of their pre-marital relationship). This passage speaks volumes about his perception of her as an artist of equal if not superior vision, as well as her confidence to offer constructive criticism and express her own aesthetic ideas that conflicted with her husband's. She assesses his painting without the hyperbole and flattery more typical of feminine praise of a famous male artist's work. This entry records Mary asserting her own voice through (a traditionally male) artistic discourse – the sophistication, conviction and detail of which reflects her formal art training at the Slade. Her exclamation and underlining of the word 'dare' suggest her excitement and pride in recording her transgression of traditional femininity and her active role in her husband's artistic process. The large-scale, high-relief, carefully wrought wings of the angel in Mary's *Death Crowning Innocence* – arguably the most impressive aspect of her *Aldourie Triptych* – show her particular talent for representing wings, which explains her specific criticism of the wings in George's *Promises*.[3] As early as 1887, he asks her to assess the 'crimson wing' in his famous painting *Love and Death* (10 October). Such entries challenge the concept of a 'unified "conjugal gaze" in which men and women – and the visual burden is mostly on women – learn to align their views' (Michie 2006: xv).

Another, more radical, gender-role inversion and subversion of patriarchal power relations occurs when Mary assumes the role of 'taskmaster' who expects George to meet her high aesthetic expectations:

> He calls me in to look at his work . . . he has got the sky & foreground now to his satisfaction & mine, but I miss and still insist on his trying for the spark[l]ing . . . clear cut iridescent character of the icy peaks, once got but lost long ago at Brighton – 'Now you've depressed me' he says, & I feel a brutal task master – but I tell him he [showed] it to me once so I can't be satisfied with less. (1893: 27 February)

Mary's interesting use of the term 'master' as a self-description (if somewhat tongue-in-cheek) suggests her awareness that she has, if only temporarily, assumed the dominant, powerful and traditionally male role of teacher in their relationship. This subverts the apparently inherent connection between the relations of man/woman or husband/wife and master/student or master/servant that existed in the ideological structures of the Wattses' own time. Mary's conscious adoption of a male persona as 'master' exemplifies the subversive Victorian 'gender crossing' adopted as a New Woman strategy in professional women's struggle for gender equality or greater freedom; it demonstrates her recognition, on some level, of the fluidity and performativity of gender, and enacts a destabilisation of the traditional gender binary. The role reversal is ironic given many young women artists – including Mary herself in her early days of portrait painting – looked to the famous George Watts as master, referring to him as 'Signor',[4] and were grateful to follow his teaching. Mary's diaries reveal her to be the driving force behind the creation of some of George's famous artworks (perhaps more than she records) which were only finished when they were to her satisfaction. She encouraged him to capture something of her creative vision as well as to fulfil his own artistic potential, which resulted (among other works) in George's visionary alpine landscape: what Mary refers to as the 'Ice Mountains' is possibly *Sunset on the Alps* (1888–94). Such paintings can be seen for the first time as collaborations of his skill and her vision.

However, Mary's diaries reveal that her strong-mindedness was not always appreciated by her husband, and this further complicates any straightforward view of their relationship. While it is not unusual for a married couple to experience the tensions of togetherness, George's occasional criticisms of Mary's character and work approach the very patriarchal discourse that he generally eschews, voicing the deeply ingrained principles of his time. When the couple had not yet been married a year, Mary records in her diary,

> My loved one said to me today that I did not quite help him as I ought, to be better & more kind in spirit – 'How could I', I said 'unless I were to become quite an angel!' & 'then wouldn't you want a little devil sometimes to play with[?]' – He tells me [he] thinks he could play with angels, & not find them monotonous –
> He says to me 'Charity thinketh no evil'. I say 'Yes, but Charity's wife does' – (1887: 9 August)

George criticises Mary's strong-spiritedness, tells her how she 'ought' to behave and voices an explicit desire for her subservience. Yet she does not silently acquiesce in self-criticism or shame, but rather contests his authority and mocks him with her witty retorts; she meets his moralising comments with subversive humour. Her very record of this rebellious episode marks an unapologetic enjoyment in playing the transgressive role of the wicked 'little devil' – the antithesis of the angelic role she was expected to play as the wife of a great artist. Elsewhere, too, she refers to her 'angel husband' and to herself as his 'wicked wife' (1891: 1 January). While Mary has been perceived as 'the archetypal Victorian woman, the "angel in the home"' in that she 'fulfilled the duties of a Victorian wife, caring for her husband' (Unwin 2004: 246), her diaries show that she does not fit Virginia Woolf's description of the self-abnegating 'angel in the house' who 'never had a mind or a wish of her own, but preferred to sympathize always with the minds and wishes of others' (Woolf 1942: 237). Mary's record of her response, in which she directly quotes herself, suggests her pride in her secret rebellious spirit. Indeed, the 'life-writing potential of the diary' has been 'identified as a site for specifically female rebellion' and resistance; within its private pages a woman could 'challenge patriarchy in an attempt to recover her self-worth' (Delafield 2009: 16, 18).

Early in 1887, Mary records her 'horrible dream' that after her marriage to George,

> he took a new wife to himself, a staid excellent woman with brown curls in combs . . . she was so much better than me too, that was the worst of it. [. . .She was] all virtues. Already we speak of 'Brown Curls' as a third party who does what is right and admonishes. (1887: 22 January)

From the very beginning of their marriage, then, the 'angel in the house' existed only as a dream, spectral, ideal figure distinct from – and rejected by – Mary herself. Nonetheless, she was evidently haunted by the ideologically dominant Victorian image of woman as the 'angel in the house'. This was conceived by Coventry Patmore's popular titular poem (1854–63), portrayed by George Elgar Hicks's painting *Woman's Mission: Companion of Manhood* (1863) and championed by John Ruskin who recommended 'true wifely subjection' on the part of 'her who was made to be the helpmate of man' (Ruskin 1916: 83). Evelyn De Morgan was described by a biographer as William's 'guardian angel' (Barrington *c.*1922: 27) – a description which, though more palatable for a contemporary readership, simplifies the complexity of her role and relationship. The De Morgans, like the Wattses, viewed themselves as equals in art.

Mary's diminutive descriptions of George in her diaries as her 'sweet', 'frail and delicate' (1891: 21 December) 'little darling' (1896: 1 September) and 'darling child' (1887: 17 June) reinforce the gender role reversal recorded by her anecdotes. These affectionate terms of endearment imply George's gentleness and Mary's closeness to, rather than reverence for, her husband. They connote a smallness and sweetness traditionally associated with childhood and femininity that contrast with the patriarchal connotations of 'Signor' and signify her matriarchal role. Mary's description of George's sensitive nature and delicate disposition in her diaries – reinforced by Josephine Butler's description of him as 'small . . . and thin . . . so gentle . . . very delicate' ([1954] qtd. in Ormond and Ormond 2012: 82) – undermines the patriarchal power he seemingly represented as a world-famous Victorian artist, instead suggesting an effeminacy at odds with his grand, monarchical image and status. Mary's description of her husband's 'little head – the forehead like a shell, with white soft flames of silver hair, that ethereal look [. . .giving the impression] of some beautiful childs [*sic*]' (1896: 26 October) presents an infantile, angelic image of him. Commenting on his 'neatness, politeness and unobtrusiveness', Shelagh Wilson goes so far as to say that

> for his female admirers it was [George] himself who was the 'angel in the house', bringing beauty and spiritual purity to the domestic sphere . . . In other words, there was a partial reversal of 'masculine' and 'feminine' roles, but one which paradoxically entrenched the ministering feminine ideal. (Wilson 2004: 170)

Yet Wilson fails to see the implications of her own evidence here: she perceives the departure from Victorian masculinity embodied by George, but apparently not the departure from Victorian femininity embodied by Mary. While Millais was 'happiest smoking in gentleman's clubs or shooting on the grouse moor . . . interest[ed] in the marketability of his paintings', George 'preferred a domestic life, painting in his studio or decorating the homes of his female supporters' (Wilson 2004: 170); outside his studio, George was 'nervous and hypersensitive and unbusinesslike' (Gould 1998: 30). He became increasingly fragile, dependent on Mary, and confined to the domestic sphere in his illness and old age. Although George is best known as a portraitist, throughout the 1850s his central concern was with wall decoration, inspired by the Sistine Chapel, which he painted primarily in domestic spaces (Unwin 2004: 240); while Mary is best known as a craftswoman, she initially specialised in portraiture. A gender-role inversion is thus manifest in the Wattses' characters and creative practices.

Mary, having revelled in her mischievous rejection of the angelic role prescribed by society and expected by her husband, proudly records her subversive humour on another occasion later in the diary. When George scolds Mary for failing to replace the matchbox beside the bedroom candle, saying 'My dear child, I do wish you would try to be a little more precise', she confesses and replies 'penitently' while determining to play 'a little joke' on him. Armed with George's 'pair of white flannel drawers' that he had carelessly left in the hall in his hunt for the matches, she follows him to their bedroom and 'very gravely' says, '"Signor . . . I want just to ask you to try & be a little more precise." I then held up the convicting and very voluminous articles, spreading their hinder parts . . . I had scored' (1887: 17 November). Her mimicking of his patriarchal discourse undermines its authority, and her strategy of double exposure – revealing his own imprecision whilst spreading the hinder parts of his drawers – deflates his sense of superiority. They subsequently 'laugh for ten minutes', showing how her humour effectively challenges patriarchal order, breaks down the hierarchy he attempts to establish, and rebalances power relations in her marriage. Indeed, subversive humour was recognised as a powerful tool and utilised in suffrage propaganda. This diary entry demonstrates the Wattses' 'perfect liberty of thought & action with each other' (1887: 3 May).

Though Mary generally displays humour and resilience in such instances, George's disparaging and demeaning remarks sometimes adversely affect her. He patronisingly refers to her as a 'foolish little wife who is very dear though she chooses to be deceived' (1887: 9 June), and tells her, 'I believe nature intended you only for a dreamer' (1893: 7 January), typifying patriarchal perceptions of women as essentially subordinate and 'sensitive–intuitive–dreamy' (Cixous 1976: 878). When Mary is inspired to draw her sister-in-law 'sitting by the fire, behind her the low red sun – lighted up her hair, with a coppery sort of [aureole]', which reminds her of an early Millais, and excitedly calls George 'to come & see it', his disapproval leaves her deflated:

> I tried to make a sketch – alas, I have no powers – when it was fairly finished, Signor looked at it coldly & said the face should have been darker than the red wall behind, & I tried to alter it with the usual result of spoiling it. I am not strong enough to be independent in my work, & when I try to lean on him I fail entirely. Of course he sees things quite differently from me. (1893: 4 January)

George supported and fostered Mary's creativity but also sometimes fuelled her insecurities about her artistic ability – either out of a tactlessness, sense of rivalry or keenness to reinstate his authority – convincing her of her inadequacy and failure. This highlights an important contradiction in the behaviour of Victorian male artists towards younger women artists: many encouraged women to make artistic contributions and yet forced them into a role of dependence; even 'the kindest of men expected deference and obedience from his spouse and this was assumed to be the natural order of things' (Jan Marsh qtd. in Peeters 2002: 25). Yet the Wattses' creative partnership necessarily entailed criticism as well as encouragement of each other's work, and some of Mary's reviews of George's work are equally 'cold'. She says she suffers 'the sorrows of the artist's wife' when George overworks Walter Crane's picture, turning it from an 'entrancing . . . work of genius' to 'nothing more than [an] ordinary portrait'; though George immediately carries out her suggested alterations to the eyes and chin, she feels 'he will never recapture what he once had' (1891: 6 October). Nonetheless, George's portrait of Walter Crane is now considered 'one of his best, most insightful likenesses' (Greenhow 2016a: 11), testifying to Mary's rigorous tuition.

Mary's later 1896 diary further reveals her rejection of patriarchal notions of femininity, as well as her husband's tacit approval of her progressiveness. In one entry describing her interaction with a male sculptor who visited the Wattses' home to have his portrait painted, Mary writes,

> as I sat & talked to [Sir Alfred Gilbert], I perceived more crankiness developing – women must not bicycle, girls should be kept in glass cases, & he harped unpleasantly to me on the subject of the physical difference between men & women. (29 September)[5]

Ten days later, Mary writes, 'A lovely morning [. . .I] walked out with the dear beloved, stepping along so lightly to look at a Bicycle I thought would do for us' (8 October). Less than a month later she had bought a bike and was determined to ride it, to her own and her husband's delight: 'My love very happy this morning because I had my 1st turn on my bicycle . . . I feel sure it will give me new power' (3 November).

The bicycle is widely perceived to have endowed Victorian women with new freedom and independence; the inclusion of women cyclists in suffrage campaign activities (including the 1913 Suffragist Pilgrimage in which Mary participated) is well documented, and it has even been suggested that 'cycling brought the sexes together on equal terms more completely than any previous . . . pastime' (Rubinstein 1977: 68). William De Morgan invented 'a twin speed bycicle [*sic*] of a compact and handy sort' (E. De Morgan 1904: 3 June) that may have been used by women. Mary's 1896 diary was written during the cycling craze, and in 1898 she records her enjoyment in cycling publicly around the village with her ward Lily and alongside male relatives. She thus defied restrictive feminine norms and what she recognised as outdated patriarchal notions of sexual difference that enforced female passivity, captivity and subordination. It is clear that her swift acquisition of, and determination to ride, a bike – which she describes with obvious pleasure – was a conscious act of protest rather than a merely practical purchase. George's presence at, if not participation in, its purchase and test drive suggests he shared Mary's progressive views rather than those of his male sitter. This is a prime example of how personal and socio-political matters meet in Mary's diaries, as in later autobiographical suffrage writings which 'grounded public debate in personal experiences of oppression and resistance' (Green 1997: 5).

Other entries offer more explicit statements of Mary's support for women's rights and culture during her marital years. Her claim to be in favour of 'feminine influence in politics' in her husband's biography is a brief, sanitised public statement compared to her passionate diary entries which reveal the strength and evolution of her feminist feeling. In 1891, Mary attended a rousing lecture by controversial British philanthropist, temperance leader and women's rights campaigner Lady (Isabel) Henry Somerset (niece of Julia Margaret Cameron and cousin of Virginia Woolf's mother), commending her 'great work', 'strong nature' and oratory. Such powerful, persuasive speeches may have influenced Mary's increasingly confident feminist voice and views. Isabel sought Mary's advice on clay for her Duxhurst pottery in Surrey (Black 2010: 80), where she established a rehabilitation centre for female alcoholics. She was a high-profile suffragist who delivered the first speech at the Albert Hall at the end of the 1908 NUWSS procession and was pictured in the *Illustrated London News*. In 1913 (the year that Mary gave her own suffrage speech) she was voted by readers of the *London Evening News* as the woman they would most like as the first female British Prime Minister (Black 2010: 2). Inspired by Isabel's lecture, Mary writes in her 1891 diary,

> I felt very proud of 'woman', for her clear round voice, her fluent earnest speech, left all the male speakers far behind. Two Members of Parliament were amongst them – She touched on woman's influence in legislation, & its moral action, . . . and how they will not stand having immoral men making laws for them as they do . . . I heard 3 charming women speak on that platform . . . & more womanly, or charming, the impression of all three could not be – they spoke to the purpose, & saw the truth clear & directly. . . . How I wished that my dear one could have been there & could have heard. (1 May)

Mary's reference to her husband implies the Wattses' shared sympathy for women's causes. Yet while George painted portraits of Isabel and her family, his absence from the lecture signifies his lack of active support. Mary's pride in 'woman' as a strong speaking subject with intellectual and social presence and power, and her description of the speakers' 'womanly' impression (echoed by her endorsement of 'feminine qualities' in her 1913 suffrage speech), implies her acknowledgement of sexual difference, but one that involves a perception of women's capability rather than inadequacy. According to the NUWSS, sex and gender differences should be 'acknowledged and appreciated' (Wingerden 1999: 102). Mary, like other suffragists, argued for the benefits of the emancipation of womanliness into public life, since 'if the different natures and responsibilities of the sexes were part of the rich diversity of life . . . it was surely reasonable to make the political system more representative by encompassing them both' (Tickner 1989: 156). Mary's conception of 'womanly' associated with agency, eloquence, directness and clarity is distinct from the uncontrolled emotion, dreaminess, hysteria or silence traditionally associated with Victorian femininity: she admired the New Woman of the late nineteenth century. Mary's diary entry is comparable with Constance Lytton's recollection of Christabel Pankhurst's political speech in her autobiography, showing how suffragettes and suffragists admired similar qualities: 'her nature being so essentially a woman's, there was a vein of tenderness throughout her speech, and her strength lay in her steadfast, resourceful and brilliant intellect' (Lytton 1914: 29).

Mary's diary of 1904 traces the deterioration and death of George (aged 87) at their London home Little Holland House – the full details of which are omitted from her *Annals*. It thus offers an unprecedented insight into the Wattses' final moments together, and George's physical and psychological state on his deathbed as he hovers on 'the borderland between life & eternal life' (1904: 16 June). Mary feels 'the All Pervading [is] about [them]' (1904: 30 June), alluding to George's painting *'The All-Pervading'*, and George's last words allude to his painting *The Messenger*. For George, the messenger of death was maternal: 'that kind nurse who puts us all as her children to bed' (G. Watts qtd. in Macmillan 1903: 245). Mary assumes the role of a soothing mother putting her child to bed when, in a final gender-role inversion, George begs her to read to him. This is fitting and poignant given that their evening readings were among their happiest times at Limnerslease. She writes,

> I had not been there many minutes when quite strongly he called 'Mary Mary Mary come to me' – I sprung up & was quickly holding his beloved hand once more – I had my bed (now nearly a month away from his side) pushed up once more & lay beside him – & when he slept I slept my last sleep at his side. [. . . He said] suddenly to me 'Read to me' – I had no book – but said the verses of the opening of [Alfred Tennyson's poem] In

Memoriam – 'Strong Son of God Immortal Love' I could not remember them all – but he must have heard & liked it for he said 'Say it again' . . . I read again 8 verses . . . 'what more is to be said' he seemed to say – 'I want you to be happy' he said later . . . 'Why, why don't they come?' he cried after – meaning the great messenger he had so implored to come a few days before –

    The End. (1904: 30 June – 1 July)

Mary's diaries also record the Wattses' earlier, light-hearted discussions about death:

We came to talk of <u>death</u> somehow – the losing hold of all material things . . . 'Ah, but sweet' I said 'you will save with you a paintbrush when you get to the new life' – 'That I am sure I shall' he said laughing. (1893: 20 February)

Yet the moment of George's death is a very solemn and self-conscious occasion for them both. This is suggested not only by Mary's readiness to recite the famous elegy by Tennyson, but also her use of the narrative convention 'The End' to mark the conclusion of her diary entry and simultaneously their life together – though not her diary-keeping or artistic practice. Indeed, with characteristic resilience and optimism for the future, Mary resumed her artwork only a month after George's death. She finished the interior decoration of the chapel, worked on pottery designs and planned a retrospective exhibition of his work for the end of the year.[6] Given the cultural and literary fascination with famous figures' last words, Mary's life writing recording the death of 'England's Michelangelo' is of great public interest and cultural importance, and she would undoubtedly have been aware of its value as a domestic memorial. Her focus on her own central role in his final moments and her rapid return to work suggest she recognised her statuses both as his wife and his widow as creative opportunities and career-furthering strategies.

Acutely aware of her husband's reputation and legacy, as well as her own by association, Mary may have written her diaries with an awareness that they might one day be read and published. Illustrating her personal interest in life writing, she mentions in her diaries the infamous *Marie Bashkirtseff: The Journal of a Young Artist 1860-1884* (published 1887, translated into English in 1889); Margaret Oliphant's *Memoir of the Life of Laurence Oliphant and of Alice Oliphant his Wife* (1891); and Mrs Sutherland Orr's *Life and Letters of Robert Browning* (1897). She compares her life writing to that of her female contemporaries: 'Reading [Georgiana Burne-Jones' *The Memorials of Edward Burne-Jones* (1904)] – I envy her all the precise & clean history she has of her beloved – of mine I can but garner here & there facts out a mist!' (1904: 30 December). Queen Victoria's *Leaves from a Journal of Our Life in the Highlands* (1868), memorialising her dead husband, was hugely popular, and Mary would also have been aware of published diaries by her female predecessors such as Frances Burney and Emily Shore. Consciously or unconsciously, her readings must have influenced her writing, and her ambition to publish her diaries is suggested in the very first one: 'We [she and George] took up Fatima & read some of the notes & hope to work them out & put them into better form one day' (1887: 3 April). Unlike other Victorian women who committed their thoughts to diaries not intended for public consumption, Mary perhaps shared fellow artist Marie Bashkirtseff's intention to have her journal – 'a monument of human and literary interest' – published. While Marie's journal displays a narcissism absent in Mary's and Evelyn's diaries, Mary's can likewise be described as a 'record of a woman's life, written down day by day . . . as if no one in the world were ever to read it, yet with the purpose of being read' (Bashkirtseff 1884: iv, viii).

In the newly published *Diary of Mary Watts*, editor Greenhow claims that 'Mary wrote it for herself, not anticipating sharing it with the world or with anyone else. This is clear by the tiny, difficult handwriting, and its voluminous nature' (2016a: 9). However, a consideration of the possibility that Mary's diary writing is a self-consciously performed narrative in which she assumes roles or author-characters for a future audience allows it to be read as a canny self-fashioning and even self-promoting strategy through which she aims to (posthumously) challenge public perceptions of her as a submissive angel-wife, as well as wider patriarchal concepts of femininity. There certainly seems to be a performative aspect to her anecdotes, especially in the use of quoted dialogue in the recreation of scenes. Popular critical arguments that 'keeping a diary must entail an imagined reader, whether actual, eventual, or altogether imaginary' (Steinitz 2011: 80) support the idea that Mary intended there to be an eventual external audience for her diaries and adapted them accordingly, inscribing her artistic and authorial agency as well as her dynamic character and rebellious spirit. 'Truly private diaries' reveal so little about their content (being largely incomprehensible to others because written for the self) that they necessarily 'exclude the reader' (Bloom 1996: 25). Contrastingly, though written in tiny writing, Mary's highly detailed and descriptive anecdotes are not encrypted in code like the diaries of Anne Lister, or indecipherable due to use of excessive shorthand, but rather carefully recorded and perhaps just as carefully selected for public consumption. This supports the idea that they were written to be read.

The *Annals* show Mary's unwavering devotion to George and admiration for his work, portraying a somewhat idealised account of their relationship. Mary's diaries paint an alternative, more nuanced and arguably more accurate portrait of her marriage and of herself, undermining longstanding perceptions of the couple and patriarchal concepts of gender as well as assumptions about Victorian marriage. She publicly revered her husband but privately challenged him, transgressing feminine norms in word and action. Using her narrative of togetherness to highlight her own significant interventions and interactions with Victorian Britain's most famous and respected artist, she reveals herself to be an active and influential creative partner or 'significant other' rather than a passive and peripheral wife who unquestioningly worshipped her husband and praised everything he produced. The development of her artistic identity and feminist voice can be traced through a reading of her diaries in which power struggles, sexual politics and gender-role inversions in the Wattses' partnership are registered. The publication and study of Mary's diaries will ensure the recovery and revival of her marginalised life/writing, and the reclamation of her as a remarkable writer as well as artist.

Evelyn's Diary: Adolescence, Anger, Art

Mary's diaries can be compared with Evelyn's daily diary of 1872, written in her adolescent years when she was sixteen and seventeen, which offers insight into her thoughts and feelings as a maturing woman and artist. While it was written long before her marriage to William, and thus contains no record of their interactions, it sheds light on Evelyn's attitude to art, society and femininity. Highlighting debates about female adolescence in the Victorian period, Sarah Grand wrote in 1894, '[i]n the present aspect of the Woman Question, the position of the young girl becomes an important as well as an interesting consideration . . . what girls were, are, will be, and should be is the constant question' – one with which Evelyn was only too familiar. Though her exploration of the 'woman question' is not as explicit as in Mary's diaries, her diary shows she was most certainly a 'modern girl' in that she thinks for herself, revolts against restraint, eschews feminine education in favour of art education, and wants 'more life and fuller' (Grand 1894: 706–7, 713). Offering Evelyn's diary as a case study, and using the diary as 'a way of investigating how young middle[-upper-]class women viewed the choices and constraints they faced in the late Victorian period' (Lewis 1983: 143), this section explores how diaries 'contributed to the evolution of a generation of Victorian girls into the New Women' (Hunter 1992: 54). It further reveals how, for budding women artists, diaries were sites of struggle rather than submission, and private records of professional creative development.

Evelyn's diary registers the problematic nature of the transitional time between childhood and womanhood, and the pull between competing identities. Her diary itself functions as a 'transitional object', 'useful in the [process] of adolescent separation' (Katherine Dalsimer qtd. in Hunter 1992: 65) – that is, as a tool for reorientation of girls to women, from birth family to independent self, just like Mary's honeymoon diary can be seen as a transitional tool for reorientation from the birth family or singular identity to conjugality (Michie 2006: xv). If Mary's diaries can be read together as a fragmented *künstlerroman*, Evelyn's diary is a stunted or truncated *künstlerroman* which stands testimony to her artistic achievement even as it persistently denies it. Frustration is the keynote of Evelyn's diary, in its tone and articulation of adolescent strife, and in its unfulfilled narrative about her artistic growth to maturity. Yet, though her career was still embryonic at this time, Evelyn's early artistic drive and dedication is conveyed by an entry on her seventeenth birthday:

> At work a little after 7 . . . 17 to-day, that is to say 17 years wasted . . . in eating, dawdling and flittering [*sic*] time away . . . At the beginning of each year I say 'I will do something' and at the end I have done nothing. Art is eternal but life is short . . . Now I must do something, I will work work . . . I will make up for it now, I have not a moment to lose. (1872: 30 August)

This significant diary entry marks Evelyn's conscious private resolution to rebel against parental and patriarchal authority by dedicating herself to professional artistic practice. It conveys her earnest and eager approach to art, as well as her self-motivation and determination to assert herself in a male-dominated discipline despite the strong opposition in her family and wider society. Other entries record her intense frustration and bitter despair at how much time was 'fritter[ed] away' on tedious social conventions such as 'needless[ly]' 'chang[ing] [her] dress' (19, 17 August) for 'mortally dull' breakfasts, luncheons and dinners that 'lasted [a] century' (4 December). These express not only a typical teenage boredom, hyperbole and cynicism, but also her conscious contestation of the feminine conventions and social pressures that typically prevented women of her class from pursuing serious careers. She rejects Victorian ideals of aristocratic or bourgeois domestic femininity (fashions, manners and customs she conflates with frivolity and passivity) in favour of a 'masculine' artistic ambition and desire to be 'more industrious' (24 August). Mary, too, notes that she was 'very proud' to be called an 'industrious woman' (1891: 20 April). In writing, drawing, modelling and painting, Evelyn retaliated against what she called her 'insufferable' 'enforced idleness' (18 September), and refused to be detained by patriarchal notions of womanhood.

In a rare discussion of Evelyn's early life, Deborah Cherry argues,

> The diary centres an author-character, unifying in its textual work the fragments and contradictions in which subjectivity was forged. A coherent sense of self was constituted in the narrative of personal struggle against adverse circumstances and massive obstacles, a self-representation in which a resistant and oppositional subject position was formed. (Cherry 1993: 32)

Like Mary's diaries, these 'fragments' trace the emergence of a defiant, distinctive, assertive female voice, recording a 'personal struggle' for a 'coherent sense of self' in the form of artistic identity. Yet, while Mary's diary narrative 'ultimately tells a story of success' (Tromans 2016: 7), Evelyn's diary is by no means a straightforward narrative of triumph over difficulty, or of obstacles overcome. She obsessively records how much time she spends working – or rather wasting – each day, and there is little divergence from this pattern; this suggests the inescapable monotonous daily regime of the bourgeois household that restricted her artistic progression. A typical entry reads, 'worked for an hour before breakfast, worked 3 hours and a half at Grosvenor Square, after luncheon worked again for an hour . . . Another week gone and I have done nothing, have worked even less than usual' (18 August). Comments like 'what an immense deal of time I have wasted' (28 August) pervade her diary, and conclude a large proportion of entries. Evelyn's diary paints a graphic portrait of her girlhood that concurs with a Slade school-friend's memory of her as a 'very serious worker . . . always very absorbed in her work, and quite indifferent to . . . dress . . . she had splendid concentration, and fire enough and genius enough to soar very high' (Lady Stanley qtd. in Stirling 1924: 210).

Evelyn resents rather than enjoys leisure activities like games of chess, and any activity that tears her away from drawing, painting, modelling or reading makes her feel 'unsettled' (19, 16 August); Mary similarly 'fidget[s] to be at work again' (1891: 10 December). Visitors and meals interrupt Evelyn's work; the flickering gas lights strain her eyes and give her headaches; and she angrily records how she 'worked till five but unsatisfactorily as no-one would SIT [for her] and made [her] lose time' (13 September). Inscribing her transgression of the domestic space that obstructed her artistic activity, Evelyn records practicing perspective outside, studying at the British Museum, and visiting the National Gallery and Dudley Gallery – where her future husband William exhibited his own watercolours in the 1860s. Evelyn produced several large, ambitious paintings around this time, including *The Angel with the Serpent* and *Mercury* (pre-1873), for which her brother Spencer was the model; she drew on biblical, literary and mythological sources from an early age. Evelyn's diary reveals an 'author-character' that prefigures her paintings of imprisoned yet resistant women standing at windows, in pivotal positions or at crucial moments (especially *The Gilded Cage*). Her diary was instrumental in the development of her artistic focus and identity, since 'diary-keeping contributed to the process by which late-Victorian girls amassed fragments of experience into identity' (Hunter 1992: 52) in an exploration or construction of an independent (if not 'coherent') self.

Evelyn's diary is comparable with other Victorian women's accounts of their 'struggles to be better' and exemplifies the Victorian 'girlhood diary [as] a document in self-discipline' (Hunter 1992: 64). Yet crucially, she strives for self-improvement and self-discipline in artistic practice rather than genteel femininity or religious devotion. Her diary to some extent conforms to the familiar 'program of reflection, . . . self-admonition, . . . and resolve' (Hunter 1992: 72) in Victorian girls' diaries, yet it is atypical in that all elements pertain to art. Rather than attempting to repress her artistic impulse, passion and potential in a 'narrowing of possibilities . . . action, thought' (Hunter 1992: 63), she resolves to express, advance and fulfil it in a radical redefinition of feminine duty. Instead of affirming her conformity to expectations of appropriate feminine behaviour, she explicitly asserts her 'masculine' artistic ambition. While the confessional, self-berating nature of her diary is comparable with the confession familiar in other Victorian women's life writing (Hunter 1992: 67), her daily confessions about her lack of artistic work or progress inscribe a very different kind of repentance and resolution to that desired by her parents (that is, the relinquishment of professional artistic practice). Since artistic practice was itself a form of rebellion (in her social and familial context), this is a dangerous and disobedient rather than dutiful daughter's diary fit for family reading, and it is as confrontational as it is confessional: it flouts parental authority, social conventions and gender norms in its private pages.

Sarah Grand points out that parents 'frequently compel their . . . daughters to lead an idle, useless, and irksome existence in accordance with their own prejudices, and quite irrespective of the girls' abilities . . . until it is too late for them to make a career for themselves'. She continues, 'daughters of rich, idle . . . mothers . . . are more hoodwinked and imposed upon than girls in any other class', and Evelyn was thus one of the 'most sedulously "protected"' (Grand 1894: 708, 711). Discussing the 'leisure class', Mary Watts expresses similar sentiments in her diary:

> Lives with no end or aim, lived in ministering to one domineering spirit. The very conventions of the life demanding silence, no resistance, a lifelong martyrdom, where all looks luxurious & happy. It is a suffering that naturally I feel a great sympathy for. 'Oh, mothers,' I feel inclined to say, 'make your children live their own lives, not yours. The Home tie is often a halter.' (1891: 11 January)

Echoing Mary's discourse of captivity, Evelyn's sister recalls her saying, 'No one shall drag me out with a halter round my neck to sell me!' (Stirling 1922: 181), and her mother's desire for 'a daughter, not an artist' encapsulates Mary's concern. Yet Evelyn's awareness of her circumstances, recognition that 'the happiness of her whole life depend[ed] upon the early choice of [an artistic] career', and obsession with maximising her time meant she avoided the familiar female fate of being 'doomed to stagnation at home' (Grand 1894: 713). When forbidden to paint, she continued to work secretly, before the family breakfast, at dawn or in the dark when she struggled to see, locking herself in her room and hiding her artistic materials from her mother (Stirling 1922: 173–5). Though 'trained in the rituals of gentility' (Cherry 1993: 32), Evelyn refused to conform to the social routine of balls and dances in order to secure a financially advantageous marriage leading to motherhood. Evelyn's private diary, inscribing resistance to domestic captivity, functions as 'a "compartment" for exploration and release within the context of the family home' (Hunter 1992: 70), allowing her to vent frustrations that could not be openly articulated, and to assert her personal autonomy distinct from the wishes of her family.

Despite working for hours at a time, Evelyn constantly rebukes herself for being 'diss[i]pated', 'lazy', 'appallingly idle' and 'always dawdling' (16, 20, 29, 27 August). Her self-scrutiny and self-flagellation show the damaging impact – and perhaps partial internalisation – of Victorian notions of female inadequacy. Mary is also at times ashamed by her own unproductivity, 'lazy inclinations' and 'lapse[s] into idleness' (1887: 2 April, 2 September), and resolves to 'use all daylight possible . . . be punctual . . . not dawdle!' (1904: July), using the same self-critical lexis. Mary's high expectations of herself are conveyed by entries such as, 'the ceiling was all up & I saw my work for the first time complete – though I would like to begin it again & do it better in every way'; and 'let me always expect ten times as much of myself than I do of others' (1891: 17 April, 31 August). Evelyn sees 'a thousand faults' in her works (26 August), admonishes her 'unsatisfactory' progress (16 November) and laments she 'never can get the work [she] want[s] done' (21 August). She is her own harshest critic and 'brutal taskmaster', who is never 'satisfied with [her]self' (20 November) and always 'cross with [her]self' (11 December).

As a fellow woman artist, Mary empathised with Evelyn's frustrated feelings, and both register a conflict between – and struggle to reconcile – domestic duties and artistic practice in their diaries. Unwin points out that because Mary's work took place within the home environment rather than a geographically distant studio, her ability to work was not limited by physical access or compromised by the increasing demands of her role as a wife and nurse to an ailing and elderly husband (2004: 245). Yet Mary spent much time caring for George during his frequent bouts of (at times grave) illness, and was restricted in artistic activity by 'the many small dull things upon the road of life, always needing [her] thought & care' (M. Watts 1891: 10 July). The necessity of a famous artist's wife to do 'things of the house' – enduring 'afternoons of drudgery' (1891: 13–14 June), sending letters, writing visiting lists, 'spending afternoons leaving cards on people' (1891: 23–6 June) and entertaining an almost continuous influx of visitors – prevents or interrupts her work. Her unfinished sentences, aposiopeses and ellipses testify to 'the old misery of constant intrusion' (1891: 5 July).

Articulating woman's process of artistic production against adversity, Mary writes that her banner is 'having a hard struggle for existence' (1906: 1 August), and that 'the days pass, & [she seems] only to take small steps towards any of [her] goals' (1891: 15 December). She suggests the greater difficulty for a maternal figure to be an artist when she cares for her young niece and nephew, writing, 'the darlings take up much of my time – "All your time" [George] says a little reproachfully' (1893: 17 April). She also suggests the difficulty of sustaining an artistic career as a married woman when she writes in her diary, 'My days slip by without a scrap of artistic work being done. Why women fail in art is answered to myself "because of the little things in life"' (1893: 15 April). This fleeting, seemingly superficial diary entry can be read as a serious social comment on the domestic pressures militating against women's artistic activity. Entries in Evelyn's adolescent diary concur: 'Somehow or the other I am wasting all my time' (17 September); 'this year every imaginable obstacle has been put in my way, but slowly and tediously I am mastering them all' (30 August). While Evelyn's diary confirms that 'femininity was one of the great obstacles facing the aspiring woman artist' (A. Smith 1996: 41), she refused to be content with amateur status and the limitations imposed on 'lady artists'. As in Mary's diary, Evelyn's use of the term 'master' has double connotations of gaining control and improving artistic skill, challenging the patriarchal power of the 'Old Masters' and the traditional association of artistic mastery with masculinity.

Self-reproach verging on self-loathing often surfaces in Evelyn's diary entries: she 'feel[s] very disgusted' with one of her paintings which she calls 'a parody [of] the original' (26 August), and believes she left another work 'worse even than [it] was before' (17 September) after spending four hours on it. Evelyn's sister writes that 'work, to her, was the joy of existence, and she laboured – voluntarily, unceasingly – from the cradle to the grave' (Stirling 1922: 12); yet Evelyn writes in her diary, 'each minute idly spent will rise, swelled to whole months and years, and haunt me in my grave' (30 August). Journal entries by better-known British diarist Emily Shore (1891) aged sixteen and seventeen are strikingly similar to Evelyn's expressions at the same age. Emily writes that she will 'look back with great regret on . . . the seventeenth year of [her] life, thus apparently wasted, as far as study is concerned', and on her seventeenth birthday she writes, 'I truly hate myself' (1836: 15, 25 December). She berates herself for her idleness and incapability, though it is clear she is an avid reader, sharp thinker and ambitious writer. Similar expressions are recorded in Mary Watts's diaries: she 'remember[s] feeling very old at 16' (1891: 7 November) and admits 'wishing [she] never was born - trying to draw & not able to please [her]self' (1887: 1 September); George also 'remembered at 16 being <u>ashamed</u> to think he was so old & had done nothing' (1887: 9 June) and at seventy-four he says 'there is not an hour left that I can afford to lose' (1891: 24 February). Self-criticism engendered by an acute consciousness of irrevocably lost time and a sense of insufficient artistic output was a particularly pertinent issue for professional Victorian women artists in their struggle to reconcile domestic and artistic matters, feminine and professional identities. Despite their ability and achievements, Victorian women diarists Emily, Evelyn and Mary were tormented by an imagined inertia and shared a deeply ingrained sense of inadequacy that was a wider condition of the Victorian woman creator (writer and/or artist) subordinated by patriarchal society. They shared an early feminist discourse of struggle, dissatisfaction and frustration, voicing specifically female experiences and concerns. Yet for Mary and Evelyn, both self-criticism and self-belief were integral to their success as ambitious professional artists.

Towards the end of the diary, Evelyn's tone becomes less frustrated as her artistic activity increases and she works more 'steadily', although her low spirits in this year permeate her writing. One entry reads, 'worked 1 hour before breakfast, <u>real[l]y worked</u>, only 4 hours at [the South Kensington], read 1 hour in Reading Room, modelled 1 hour in evening' (29 October). Another reads, 'worked steadily and successfully at Kensington', although it ends with the familiar remark, 'did nothing after dinner, miserable, I am always wasting time' (25 November). Her diary traces not her artistic progression but rather (what she sees as) her artistic stagnation, as shown by these three successive entries: 'very tired [and] depressed, did not sleep last night, I cannot work as I want to' (26 November); 'worked steadily at Kensington but not brilliantly, 3 hours modelling, dissatisfied – do not progress' (27 November); 'did nothing marvellous, tired depressed dull' (28 November).

Presumably, Evelyn's suffering from 'that feeling of depression' (M. Watts 1891: 20 July) and artistic frustration was alleviated by her attendance at the Slade School of Art the following year, where she excelled, before spreading her wings to study in Italy. Both Evelyn's and William's depression was apparently remedied by marriage, which gave them each new life: William's cousin (a woman artist) recalls that he was 'subject to states of serious depression – but only *before* his marriage. Evelyn cured all that. She would never allow him to mope. She gave him new vigour, and brought into his life just what he wanted – her own splendid courage' (Stirling 1924: 225 [original emphasis]). William, remarking on the cruelty of life, told a friend, '[i]f it were not for Evelyn I should like to get out of it all' (qtd. in Barrington *c.*1922: 6). Similarly, Mary records her discovery of 'old notes' of George's showing his 'deep sadness & dejection' (1887: 5 December), before his marriage to her brought him happiness and renewed enthusiasm for life. This shows the profound impact Mary and Evelyn had on their husbands' psychological states as well as their works.

Mary's criticism of her diary writing is more extreme than that of her visual art. Echoing Evelyn's daily resolutions to do better in art, Mary writes, 'I woke thinking of the precious thoughts I let go! alas . . . I must try to keep my Fatima better (1887: 2 October). She records her struggle to write: 'Fatima like the grasshopper becomes a burden to me at times, the moment I take her up, my brains lie down like naughty boys & kick – I am like the unfortunate nursery maid trying to deal with them' (1891: 17 March). This intriguing entry simultaneously reveals her androgynous self-perception, rebellious spirit and determination as a diarist. Mary became increasingly aware of her older husband's mortality and her heavy responsibility as the sole recorder of their life together. She writes,

> Each morning as I sit up to write, I feel a pang of grief for the barrenness of mind that comes to seize me when I take up Fatima. I am aware of my stupid dreams out of which I have just come . . . I look back over another day of my life with him, <u>gone</u>, & I feel miserable at my brain numbness & the dull record becomes more & more impossible. (1891: 10 July)

Mary's use of frustrated or painful maternal metaphors in her description of her 'barrenness of mind' and keeping 'Fatima in these days of labour' (1891: 25 March) prefigure Cixous's metaphors for literary composition as childbirth. Cixous links woman's 'gestation drive' with the 'desire to write: a desire to live self from within, a desire for the swollen belly, for language, for blood' (where blood and milk are associated with ink) (qtd. in Jones 1993: 457). Mary's numerous self-reflexive entries berating herself for her bad memory and poor diary-keeping, 'mad at [her] own stupidity' and 'unrelieved dulness, idioticy! [*sic*]' (1891: 28 June, 25 March), suggest her anxious attempt to 'catch & keep . . . the silver stream of [George's] delightful talk' (1891: 28 June) as though recording it for posterity (and publication). She reviews her own writing: '[I] have been looking back through Fatima – glad of what there is, tho' it is but a poor shadow of the blessed substance' (1891: 12 July).

Her sometimes problematic relationship with writing is expressed in other diary entries: 'we seem to need better & more expression' (1891: 18 June); 'I write write write, each morning increasing the errors' (1893: 15 June); 'I [am] feeling too stupid to write or think . . . what is the use of trying to write with a sodden brain like mine' (1893: 30 March); 'My day to write! I sometimes wish pens were at the bottom of the sea!' (1896: 22 December).

Both Mary's and Evelyn's diaries express a sense of creative frustration and artistic urgency, illuminating the tensions and anxieties experienced by professional Victorian women artists, writers and diarists. They both convey woman's struggle to write within the confines of a male-constructed linguistic system and to create within the limitations of a male-dominated art world, as well as the difficulty to overcome internalised patriarchal notions of women's inability and inferiority. Cixous suggests that 'silenced women must finally find ways to cry, shriek, scream' (Gilbert 1986: xi) in writing, and indeed, Mary records the cathartic, empowering effect of privately expressing female pain in her diary: 'what a blessing for women that they may cry & howl, it clears away so much . . . I cried . . . & was able to rise again, comforted and healed' (1893: 10 June). This entry offers valuable insight into her private heightened feelings at a time when feminine emotion was suppressed, controlled and kept within social bounds. Although no such comfort is visible in Evelyn's deflated diary, its lamentation of lost time and expression of artistic ambition shows its similar function, offering unprecedented insight into her emotional and psychological interiority. As women writers and artists, Mary and Evelyn represented a radical challenge to phallo(go)centrism as active creators of meaning and cultural producers. Their diaries explicitly reveal the agency, intent and determination involved in their resolution to depart from gender conventions as professional women artists asserting themselves in male domains and traditions.

Despite the similarities, there are also crucial differences between Evelyn's and Mary's diaries. In its primary function as an activity – or rather inactivity – log (recording the exact number of hours spent working or wasting, at church and galleries), Evelyn's largely factual diary privileging artistic concerns resists the 'feminine gush', conversational style, intimate detail, excited recording of visitors and writing of the female body found in other Victorian women's diaries (including Mary's), which tend to focus on family affairs, friendships and domestic details. Critics have noted that for some Victorian teenagers, 'the diary's primary purpose seemed to be to provide a safe ground for documenting, exploring, and disciplining nascent sexuality' (Hunter 1992: 68). By eschewing emotional excess, a discussion of physical female development (including any mention of menstruation) and a focus on the (changing adolescent) body, Evelyn's diary subverts expectations of a Victorian teenage girl's diary and women's life writing more broadly. She perhaps consciously resisted traditionally feminine or female modes in her private writing as she did in her professional fine art practice. Although Evelyn's diary makes no explicit references to sexuality, her documenting, exploring and disciplining of her nascent artistic identity can be seen as a form of sublimation. Despite the lack of excessive or fluctuating emotion and physical description, it is in fact saturated with an insatiable, insuppressible desire and passion for artistic activity, inextricably linked with a sense of urgency and a yearning for more time to dedicate to art.

To conclude: while Mary's and Evelyn's sense of self is similarly defined in relation to their (traditionally male) roles as artists, Mary's is also defined in relation to her female role as wife (but not as 'angel in the house') whereas Evelyn's entails a rejection of genteel femininity. Evelyn's largely non-gendered budding professional artist's narrative is an even less conventional example of Victorian women's writing than Mary's, and is arguably more gender-radical. Mary represents herself 'relationally' or 'contextually'; her anecdotal, dialogue-heavy diary presents a generally positive or optimistic relationship to domesticity as it is entwined with creativity. Evelyn's sense of self is separate and individual (traditionally 'masculine'); her diary documents only her internal dialogue and profound sense of dissatisfaction with domesticity. This perhaps also reflects her unmarried status and her sense of isolation as a female fine artist who stood out in both the upper-middle-class household and the male-dominated Victorian art world. Nonetheless, a single-mindedness, strong artistic identity and autobiographical 'I' emerge in both Mary's and Evelyn's diaries. Both are sites of struggle that record their secret rebellious spirits, protests against patriarchal (conjugal or parental) authority, and attempts to reconcile domestic and artistic, private and public, modesty and ambition, feminine and feminist. Mary's and Evelyn's diaries trace the emergence of their assertive New Woman voices and (proto)feminist convictions that formed the basis of their later suffragist activism.

Notes

1. These are the only extant diaries owned by Watts Gallery and the De Morgan Foundation; it is assumed that others once existed (Mary's 1902 diary begins 'Fatima 16th') but have been destroyed, or may be in the possession of unknown relatives. Mary's diaries were not completely transcribed until 2016; I transcribed 1896, 1902, 1904 and 1906–8, and revised the 1887 transcription. Mary's unedited diaries exceed 300,000 words; the full text is available at Watts Gallery Library and Archive. Many pages from Mary's diaries are missing, having been cut out allegedly by the Wattses' ward Lilian, presumably in an attempt to censor intimate or radical content, to preserve the family's reputation or to hide her own parentage.

2. Edward Burne-Jones's painting depicts Mrs Bluebeard of Charles Perrault's 1697 fairy tale.

3. See also Mary's Limnerslease ceilings, memorial headstones and chapel designs.

4. George's many female admirers and ladies who devoutly worshipped him called him 'Signor', meaning 'Master', originally given because of his courteous manner and the time he spent in Italy. Mary sometimes affectionately refers to George as 'Signor' in her diaries.

5. Mary is probably referring to the English sculptor and goldsmith Sir Alfred Gilbert, R. A. (1854–1934), whose portrait was painted by George Watts in 1896.

6. Like Mary, Evelyn returned to work in her studio soon after William's death, and began to make a design for the monument for his grave, which she modelled in clay from her drawing before it was worked out in marble (completed 1918, about eighteen months after his death).

Chapter 5

Inscribing the Female Body

Drawing on extensive archival research, this chapter studies various neglected writings – private and published – by the Wattses and the De Morgans. Exploring questions of authorship and authority, it analyses collaborative and individual writings that focus on and inscribe the female body: Evelyn's unpublished juvenilia, William's neglected novels (written and published in partnership with Evelyn), and their anonymously published automatic writing; George's anti-corsetry article (conveying both his and Mary's views, republished in Mary's *Annals*), Mary's private experimentation with poetry, and her published guide to her symbolic decoration *The Word in the Pattern*. With the exception of William, who embarked on a second career as a novelist, these figures have never before been appraised as literary as well as artistic figures, and their writings are largely unexplored. I will analyse and compare the representation of women in their writings, showing how they explored women's place, engaged with contentious early feminist debates, and supported or promoted women's liberation in both their literary and visual works.

The De Morgans: Juvenilia, Novels, Automatic Writing

In addition to her diary, Evelyn wrote stories, poems and plays (*c*.1860s–70), a magazine called *The Reader* (1869), *The Child's Own Book of Fairy Tales* (monographed in the Preface) and the beginning of a novel titled *Nora De Brant* (1869). These childhood writings currently reside unpublished and untranscribed in the De Morgan Foundation archives, and have never before been studied. While these have been entirely disregarded and dismissed as trivial juvenilia, many reveal the 'remarkable, if somewhat grim, imagination and beauty of vision' (Stirling undated)[1] – as well as the progressive and (proto)feminist thought and feeling – of the self-proclaimed 'Authoress' (E. De Morgan notebook 1869: NP). Many of her writings parallel or prefigure her paintings in theme and focus on the female figure, and those with identical titles (for example, her poems and paintings titled 'Love the Misleader', 'The Angel of Death' and 'The Valley of Shadows') can be read as 'double works', for which her Pre-Raphaelite predecessor Dante Gabriel Rossetti is famed. Her literary and visual texts share a vocabulary of spirits, angels, death, rebirth, nature, prisoners, the sea, mermaids and mothers, and can be read alongside each other to enhance an understanding of the ways in which Evelyn explored the role and representation of women in her work from a young age.

As a teenager, Evelyn was dissatisfied with the lack or quality of 'recreation books for the young' and so, as she explains in the Preface to her novel *Nora de Brant*, she 'entered the lists with so many of her country-women to endeavour to supply the young folks of the present day with amusing and at the same time instructif [sic] tales'. She adds, wryly, that 'though some may smile at the idea of anything instructif [sic] being contained in a novel, the authoress hopes to prove that it is by no means impossible' (1869: NP). *The Girl's Own Paper* (1880–1956) shows young women writing stories for girls, revealing how Evelyn's work fits into a female literary culture. She was perhaps frustrated or bored by romance novels, devotional works and mass-produced cheap reading material, and quite literally took matters into her own hands, addressing gender-related issues in her writings which often portray active, adventurous, thoughtful and unconventional young women. The female protagonist of her novel, who had 'an energetic disposition', 'could not bare [sic] restraint' and 'mean[t] to break through every sense of propriety', embodies something of Evelyn's own diary author-character. Echoing her diary as well as early feminist writings calling women to action, Evelyn's novel condemns the 'idleness that pervades the minds of the greater part of the rising generation' and imagines what could be achieved if 'the number who are dreamily sighing . . . would but rouse themselves from their lethargy'.

In her handwritten magazine *The Reader*, Evelyn addresses forced mercenary marriage in a short story, engaging with a central feminist issue of the mid-Victorian period. The female character, eighteen-year-old Helen, is told not to consider her own 'likes and dislikes' and instead to adhere to her parents' plan for an 'advantageous' marriage to the 'very rich' Mr Merton. When Helen expresses her opinion that 'one ought to marry for love and not for money', her mother angrily retorts that she shall do as she is told. Helen, stripped of her freedom of choice in marriage, throws herself into her work with 'renewed energy' (E. De Morgan 1869: 1). Biographical parallels can be detected in the conventional, pushy mother and the rebellious, hardworking daughter (though not in the arranged or forced marriage). Evelyn, as 'authoress' of this one-penny 'weekly magazine', writes imagined press reviews of it on the back page, where various newspapers praise her work; this is reminiscent of the format of the popular art magazine *The Studio* which Evelyn almost certainly read.[2] *The Times* calls *The Reader* 'the <u>best</u> and <u>cheapest</u> periodical of the present day'; the *Morning Post* 'cannot fail to recommend to the public this interesting magazine – the tales are moral and instructif [*sic*] without being tedious'; and the *News of the World* calls it 'the best most exciting most interesting most moralising and most instructif [*sic*] of Magazines'. Echoing artist Marie Bashkirtseff's famous teenage journal which Marie herself calls 'the most useful and the most instructive of all the books that ever were or ever will be written' (1889: 24), Evelyn's reviews of her own writing evince her early literary ambition. Her private writing was evidently an imaginative and intellectual outlet where she could experiment with ideas and develop a distinctive voice. Her exploration of gender-related and woman-centred issues – and particularly the tension between female captivity and liberty – in her writings prefigured her visual texts.

Evelyn was largely responsible for William's successful second career as a novelist, whose nine works were motivated and overseen – and in two cases completed and published posthumously – by her.[3] Stirling claims that 'to her alone it was due that he did not actually destroy certain of his books' (1922: 308). In 1901 he wrote two chapters of a novel – which later became *Joseph Vance* – 'just to see what [he] could do', but was 'so little impressed' with his own work that he 'nearly burnt it' and 'put it away in a drawer and forgot all about it' (W. De Morgan qtd. in Stirling 1922: 233). When Evelyn later found the abandoned manuscript, she encouraged him to resume it: impressed by its 'graphic, sordid realism', she 'laid it by his bedside, with a pencil temptingly adjacent' (Stirling 1922: 233) – which he once again took up. Evelyn wrote to a publisher about his first novel, and although it was refused by one publisher before being accepted by Heinemann, she apparently never doubted its worth. His first completed novel *Joseph Vance* was an immediate success when it was finally published in 1906; it was subsequently reprinted in September 1906, three times in 1907 and three times in 1908. His novels were likened to those of Charles Dickens (whom

William greatly admired) in their 'exceptional powers of observation and insight into character' and ability to 'portray the touching woes of the helpless' with 'real pathos' (Barrington *c*.1922: 35).

William's last two novels, *The Old Madhouse* (1919) and *The Old Man's Youth* (1921), left unfinished on his death, were completed and published posthumously by Evelyn in a literary collaboration that stands further testimony to their creative partnership.[4] This posthumous collaboration is comparable with the Wattses' Tennyson statue. Yet Evelyn, while apparently attending to William's legacy, also assumed the position of writer-creator in a usurpation of ultimate authorial and editorial authority, subverting male supremacy and disrupting phallogocentrism. There is a clear distinction between William's and Evelyn's writing in *The Old Madhouse* since William's writing stops mid-sentence and Evelyn continues the narrative on the next page, describing what 'the story would now have told' (De Morgan and De Morgan 1919: 556) over the next ten pages. She pieces together disjointed material to form a coherent whole, revealing the plots that William had shared and constructed with her. This intimate knowledge of her husband's ideas enabled Evelyn to complete and publish the two unfinished works, which not only shows 'how entirely she was one with him in his work' (Barrington *c*.1922: 72–3) but also how she assumed the traditionally male role of writer and powerful position of Author-God. When 'long columns of rapturous enthusiasm for his book arrived' (Barrington *c*.1922: 73), Evelyn had indirectly achieved the literary success she longed for and imitated in her reviews of *The Reader* as a child.

The De Morgans' contemporary Sir William Richmond recalls how William always 'spoke of [Evelyn] with a mingled pride and reverence' (qtd. in Stirling 1922: 308), and Stirling records the couple's collaborative reading and writing practice:

> [William] systematically referred all that he wrote to his wife; and he often stated that he never began any story till she had given him the keynote in an opening sentence. . . . she was an excellent critic; and as she had been the mainspring of his imagination, so hers remained the final verdict against which, in his view, there was no appeal. (Stirling 1922: 308)

This version of events is verified by Evelyn in 'A Few Last Words To the Reader' concluding *The Old Madhouse*, proudly explaining how she was centrally involved in William's creative writing process as the first reader and reviewer of each new novel:

It was his usual practice to read out aloud to me every Sunday evening all he had written during the week. When the novel was completed we read it aloud again straight through from the beginning to the end . . . As the story was always read to me while in progress I too got to believe in the reality of the characters . . . and I have frequently asked him when he came down to lunch, or had finished writing for the day, such a question as, for instance, 'Well, have they quarrelled yet?' . . . towards the end of the book when an intelligible winding-up of the story became imperative, the plot was taken up and carefully considered, all the straggling threads gathered together and finalities decided upon . . . it happened that on that last Friday night in December, when my husband laid down his pen in the middle of a sentence never to be completed, he had told me as much as he knew himself of what the ending of the book was to be. I am therefore able to give a short synopsis of his ideas . . . (De Morgan and De Morgan 1919: 566–7)

This practice whereby William read his work to Evelyn in the evenings, leading to lively discussions between them, is comparable with the Wattses' evening reading practice which also sparked stimulating discussion in the privacy of their studio-home. A contemporary tribute to the De Morgans hails Evelyn as 'the presiding genius who encouraged and stimulated her husband in his writing' with her 'discriminating incitement'; '[William] when nearing the age of seventy, was far too diffident of his powers in this new line of activity to have carried through one story had it not been for the inspiring companionship of his wife' (Barrington *c*.1922: 72–3). She supported his literary career intellectually, offering constructive criticism and alternative plots; she helped him revise that of *Somehow Good* (1908) which 'of all his novels . . . has the most orderly and best-constructed plot, and . . . is his masterpiece' (Phelps 1917: 442–3). Thus, in both the Wattses' and the De Morgans' partnerships, the female figure had an active, authoritative and crucial (if largely unrecognised) role in her husband's creative process and production, and they painted or penned works together, subverting traditional dynamics between the sexes. In the light of Evelyn's considerable influence over her husband's work, William's writings that address gender-related and feminist issues can be seen to reflect and express both his and her own progressive socio-political views.

William's novel *An Affair of Dishonour* (1910) directly addresses the place and treatment of women in what can be read as a serious critique of patriarchal Victorian society. Despite being set during the Restoration in England, William writes that the novel's heroine Lucinda 'lived in a day when women condemned women and applauded men, even as in our own' (41). Rhetorical questions such as 'were not the world and its ways, its gains and its glories – and its women – for men?' (93–4) seem designed to make readers reassess masculinist assumptions and ideologies. The novel addresses and condemns the objectification, ownership, use and abuse of woman by man, echoing and joining early feminist discourse. The description of villainous Sir Oliver's affairs with women details how 'he had tired of them and flung them away, much as a child discards the toy it cares to possess no longer!' (70). Describing the relationship between lovers Sir Oliver and Lucinda, William writes,

> For this was the way he treated women, doing all he might, without overmuch trouble to himself, to keep them cheerful, brilliant, and beautiful, for his own sake. In doing which he no doubt studied in a sense their happiness, just as it might be said that he studied also the happiness of his horse. But when at last his horse failed him . . . he would turn him forth to the knacker without remorse, unless he thought there was still service in him . . . And the like held good, in its degree, when women were in question, and no lesser beasts of burden. (W. De Morgan 1910: 62)

The omniscient narrator offers insight into the male character's mind and implicitly condemns his use of women for self-gratification. The analogy between the woman and the horse highlights her subservient status as male property, and the reference to the knacker's yard has dangerous, violent implications for women while presenting man as a ruthless master. Such passages suggest the author's dissociation from or disidentification with patriarchal perceptions, which are presented in the text only to be challenged, attacked and ridiculed by the narrator who voices William's antiphallocentric views. A contemporary review hailed this novel 'a powerful story, told with great art; destined . . . to have a permanent place in English fiction' (Phelps 1917: 446).

Although William's engagement with feminist issues in his novels might not be immediately obvious, his attack on hypocritical masculinist society is at times strikingly direct and explicit:

> a society of liars and hypocrites bestows [brutal epithets containing falsehoods] so freely on the woman who transgresses laws womankind have had no share in making, with only a lenient word of formal blame for the male transgressor, of whom she may have been the half-unwilling victim. (W. De Morgan 1910: 167)

This prefigures his letter to Lansbury in support of women's suffrage – showing how his feminist ideas took shape – and complicates the popular yet simplistic contemporary view that in literature 'he was a humorist, he was no cynic, he was a playful, wayward optimist who . . . was much nearer comedy than tragedy' (Richmond qtd. in Stirling 1922: 10). Lucinda might seem to be a victim rather than an active agent for change in that she is accepting of her submissive role to the wicked libertine figure of Sir Oliver and continues to love him throughout her tribulations. Yet her indignant statements like 'treat me not like a fool, because I am a woman' (W. De Morgan 1910: 109) undermine an interpretation of her as a mere submissive victim. William engages with sexual politics both implicitly and explicitly, indirectly and directly in this text; his strong sympathy with woman and condemnation of man can be seen to reflect his feminist position. William addresses marriage conflicts and social issues involving women in his other novels (including *Somehow Good*), and 'qualities of sharp intelligence, determination and independent thought' are characteristic of the female figures in *Alice-for-Short* (1907); this novel contains 'a new type of De Morgan woman: ambitious, scheming and ruthless' (Cain 2012: NP).[5] Though most of William's novels are now largely unknown or dismissed as awkward or unremarkable, one contemporary critic claimed 'William De Morgan has had more influence on the course of fiction in the twentieth century than any other writer in English' because 'he gave new vogue to . . . the "life" novel' (Phelps 1917: 444). His novels are culturally important in their engagement with gender-related issues and early feminist debates, and as examples of male-authored antiphallocentric writing and conjugal collaboration in literature.

Around the time of their marriage, Evelyn and William embarked upon a long-term collaborative project with 'automatic writing', consisting of letters purporting to come from spirits of the mediums' friends and from angels. The collection of 'spirit messages' was published anonymously by the couple in 1909 under the title *The Result of an Experiment*. This text can be read in various ways: as interwoven biographies of their dead friends; as conjugal creative writing containing characters (as in William's novels); and as a record of Evelyn's internal dialogue or monologue. Evelyn was preoccupied with psychical investigation, and the Wattses were also interested in spiritualism: George was elected to the Society for Psychical Research in 1884, and Mary writes in her diary that the 'love of the mysterious [is] an essential & valuable part of the human mind, far from being . . . an impediment to progress, it [has] in the main been the stimulus towards something better than man's best effort' (1891: 22 August). While the De Morgans' long-forgotten text has never before been studied, a feminist reading illuminates its cultural importance. Previous scholarship has recognised the connections between psychical research and feminism (Cherry 2000: 207). E. L. Smith argues that Evelyn's agenda was twofold in that her artworks reflect both spiritualist and feminist concerns (2002: 17), and these two discourses are complementary in their focus on transfiguration and liberation. *The Result of an Experiment* exemplifies how spiritualist discourses were used as vehicles for the expression of feminist ideas in the nineteenth century.

The De Morgans conducted this controversial experiment in automatic writing together when they were alone, and their description of a double writing evokes the plaster cast of the Wattses' clasped left hands as well as the De Morgans' own collaborative novelistic practice:

> One person holds a pencil as though writing, and the second places his or her hand on the wrist of the writing-hand of the first. The point of the pencil of course rests on a blank sheet of paper. Under these circumstances the hands usually move after a while; each operator believing in most cases that his or her hand is pulled by the other. If the experiment is persevered in, writing not infrequently results. (De Morgan and De Morgan 1909: xii)

While the hierarchy of hands is unclear, the order of persons in the opening lines of their publication (subsequently repeated) suggest that Evelyn was the leader of this project as she was in William's novel-writing process: 'The following pages contain the outcome of a prolonged experiment tried by two persons, a lady and her husband' (xi). Indeed, some 'spirit letters' are reminiscent of Evelyn's diary entries, and several allude to (her own experience of her) professional artistic practice: 'Art is more important than you think. But it must be earnest . . . the strength of one's arm, and the whole power of one's being is to be given to it' (11). Another reads,

> Art is hard, and the flesh a burden, and many are swept back by the angry flood of adverse criticism. It is best to do as you do, quietly to work [. . .] to shun the public with its ever-vacant stare, to hide your innermost thoughts from view till they grow and become strong. Continue. And now I bid you prosper. (6–7)

Here, Evelyn as writer seems to address Evelyn as artist, expressing her private thoughts or internal dialogue. The automatic writing process she records can be seen to reflect woman's struggle to write within phallogocentrism: 'At first nothing but scribbles came, then a few words were written, then a phrase; the phrase often being repeated all over the page. After many months the writing became stronger and clearer' (xii).

The self-berating voice in Evelyn's diary is also recognisable in 'spirit letters' which seem to express her own artistic anxiety and ambition: 'I am not in any most certain state of mind about my life-work. I mean that though I did my best I am fully aware I might have done better' (8); 'to be idle is fatal' (20); 'apparent failure [was] stamped on all I did. I made as I thought no progress. I felt my life was wasted' (45); 'life on earth is short' (46); 'When you rise in the morning say aloud: – This day I will work with a will' (51). Another speaker's warning to the couple 'not to put [their] strength into fool-ish dinner-parties' (50) echoes Evelyn's lamentation of dull dinners and social events in her diary. The spirit messages, which are generally hopeful, encouraging and reassuring, are perhaps Evelyn's self-moti-vational mantras that she used as a mechanism for coping with the work and time-related anxieties expressed in her diary. They could also be William's words of consolation to her: 'at night when you go to rest ask yourselves if during the day just ended you have done the best you had in you to do . . . Then rest in peace' (51). Indeed, they echo his philosophy that 'all men and women have within them the possibility of eternal development' (Phelps 1917: 446), which underpins his novels.

Yet crucially, the De Morgans 'could only get [the automatic writ-ing] together'. Their dual authorship or bi-narrative, in automatic as in novel writing, raises the question of authorial and gender iden-tity, subverting any notion of clearly demarcated gendered writing. Like the Wattses who read together every evening, the De Morgans 'decided to devote a certain time every evening to writing, and to admit no one into their secret' (De Morgan and De Morgan 1909: xii). The couples' collaborative, interdependent reading and writing practices involved an intimacy that was perhaps to some extent eroti-cally charged. While the Wattses' private reading alcove has its own erotic connotations and symbolism, the De Morgans' solitary secret 'experiment' necessitating physical contact in order to conduct spir-its through the medium of the body in an uncontrolled trance-like or transformative state has sexual undertones. It can also be seen as a liberatory writing of the female body (with its erotic energies) as conceptualised by Cixous. Indeed, the repetitive, elliptical, non-chronologically ordered writing apparently led by Evelyn assumes multiple characters (signified by varied voices and handwritings) and 'became often very fluent and rapid, pages being covered without any pause' (De Morgan and De Morgan 1909: xiii) or punctuation, featuring stylistic and formal tendencies of *écriture féminine*.

In the De Morgans' text, 'Angels' (named 'Hope', 'Freedom' and 'Courage') and 'Spirits known to the Mediums when in the flesh' – which may well have included the (supposed) voice of George Watts – discuss their 'social views' (14) on controversial contemporary topics such as vivisection (41), Mammonism (45) and temperance (49). They speak of 'the threshold' (71), a 'future life' (1), a 'glorious awakening' (2), and 'rejoice in the full fruition of [a] life of struggle in the flesh' – an 'upward struggle' (6) 'into the light' (8). Echoing the early feminist iconography of Evelyn's paintings, spirit messages refer to 'ropes' (74), 'chains' (71) and 'dark prison[s]' (64) as well as 'freedom' (8) and growing light (90). One reads, 'strive upwards . . . break the last chain that binds you, and rise upwards into the dawn' (25), paralleling the transformation from captivity to liberty in her visual art. To some extent, this text can be read as a companion piece to Evelyn's paintings, which visually depict her ideas on spiritual and socio-political evolution.

Envisioning a world of liberty and equality, spirit messages describe a 'glorious' world of 'no physical drawbacks, and a great . . . extension of perceptions and powers', telling the mediums, 'You are on the right path. Your work is all right and you are both growing fast . . . Continue . . . that hard incessant struggle' (10–11). This perhaps refers to their labours as both creators and suffragists. The speakers express the potential for the achievement of a utopian world, and commend the De Morgans' 'most modern' 'sympathies, . . . art, . . . way of seeing life' (48), telling them 'You are ahead of your time' (72). Among the letters purporting to come from Angels is one telling the couple, 'You are in the mire but on the verge of a new birth, and light is breaking . . . You must learn, and hope, and strive, and struggle' (32, 35); and the Angel of Hope says, 'remember that in your toil and striving lie the seeds of the future growth' (72). Using the early feminist discourse of struggle and hope, these messages seem to convey and encourage the De Morgans' shared suffragist spirit and dedication to the women's cause. Another Angel tells them, 'You . . . must do your best, units of a big whole' (48); 'you will not fail in the fight' (50); 'be brave' (54). The wise, kind Angels are consistent with Evelyn's as well as the Wattses' visual representations of maternal Angels of Death, and with early feminist angelology.

One particularly striking statement alludes to the De Morgans' interests in art, politics and spiritualism, and seems to comment on the progressiveness of Edwardian society in its move towards women's suffrage: 'Now you have . . . Art of a growing sort, and a great striving for social growth, and underlying all a dim perception of another world. Never was there a greater age in the history of the world' (48). This echoes Mary's diary entry: 'We are on the verge of great changes, perhaps the greatest the world has known' (1887: 15 May). The Wattses' and the De Morgans' shared feminist vision is expressed in their writings as in their visual works.

The Wattses: Articles, Poetry, the Word in the Pattern

The Wattses publicly supported female emancipation as leading figures in the late nineteenth-century dress reform movement: they were Vice-Presidents of the Healthy & Artistic Dress Union, founded in 1890 to promote dress reform. Debates surrounding fashion and clothing elucidated conflicts central to early feminist debates about the female body, gender roles and characteristics, boundaries between separate spheres, and the relationship between nature and artifice. Art and politics met in this movement, which intersected with the women's suffrage movement in its promotion of greater female freedom. Members and supporters of the Healthy and Artistic Union were active in the suffrage movement: Laura Elizabeth Morgan-Browne was a member of the committee in 1892 before becoming an executive in the Central National Society for Women's Suffrage in 1896; and militant suffragette Frances Elizabeth Rowe published an article titled 'Healthy and Artistic Dress' in *The Dress Review* in 1908 (Crawford 1999: 48, 609). The Union's pamphlet written by E. M. D. Wheeler, illustrated by socialist and 'mentor of radical activists' (Crawford 1999: 519) Walter Crane, clearly lists 'Mrs G. F. Watts' as one of its Vice-Presidents alongside Crane, prominent suffragist artist and writer Louise Jopling, and New Sculptor Hamo Thornycroft. Illustrator and close friend of the De Morgans, Henry Holiday, was President of the Union.

This highlights Mary's important role in a forward-thinking artistic community and feminist reform circle. Together these famous figures openly stood against oppressive norms of feminine beauty and restrictive Victorian feminine fashions such as corsets, crinoline and bustles. They criticised this multi-layered, physically constricting clothing, and particularly the hourglass figure achieved through the wearing of the corset, which can be seen as a nineteenth-century symbol of women's literal imprisonment in their bodies. Normative male ideals of feminine beauty were enforced through the widespread corseting of the female body, which clinched in the waist, exaggerated the hips and pushed up the breasts. The leaflet's aim was to persuade ladies to abandon the corset and instead wear comfortable, loose-fitting clothing, though this was not in line with the current mode of dress.

George was elected President of The Norwood Anti-Tight-Lacing Society, and his condemnation of corsets in his public diatribe 'On Taste in Dress' was published in the *Nineteenth Century Review* in 1883. Mary (who encouraged George to write articles on aesthetics) republished it in her *Annals* in 1912, suggesting her approval and recognition of the appropriateness of its message during a time of rising feminist feeling. It joined the chorus of outcries against various forms of female oppression. George's passionately written article places strong emphasis on female physical freedom: he argues that the 'fashionable lady's gown fits so closely to her person that freedom of movement becomes impossible' (1912: 203); stays restrict 'freedom of movement' (220); the neck should be 'left free'; and a dress 'should be so cut as to leave the arm at the shoulder as free as possible' (211). This can be seen in Mary's own practical style of dress in her 1882 self-portrait, and Evelyn De Morgan – determined to escape 'young-ladyism' – longed to dress like a poor art student (Stirling 1922: 178).

George's argument that women conform to the wearing of corsets in 'obedience to a stupid conventionality' (221) and only admire a tiny corseted waist 'because modern men and women grow up accustomed to such departure from nature' (204) suggests his recognition of the cultural construction and performance of femininity: 'the passing show' (204). He seems to acknowledge the social conditioning that dictates and perpetuates ideals of feminine 'beauty', which he claims is in fact 'hideous deformity' (217). He champions the 'organic' over the 'ornamental' and the 'natural' over the 'unnatural' (210) in a condemnation of excessive beautification and feminisation. While women who 'self-impose weakness' by wearing corsets, tight gloves and crippling shoes provoke his contempt because they are somewhat complicit in their own oppression, he also expresses his sympathy with women who 'from long custom of wearing these stays, are really unaware how much they are hampered and restricted' (215, 219). His recognition of women's 'unconscious slavery' to the 'tyranny of fashion' (225) is remarkably radical for a man of his time, pre-empting more recent feminist discourse and gender theory on women's enslavement to oppressive patriarchal ideologies and the beauty system.

George's sympathy specifically with women is reinforced by his claim that 'for one boy injured by football or other games, there are many thousand girls whose lives . . . suffer from a fashion' (225). As well as urging women to rebel against prevailing feminine norms, he entreats men not to objectify women and perpetuate male ideals of femininity which women suffer to achieve: 'Let the man who admires the piece of pipe that does duty for a [female] body picture to himself the wasted form and seamed skin' (219). George thus demonstrates how forms of writing were not only significant vehicles for constructing ideals of femininity in the Victorian period, noting that 'tiny feet and hands are terms constantly used by poets and novelists . . . to express . . . general delicacy and refinement' (215), but also for challenging and deconstructing them. The Wattses advocated freer, looser styles which allowed more freedom of movement and enabled women to be more active, impacting the role and representation of women in Victorian society. In the Wattses' shared agenda to highlight, critique and liberate women from oppressive feminine norms in their work, they can be perceived as early feminists. George's writing on the female body not only stands testimony to the fact that early feminist views were held by men as well as women, but also to twentieth-century feminist theory that men can produce antiphallo(go)centric texts.

In its politically charged rhetoric about the female body, George's polemical article shares a discourse with feminist journals, magazines and newspapers of the period, and with pioneering feminist writing using dress as a metaphor for female captivity. Echoing George's earlier article on women and dress, Sarah Grand criticises a prescribed feminine mould (role or ideal) 'of an invariable size and shape for all girls . . . If is does not fit, the girl is held to be at fault' and she is to be altered and taken in 'like a dress'. She continues,

> if possible she is forced into it and kept there; and in one case her spirit will be broken, her development checked, and her chances of happiness lost; in another she will outgrow it in spite of herself, but will become distorted in the effort. (Grand 1894: 713–14)

George's article can be seen to dialogise with, and contribute to, the discourse of dress used to highlight women's ideological enslavement in Victorian society.

Mary's unpublished writing – in the form of notebooks, common-place books and journals – is an expressive fusion and profusion of forms or genres that is devotional, political, poetical, philosophical and auto/biographical. Pages are mysteriously torn out or stuck together, cut out and stuck in from elsewhere; words or lines are crossed out and asterisks or arrows are added; and fragments of verse are scattered sporadically alongside preliminary sketches. Mary's unpublished writings provide evidence of her hitherto unacknowledged experimentation with poetry. The pages of Mary's pre-marital journal or 'Diary'[6] (1870–86) are full of poetry – the genre that the Wattses most admired; Mary writes, 'I say prose walks but poetry has wings' (1887: 4 December). Much of this poetry is untitled and anonymous, many are psalms or prayers, and some are copies of famous poems; yet some are her own poetic compositions. This is suggested by the combination of ink and pencil (the pencil sometimes rubbed out after being written over in, but still faintly visible beneath, the ink), unfinished lines and stanzas, crossed-out and altered words, and extra lines squeezed in between lines; it is confirmed by Mary's inscription of her initials 'M F T' beneath several pieces of poetry, as in the corners of her self-portraits. Evelyn also signs her early poetry 'M E P', similarly inscribing her private pre-marital poetic identity.

An untitled poem of 1874 is apparently Mary's own composition, as evidenced by her rewriting of the final line: 'the blue is our paradise' is crossed out and replaced with 'behold the blue our paradise' (1874: 13 December). This is reminiscent of the final lines of George Eliot's poem 'Blue Wings' (a song from *The Spanish Gypsy* [1868]), which is copied out by Mary on the first page of her 1870 'Diary' beneath her own maiden name: 'I . . . Thought the little heaven mine, / Leaned to clutch the thing divine, / And saw the blue wings melt within the blue!' Mary greatly admired – and owned the works of – George Eliot (21 vols, Limnerslease Inventory 1938: 41, WG), who was commemorated by an ASL banner. Mary's reproduction and imitation of Eliot's work shows that she was inspired and influenced by contemporary professional poets, secretly experimenting with poetic composition in these private pages, which provided her with imaginative spaces safe from public scrutiny. Mary never attempted to publish her poetry, and Cixous offers a convincing explanation for her – and other women's – reluctance to do so: 'I know why you haven't written. . . . Because writing is at once too high, too great for you, it's reserved for the great – that is, for "great men" . . . Besides, you've written a little, but in secret' (1976: 876).

Cixous's theory is confirmed by lines of Mary's initialled, self-reflexive poetry written in her 'Diary': 'I know nothing, & it is best so'; 'because of the darkness I cannot order my speech' (6 August); 'alas all words are cold, & mine most weak' (15 September). Echoing Evelyn De Morgan's teenage diary written around the same time, and prefiguring elements of her own later marital diaries, Mary explores her feelings of insufficiency, stupidity and even self-loathing in her experimentation with poetry. She writes in her 'Diary', around two years before Evelyn wrote her diary,

> What do I know? Oh me a weak weak woman . . .
> How can I answer to a strong mans reasoning . . .
> How can I judge them these men of great learning
> Men with great brains & high thoughts . . .
> (*c.*1870: 15 September)

While the speaker of Mary's poem is acutely aware of gender hierarchy and seemingly submits to patriarchal authority, an ironic or sardonic and cynical tone emerges in the rhetorical question and the melodramatic exclamatory 'Oh' as well as in the hyperbolical repetition of 'weak' and 'great', which emphasises or exaggerates the (supposed) difference between man and woman. The use of interrogatives and of multiple aggrandising adjectives in association with man – 'strong', 'great', 'high' – suggests that this is a mock-glorification, and implies disingenuousness or sarcasm rather than straightforward deference. Mary's poem can be read 'slant' (that is, with an awareness of subtext) to protest against male judgement; she seems to play on dominant Victorian perceptions of the sexes in order to convey a profound sense of disidentification and frustration with them. While the subversive subtext is subtle and her writing requires ideological decoding, Mary can be seen to use the female voice to highlight (the injustice of) gender inequality, and challenge phallo(go)centrism in the very production of her verse. This she produced in defiance of any essential relation between penis and pen as well as any synonymy between femininity and metric regularity. Illuminating the subversive subtext of Mary's poem, Kaplan points out the necessity of 'accepting the contradiction posed by [Victorian] women's writing as simultaneously a historical record of their oppression and a definitive mark of their defiance' (Kaplan 1979: 65). Mary signs her initials beneath her apparently self-effacing poetry, through which she converts subordination into affirmation.

The subversiveness of Mary's poetry is further revealed when it is read in the wider context of Victorian women's poetry. Her poem is comparable with more famous verses by Christina Rossetti, Elizabeth Barrett Browning and Emily Dickinson in their similar expression and address of woman's place from first-person female perspectives. They all produced poems that describe their struggles with writing and express 'female linguistic and emotional suppression by a patriarchal authority' (Foster 1990: 73). Christina Rossetti's poems in particular 'constantly define the lyric writer as shut out, outside, at the margin' (Armstrong 1993: 346), highlighting how woman is traditionally the invisible and silent second sex, marginalised in and by phallogocentrism. The tension between expression and repression in Mary's private writing, which illuminates and critiques the limitations of the male Logos for women (or their entrapment in phallocentric discourse), is comparable with the tension between liberty and captivity in Evelyn's artwork. Through a reading of Mary's private writings, we can trace the emergence of a distinctly feminist voice that dialogises with contemporary women's writing and early feminist discourse.

While Mary's chapel has received much critical attention from art historians, the feminist significance of her antiphallo(go)centric 'language of symbols', read in relation to *The Word in the Pattern* (1905), is largely unexplored. *The Word in the Pattern* is Mary's 'written explanation as a necessary strategy to ensure that her work is neither dismissed without consideration nor viewed as entirely superficial', and the addition of this explanatory publication establishes the chapel as a 'well-informed intellectual exercise' (Unwin 2004: 242–3). While Mary's *Annals* and diaries are concerned largely with George and her marriage, *The Word in the Pattern* specifically showcases her work and shows her to be a cultured, intellectual, professional woman artist with first-hand experiences of different countries and their arts, which would have been familiar to Mary from her research, training and travelling.

The chapel is 'saturated with symbolism – every inch a message from Mrs Watts . . . a wealth of writing' (Lambton qtd. in Gould 1998: 10) on the walls. Highlighting the intertextuality of her work, which imbues her patterns with the power of speech, Mary writes, 'every bit of the decoration of this chapel . . . has something to say'; it 'has on its walls the story, or at least the fragments of the story' (1905: 5, 3). Mary used symbolic decoration as a powerful mode of expression in the chapel, and her designs combined or entwined with fragmented sentences or words acquire a poetic power. Reminiscent of the Book of Kells and the Lindisfarne Gospels, the interior decoration of the chapel suggests Mary's textual influences, and explaining her designs, Mary quotes lines of poetry by William Wordsworth and Robert Browning (1905: 19–20). The interlacing Celtic cord and organic Art Nouveau whiplash tendrils spiralling in gesso relief over the curved interior – which is freer in style, more fluid and abstract than the exterior – creates the impression of a continuous, looped lettering or mysterious, indecipherable handwriting.

The chapel is not only remarkable as an Arts and Crafts masterpiece and a unique fusion of Art Nouveau, Celtic, Christian, Romanesque, Byzantine and Egyptian influence, but also because it was conceived and created by a woman. As Mary's notebooks containing detailed sketches and writings on the chapel show, she designed the building itself despite having no training in architecture (a masculine profession), as well as all of the exterior and interior decoration (created with the help of community craftspeople). For a woman in Victorian England to undertake such an ambitious architectural project – given the scale, symbolism and complexity of the interior and exterior chapel design – was unprecedented. By her own admission she defied expectations: 'A few people sneered, & I believed it was generally thought that the attempt would fail . . . I had many fears myself, but hoped, & went on, our little chapel grew up . . .' (letter to James Nicol of Cumnock Pottery, 1900, WG).[7] Her narrative of triumph over adversity suggests her pride in her achievement. As a woman artist designing and building an ecclesiastical building, Mary can be seen to '"re-animate" the paternalistic structures of a community', radically if implicitly challenging patriarchy and phallo(go)centrism; although she appeared to fully support the 'paternalistic hierarchy of Compton's community', her entrance into it and creation of the chapel was to 'undermine its very structure' (Unwin 2004: 241). Mary's innovative palimpsest of word and image, with its decorative pattern and complex symbolism in painted gesso, disrupts phallocentric order, clarity and linearity.

The chapel pillars which 'bear the great name "I AM."' – letters interwoven with the Celtic symbol of 'God the Creator' (M. Watts 1905: 11) – can alternatively be seen to announce Mary's identity, arrival and achievement as an artist and the chapel's creator. Mary's description of her creation of the chapel's interior is strikingly and seemingly intentionally (since she quotes from the Bible) reminiscent of God's creation of the world: 'On the decorated bricks which run up all the buttresses is the "Tree of Life" . . . a climbing creation, rising from flower to fruit, from shell to fish, serpent, beast, bird;

sun, moon, stars, and angels' (1905: 5). Mary refers to Christianity while rejecting overtly traditional Christian iconography (for example, crucifixes) in favour of her own fusion of pantheistic imagery and symbols inspired by various ancient religions and worldwide civilisations. Her unique symbolic decorative programme extends beyond Christianity in its multiple religious and historic visual references; her extraordinarily rich and inventive designs combine a variety of seemingly opposed registers and styles without privileging any one of them.

Mary can be seen to develop a feminist discourse (both literary and visual) in the chapel that joined the insurgence of feminist voices in Edwardian Britain. The theme of flight and various symbols of freedom pervade the exterior chapel decoration, as Mary explains in *The Word in the Pattern*: the 'scalloped pattern' was 'suggested by the breast feathers of the mother bird' gathering her brood under her wings; it features the symbol of the 'butterfly rising with shining wings from its little tomb, the chrysalis'; above the archway is the symbol for 'loosing the chains' designed to suggest the words, 'To proclaim liberty to the captives'; the friezes feature symbolic birds representing Hope, Peace and Light; and the 'flying fish, free in both air and sea, has been chosen as the type of Liberty' (1905: 10 11, 14, 20). Evelyn De Morgan's early poem 'A Caterpillar's Song' (*c*.1869–70) similarly traces the transformation of the caterpillar 'bursting' its chrysalis to 'issue forth' as a 'bright and gay' butterfly and thus attaining a state of freedom. In a more overtly feminist use of this symbol, Ernestine Mills produced a postcard depicting 'The Anti Suffragist' in the form of a butterfly climbing back into her cocoon, saying 'I do not want to fly' (*c*.1910).[8] In addition to Mary's repeated use of the term 'liberty' in explaining the meaning behind her designs, her phrases such as 'healing after fiery trial', to 'suffer and be strong', 'ultimate . . . triumph', and being 'raised in power' (1905: 24) can be seen to have socio-political subtext despite their original spiritual or religious contexts. Through her employment of these themes, images, words and phrases, Mary can be seen to enter into and engage with the early feminist discourse of her day, organising ideas into forms that symbolise or inscribe the female body.

More recent women writers' responses to the chapel interior (Fig. 5.1) illuminate its feminist significance as a womb-like space (Lambton qtd. in Gould 1998: 10; Gould 1998: 59; Paterson 2005: 721): life-sized modelled bodies, organ-like circular symbols and heart motifs encircle the interior walls where they are surrounded by

Figure 5.1 *Watts Chapel interior*, Mary Watts, completed 1904, Watts Gallery Trust.

swirling Art Nouveau forms resembling veins, tendons or umbilical cords. Kristeva's discussion of the body as a '*territory* having areas, orifices, points and lines, surfaces and hollows' (1982: 72 [original emphasis]) can be read in relation to the diverse terrain or body of the chapel, revealing it to be a unique example of artistic and architectural antiphallocentrism. Mary's apparently androgynous life-sized 'Angel messengers' – whose widening hips, slender arms and feminine faces support an interpretation of them as female on closer inspection – 'carry the symbols of Freedom and Limit; of Union and Conflict; of Stability and Change' (M. Watts 1905: 2.33). Through her creation of these female figures in conjunction with binary structures, Mary can be seen to enter into and engage with the feminist discourse of her day which foregrounded these tensions and prioritised one side of each binary, since suffrage supporters believed that 'change' if not 'conflict' was essential to the achievement of 'freedom'. Mary's angels can be seen to embody a struggle for female (rather than non-gendered, spiritual) freedom.

Figure 5.2 *Mary Watts and students of her HAIA class decorating interior panels for the chapel in her studio at Limnerslease,* c.1902, Watts Gallery Trust.

In a photograph of Mary and students of her HAIA class decorating interior panels for the chapel in her studio at Limnerslease (Fig. 5.2), Mary 'appears to be working with and directing assistants in an atelier model more normally associated with ['masculine'] fine art practice' (Unwin 2004: 244) as opposed to craft production. The faces of the angels encircling the chapel interior are painted onto smooth gesso as though onto a flat canvas, unlike the high relief of their modelled bodies and the exterior terracotta decoration (Unwin 2004: 243–6). These painted angel faces are not only reminiscent of Mary's own early portraits but also complement the angel in George's smaller version of his painting *'The All-Pervading'* which serves as the chapel's altarpiece (added 1904). The chapel interior is, in this sense, another example of the Wattses' creative partnership. Unwin argues that Mary's approach to her professional creative practice, 'to marriage, . . . and to her husband's practice, position and reputation' can be seen to 'converge on [the site of] the Watts Chapel' (2004: 237–8). Yet in the context of the chapel, George's originally enormous, grand painting has undergone a transformation: set back rather than foregrounded, it is overshadowed and engulfed by Mary's elaborate designs, and her encircling group of large-scale angels dominates the walls. Her work thus seems to challenge her traditional position and reputation in relation to her husband. Mary's reference to her symbolic decoration of the chapel interior as her 'glorified wallpaper' (M. Watts 1912: 2.321) and her haloed appearance in the photograph seem ironic given her transgression of the domestic sphere and the feminine ideal of 'angel in the house'.

It is significant that the chapel's altarpiece is a version of George's *'The All-Pervading'*[9] (1887–90) (Fig. 5.3), one of his most obviously symbolist works and arguably his most unconventional, subversive representation of woman. An exploration of this work is essential to an understanding of its place and importance in the iconographic vocabulary and symbolic scheme of Mary's chapel, and to her inscription of the female body therein. Here, in a completely different context to the one George originally envisaged, it arguably functions 'either as a secular altarpiece or a manifestation of universal

Figure 5.3 *'The All-Pervading'*, George Watts, 1887–90, © Tate, London 2017.

spirituality' (Bryant qtd. in Bills and Greenhow 2012: 32). Indeed, it was the play of light from a chandelier on his studio walls (M. Watts 1912: 2.104–5) rather than any religious motive that inspired this painting. It has a feminist function in its resistance to patriarchal religion and in its subversion of binary structures. It portrays a winged figure hovering ambivalently in a liminal space that blurs or deconstructs the binary boundaries between life and death, the corporeal world and the otherworldly. The heavily draped and hooded figure (whose body and face are largely obscured and cast in shadow) is shrouded in mystery – not only as to what realm it inhabits but also with regard to its gender identity. The veiled anatomy and visual ambiguity of this figure's sex and gender creates a discrepancy as to whether the figure is masculine or feminine, male or female. It is precisely the gender ambiguity of this androgynous God-like figure and the potential for it to be (re)interpreted as female that makes it so subversive and provocative.

In Bills's description of '*The All Pervading*' he initially avoids gender categories by referring to 'the figure' before eventually lapsing into the same familiar gender-specific pronouns traditionally used to refer to God: 'his lap and legs' (2010: 76). Barbara Bryant claims (without explanation) that the figure is 'more female than male' (2012: 32), and there is a suggestion of breasts in the directional lines of paint on the chest which create two vaguely curved shapes just above the globe. George himself described 'the All-pervading spirit of the Universe represented as a winged figure, seated, holding in her lap the "Globe of Systems"' ([1896] qtd. in Bryant 2012: 38). Consistent with the independent view George took of religion early in life, he conceived a radically 'different idea of an Almighty God' (M. Watts 1893: 27 January). For George as for Mary, 'universality was always the key and a specific link to one religion is unlikely' (Bryant qtd. in Bills and Greenhow 2012: 38). Frances Fowle interprets the figure as female with complete certainty:

> There is something almost womb-like about the way that the woman is cocooned by her golden wings. . . . The globe seems to hover in her hands . . . her 'all-pervading' vision gives her the power of prophecy, the knowledge of the future and of infinite space. The position of her [widened] legs and the arrangement of the draperies in the lower half of the picture make her appear like a giant Earth Mother, about to deliver forth the secrets of the universe. (Fowle 2000: NP)

Woman is imbued with God-like omnipotence and omniscience as creator and ruler of the universe. She looks down at the globe she holds like a crystal ball as it rests on the unfurled 'scroll of the book of life' (Bills 2010: 76) which tells what is to come. George's strikingly similar work *The Recording Angel* (1890) depicts the figure writing upon this scroll, emphasising the angel's role as observer, interpreter and creator. The re-presentation of God as female radically challenges the patriarchal institution of Christian religion and the concept of God as the Father; that she gazes down on the globe in her hands suggests that mankind is at her mercy in a subversion of patriarchal power relations. This image challenges the notion of man as the 'unified, self-controlled centre of the universe' who defines the rest of the world in relation to him as 'man/father, possessor of the phallus' (Tong 1992: 224). This painting in which 'God the Father' is replaced with 'God the Mother' – more powerful even than the 'Mother Goddesses' of the *Aldourie Triptych* in which women are God's angels or 'messengers' – portrays a matriarchal universe and constructs a kind of matriarchal religion in a symbolic subversion or deconstruction of the patriarchal society in which it was produced (at a time when male supremacy was ideological and all-pervasive). This conception of man made by woman radically challenges patriarchal constructs and assumptions – specifically the concept of woman as constructed by patriarchal ideologies.

The re-presentation of God as female in '*The All-Pervading*' not only subverts traditional religious and patriarchal iconography but also transforms the meaning of the biblical words in the circular 'symbols of the truths' on the interior chapel walls: 'In the beginning was the Word. The Word was with God. The Word was God. The Word was made flesh.'[10] These sentences written on the walls – seemingly an acceptance of and submission to patriarchal power – can be read in relation to '*The All-Pervading*' altarpiece and in the context of Mary's 'language of symbols' as an antiphalllogocentric statement. While the Gospel of St John identifies the Logos – through which everything is created – as divine, and identifies Jesus as the incarnate Logos, the unconventional representation of God as female in '*The All-Pervading*' shifts the phallic emphasis of the 'Word', instead aligning it with the 'flesh' or body and generative power of woman. This 'powerful image of a creator that watches over and pervades the essence of everything, the Logos' (Bills 2010: 76) signifies a reappropriation of the male Logos and the role of creator by woman. This is implied by the very title of Mary's book *The Word in the Pattern* explaining her 'language of symbols'; she becomes chief messenger of 'the Word' (a traditionally male role). In this biblical allusion, Mary can be seen to employ a subtle strategy of subversion by speaking through patriarchal (scriptural) discourse in order to challenge and undermine male orthodoxies from within its own terms of reference. By combining art, craft and writing, Mary makes a subversive statement about gender specifically through the arts, and inscribes the female body.

Concluding *The Word in the Pattern*, Mary records the names of twenty-seven women out of seventy-three workers who helped create the chapel, in support of 'the new position of woman as an equal worker with men' (M. Watts 1893: 21 May). She believed that active collaboration between classes and sexes would lead to greater equality and a brighter future for all. The presence of women's names listed in Mary's book stands testimony to the active and significant if often unseen role of women in the arts during the nineteenth century; they also have a 'representative function as emblems of other more hidden lives, equally affected by gender and class discrimination' (Aaron 1991: 19). Mary thus writes 'her story' into history.

This chapter has investigated critically neglected and hitherto unexplored facets of the Wattses' and the De Morgans' *oeuvres* to reveal the broad range of their achievements and their progressive socio-political positions as early feminist writers as well as artists. It has shown how their inscriptions of the female body dialogised with and contributed to the early feminist discourse of the Victorian–Edwardian period. It has also shown how their writings can be seen to embody elements of *écriture féminine* or challenge phallo(go)centrism, revealing their subversiveness, and offering new and fuller understandings of how these figures and works reclaimed the female body and reconstructed gender. As well as 'employing a style which, in order to express a sense of "difference", separates itself from the prevailing discourse in its specific femininity' (Foster 1990: 68), Mary and Evelyn speak through and work within traditionally male discourses and structures in order to challenge and deconstruct them; their defiance is voiced from within the male traditions of art and literature and within male/female relationships.

Notes

1. This is written by Stirling (probably), on the inside cover of an exercise book of Evelyn's verses (*c.*1869–70).
2. *The Studio* was a popular magazine devoted to the arts, which typically included 'Some Press Opinions' of it.
3. William De Morgan published seven novels in his lifetime: *Joseph Vance* (1906); *Alice-for-Short* (1907); *Somehow Good* (1908); *It Never*

Can Happen Again (1909); *An Affair of Dishonour* (1910); *A Likely Story* (1911); *When Ghost Meets Ghost* (1914).

4. *The Old Madhouse* is notable for one of William's most lively, uninhibited young women, the bicycling tomboy Nancy Fraser, and for the heartless, selfish Lucy Hinchliffe, who loves neither her child nor her husband, whom she jilts in favour of his best friend (see Cain 2013).

5. In the novel, Lavinia Straker, a cash-strapped artist's model who is also a talented singer, entraps Charles into marriage and then eventually leaves him for a more glamorous high-flying life abroad.

6. This is titled 'Diary' in Watts Gallery archives but is more of a journal; it is not an annual diary like the others, and is therefore differentiated in this book by inverted commas.

7. Mary suggested that the chapel was very much a joint project when she wrote, 'A new interest had grown up for us both . . . the building of a chapel . . . his gift to Compton. He did not design it, but suggested that, if we proposed to hold a class . . .' (M. Watts 1912: 2.284).

8. The Women's Library Suffrage Collection: TWL.2002.218.

9. George presented his original, larger oil painting *'The All-Pervading'* to the Tate Gallery in 1899, but despite being publicly exhibited several times during the 1890s, it was largely unknown from the 1930s until 1997, when it was kept in storage due to the descent of George's reputation, although the smaller version was visible in Watts Chapel.

10. John I:1 and John I:14, The Bible; these words are integrated with designs on panels I, II, III, IV of Watts Chapel interior.

Part III
Artists' Readings:
Literary Sources and Subjects

Chapter 6

Feminist Readings and Poetic Paintings

As published authors themselves, the Wattses were keen readers who read regularly and widely. George's lifelong interest in literature was fuelled by his marriage to Mary, who was his intellectual equal, creative companion and reading partner. She was an avid, cultured and discerning reader who loved sitting in the reading room of the British Museum (M. Watts 1893: 23 August) where she studied the Book of Kells, and would '[come] in for breakfast, reading [a] novel' (M. Watts 1891: 22 October). As part of her husband's circle, Mary had intimate access to some of the most famous, forward-thinking writers of the day, and she was well-acquainted with their works. Her diaries show her familiarity with British, European and non-Western literature, and are filled with (admiring and critical) references to contemporary literary culture. Around 210 books were found in her bedroom (and 78 books in her dressing room) when she died (Limnerslease Inventory 1938, WG).

This chapter explores the Wattses' collaborative reading practice (in the 'niche' designed by Mary at their studio-home) and their readings (as recorded by Mary's diaries), before discussing George's social-realist paintings inspired by contemporary poetry. It focuses specifically on Mary's readings of early feminist writings and on George's paintings provoked by articles and contemporary debates on 'fallen women', female suicide and the exploitation of women. I aim to show how the Wattses were influenced by writers engaging with issues at the heart of Victorian feminism, whose views they shared, and to reveal Mary's thoughts on, interactions and dialogues with writers of New Woman fiction. This further reveals the Wattses' progressive socio-political positions, and especially Mary's keen – if largely private – interest in early feminist writing and culture during her marital years, to which she more actively contributed in widowhood.

The Wattses' Private Library: Mary's Feminist Readings

In her diaries, Mary documents and discusses the Wattses' readings in the 'niche' (1894–5) (Fig. 6.1): the couple's private reading alcove created and painstakingly decorated by Mary in symbolic painted gesso. Far from being the strictly secret, private space to which Victorian women readers were more typically relegated, the 'niche' was a joint reading space at the heart of the Wattses' Arts and Crafts home, situated beside the hearth in the 'Red Room' or sitting room at Limnerslease. Here they spent almost every evening reading together, and talking about their readings, once visitors had left. Mary wrote in her *Annals* that this alcove 'served a double purpose, for, as [George] was slightly deaf, the niche concentrated sound, and he heard better there, and so it became his favourite corner, and he chose to spend his evenings lying there, listening to [her] reading' (1912: 2.86). She writes in her diary, 'reading in the evening – & realised what the

Figure 6.1 *Mary and George Watts reading in the niche at Limnerslease, c.*1894–5, Watts Gallery Trust.

niche will be – just room for us two & the walls will help my voice to carry straight to Signor's ear – it will be a very dear little place & fit' (1891: 12 September). She records their evening ritual: 'I note the little things that Signor says [as we read] – about half an hour before going to bed, we shut [the book] & lie back talking, he on the sofa, & I my long chair' (1891: 13 January).

Mary's creation of a reading alcove for both her and her husband was highly unusual in the context of the nineteenth century, when men and women did not typically read together, and when women's freedom to read, space in which to study and access to books was limited. The 'niche' represented an alternative to – and even a radical departure from – the more conventional desk and the official, privileged reading space of the paternal library, study or office that excluded women. It thus embodied a destabilisation of patriarchal Victorian ideologies, blurring the apparently rigid boundaries between 'public and private, . . . social and solitary reading' (Lee 2008: 46). The Wattses' habitual position of recline in the 'niche' was also subversive in being more horizontal, 'free, relaxed [and] unregulated' than vertical, 'rigid, professional [and] ordered' (Lee 2008: 47). Mary's 'niche' can be seen as a female appropriation or (sub)version of the paternal library, where she educated herself under the guise of fulfilling her wifely duties by reading aloud to her husband. She thus successfully reconciled the 'conflict for women between domestic duties and reading time' (Lee 2008: 50), transforming a space of limitation (the hearth; the living room; the home) which traditionally signified domestic captivity into one of greater liberty and gender equality. While the pleasure of the early-Victorian woman reader may have been solitary, secret and shameful (Lee 2008: 46), Mary 'record[s] the joys [she and George] have in reading together (1891: 6 August), describing the 'delicious hours' and many a 'happy evening' spent in the 'niche' with her husband. She explicitly inscribes her pleasure and celebrates a mind-expanding shared reading experience: 'Tonight in the happy niche, we read the oldest books in the world . . . "I feel as if a <u>new room</u> had been opened in my mind" I said [to George] afterwards' (1893: 7 January).

The 'niche' gave Mary an opportunity to explore her own inner experience as a reader, for whom reading was one of the most formative pleasures of her life – along with many other women writers including Virginia Woolf (2008), who wrote in her later diary, 'What a vast fertility of pleasure books hold for me! I think I could happily . . . read forever' (1933: 24 August). Mary writes, having opened an old childhood book of hers,

a wave of feeling came over me – I remembered going into my own room
& shutting the door, & going away into the life of thought in books like
these, like a mortal who has reached paradise. It was a hint of my life
now. (1891: 16 August)

This is comparable with Evelyn's immersion in her secret artistic
practice behind the locked door of her teenage bedroom (Stirling
1922: 173–5). While no sexual activity between the Wattses is explicitly recorded in Mary's diaries, and their relationship is thought to
have been more companionate than passionate, their shared pleasure
in the evening act of reclined reading in the womb-like 'niche' reveals
their closeness and can be seen as a kind of intellectually if not sexually intimate practice. Indeed, it can be seen as a form of sublimation, whereby Mary's (if not George's) sexual energy was converted
into creative energy and a desire to read. The term 'niche' – meaning
'slot', 'slit', 'hollow', 'cavity', 'opening' – is itself suggestive of the
womb or vagina, which has interesting implications when read in
relation to recent critical views of Victorian woman's reading as a
liberatory erotic practice or pleasure (Lee 2008: 48).

Mary finished the 'niche' in time to present it to George as a
birthday gift (1893: 25 February), which he proudly showed visitors
and described in 1895 as 'the first page of a beautiful book' (qtd.
in Gould 1998: 32). Its cave-like walls adorned with a myriad of
richly coloured symbols not only represented the 'different aspects
and meanings of life' (Julia Cartwright [1896] qtd. in Bills 2011: 16)
but was carefully designed to symbolise and inspire their readings in
this unique space. Mary explains in her diary,

> [George] asked me what I was designing for the niche – I said I want
> it to be descriptive of the time we pass there – the things we think of
> chiefly – therefore I am trying to make my <u>patterns express</u> the whole
> range. Flowers trees birds beasts and man in his <u>double nature</u> spirit and
> flesh – sun stars moon – angels – and a light beyond . . . but that is not
> all – <u>papyrus</u> comes in for books, <u>poppies</u> for rest – & then I am trying
> to get in painting, art, science, religion, history, fiction – he laughed 'Oh,
> you <u>are</u> greedy' he said – (1893: 1 February)

Mary's gesso reliefs in the 'niche' not only reflect her ambitious creative ideas and decorative skills but also the influence of George's
paintings on her designs, which feature angels bearing mystical symbols: her miniature design of a winged figure holding a globe is strikingly similar to – but is her own stylised interpretation of – George's

painting *'The All-Pervading'*. Mary's decorated 'niche' marks a significant reshaping of the patriarchal library or 'privileged, sacrosanct space of the father's [or husband's] study' (Lee 2008: 55). Her symbols offer an exclusive insight into the impressive breadth of textual subjects and literary genres that inspired Mary's designs and George's paintings, and into the Wattses' private life and library. Mary's diaries record their readings in the 'niche' and subsequent discussions about the works of their famous literary predecessors (including Homer, Shakespeare and Milton) and contemporaries including John Ruskin, Dante Gabriel Rossetti, Robert Browning, William Morris, George Meredith and Alfred Tennyson, whose portraits feature in George's 'Hall of Fame'. At times, Mary's diary entries appear like a reading log, recording the Wattses' readings of novels, poems, articles, bibles and auto/biographies: one entry reads, 'In our evening we begin Mrs. Josephine Butlers [*sic*] life – [*Personal Reminiscences of a Great Crusade*, 1896] – a wonderful Joan of Arc!' (1896: 20 October). The Wattses' progressive socio-political views – especially on the place and treatment of women – not only informed and fuelled, but were also shaped by, their readings.

Mary's early diaries reveal the Wattses' shared interest in influential women writers, such as Mary Shelley, Elizabeth Gaskell and Jane Austen (commemorated by a 1908 ASL banner). Mary records in her *Annals* that Austen's novels were among the books George 'turned to most often when tired or unwell' (1912: 1.15), and praises their 'graphic power' (1887: 20 April), 'delicate truth & refined wit' (1891: 12 October). She notes, '[George's] love of [*Pride and Prejudice*] is delicious – like a child who likes the story over again . . . he corrected me if I missed a word' (1887: 20 April). She also records how they were deeply moved by Elizabeth Gaskell's novel *Cranford* (1853) – which she says 'belongs to the same class as Miss Austen' – and particularly by the love story of Miss Matilda 'Matty' Jenkyns, whose feelings for her former suitor are renewed when they are reacquainted, only for him to die shortly afterwards. George is moved even more than Mary – to tears: she notes, 'he held my cheek to his, & really cried for the poor tender little suffering heart, though only living in a book' (1887: 20 November). This reveals his deep sympathy with female figures and the plight of women, as well as a surprising sensitivity behind his patriarchal public image. Though Mary notes that the characters are 'only living in a book', Virginia Woolf (2008) remarks in her diary, 'the truth is these little scenes [in books] embroil one, just as in life' (1933: 24 August). The tragic love story may have caused George to reflect on his own mortality, and his and Mary's inevitable parting; their reading about the breaking of a union in a work of fiction strengthened their own in a tender private moment.

The Wattses' readings in 1891 highlight their increasing interest in, and especially Mary's preoccupation with, women's writing and issues. The Wattses were 'struck by' *Miss Blake of Monkshalton* (1890), a novel by British social reformer, public speaker and suffragist writer Isabella Ford (sister of Emily Ford), who also wrote pamphlets on issues related to socialism, feminism and worker's rights: Mary writes, 'it is very pleasant reading, delicately drawn from life' (1891: 10 January). They read *Blessed be Drudgery* (1890) by William Garnett, a clergyman and social reformer interested in women's suffrage, with a preface by Ishbel Maria Hamilton-Gordon, Marchioness of Aberdeen, a Scottish writer, philanthropist and advocate of woman's issues (1891: 28 January). They read W. T. Stead's 'very interesting' account of Mrs Annie Besant, a prominent British socialist and women's rights activist, writer and orator – who Mary thought was 'capable of great things' but wanting in 'wisdom' (1891: 17–18 October). The Wattses read as well as watched a performance of Ibsen's *Hedda Gabler* (first performed 1891) with its culturally influential self-slaying feminist heroine; Mary finds it 'interesting [. . .as] a psychical research [. . .and] always instructive', but it 'does not interest [her] as the "Dolls' House" – it is less suggestive' (1887: 27–8 April). Mary refers to Ibsen's 'setting down of [the] great questions that a complex state of society brings all about us' (1893: 18 March) in his proto-feminist play *A Doll's House* (1879). She may have found this 'suggestive' because Helmer's 'doll wife' eventually escapes domestic captivity, abandoning her wifely and motherly duties in pursuit of self-discovery and 'perfect freedom' (Ibsen 1992: 67, 71).

On the Wattses' sixth wedding anniversary, Mary's sister Christina gifted them socialist writer Edward Carpenter's *England's Ideal* (1887), which they read together. The Wattses shared the same circle as Carpenter, who corresponded with John Ruskin, William Morris and Olive Schreiner (and he moved to Guildford, Surrey, after the First World War). Mary writes after reading his book, 'much that [Carpenter] says Signor has said to me over & over again' (1891: 20 November). Yet George explicitly refused the label of 'socialist' with which Mary identified: he told an interviewer, 'my inclinations are all the other way. I love pomp and ceremony', and he found distinctive class and period differences 'picturesque' (qtd. in Friederichs 1895: 78). While George believed in progress through leadership by a visionary Victorian elite, his public anti-socialist statement shows his lifelong preoccupation with aesthetics over politics, which Mary more consciously combined. Despite a male visitor's attempts to 'convert [her] from [her] evil & mistaken socialism', Mary considered herself one of 'the "reformers"', with their 'dreams of equality' and 'balance', who believed 'that man would be very much better under different conditions & if social opinion required him to be so'. Documenting her 'views on progress', she writes in her diary,

> so far the progress of civilisation gives us reasonable grounds for hope that . . . one day an African woman in a position lower than the beast, & stronger than that will be where her European sister is – we have abolished slavery . . . we condemn cruelty to animals, cruelty to children . . . there may come a time when the extremes of difference . . . will be not more suffered in our midst . . . the history of civilisation shows that hitherto man has moved on in the direction of Justice & sympathy . . . There is no reason that we should go backwards, we must move, there is very reasonable ground for hoping that we shall move on steadily in the way we are now going – Every noble minded leader of the day points this . . . 'Mrs Watts & her party' say the coach is going up hill, a rocky road no doubt & careful driving necessary – good steering, & not spokes & drags, are what are wanted. (1891: 13, 23 August)

Mary's entry reveals her confidence in socio-political progress and 'woman's place being changed' through 'socialistic principles'. She supported the late-Victorian reform movement (advocating gradual social change rather than revolutionary socialism) despite the opposition she faced. Mary's reformist ideas – grounded in liberalism, socialism and feminism – prefigured the call for 'reform' that became central to the women's suffrage campaign (for example, electoral, educational and prison reform).[1] While George's views were more reserved, Mary's diaries show that she was a keen socialist and suffragist who looked forward to a world of peaceful co-operation and equality.

Also in 1891, the Wattses read works by New Woman novelist and suffragist Olive Schreiner, including *Story of an African Farm* (1883), a pioneering feminist novel popular among progressive Victorians. Schreiner's allegorical work *Dreams* (2008) 'strangely moved' and had 'a great power over' Mary (1891: 15 November, 23 July). On publication, *Dreams* was 'acclaimed by, and claimed for, both aestheticism . . . and feminism' (Chrisman 1990: 126). It was a favourite with imprisoned suffragettes like Emmeline Pethick-Lawrence, whose recital of it one night in Holloway prison 'attract[ed] a rapt audience' (Jenkins 2015: 123); among it was militant suffragette Constance Lytton, a close friend of Schreiner's who disguised herself as a seamstress in prison to expose class-biased treatment. Lytton recalls in her autobiography *Prisons and Prisoners* that 'the painter [George] Watts and [her] father had been enthusiastic over the poetical beauty of these "Dreams"' (Lytton 1914: 156) when they were first published, and articulates the personal impact of the parables on her just as passionately as Mary whilst highlighting their socio-political relevance. Their 'lyrical force . . . imaginative woof and warp' had impressed Lytton in her youth so deeply that she 'read them many times for sheer emotional joy', but their feminist meaning only later dawned on her:

> Schreiner, more than any one other author, has rightly interpreted the woman's movement and symbolised and immortalised it by her writings. . . . The words hit out a bare literal description of the pilgrimage of women. It fell on our ears more like an A B C railway guide to our journey than a figurative parable, though its poetic strength was all the greater for that. (Lytton 1914: 156–7)

The text had double – poetical and political – significance for Mary in the late nineteenth century as it did for suffragettes in the early twentieth century. Schreiner's allegories collected as *Dreams* were 'said to resemble [George's] pictures', and Mary concurs in her diary: 'he uses symbols which leave the mind to take what range it pleases, she uses parables which makes her idea more infinite' (1891: 14 July). Prominent contemporary writer Anne Thackeray Ritchie (step-aunt of Virginia Woolf), who wrote to Mary and whose portrait was painted by George, refers to his paintings as 'beautiful dreams' (Ritchie 1924: 264). Several of his paintings representing allegorical female figures have an ethereal dream-like quality and can be seen to convey dreams of a liberated future for women (for example, *She Shall Be Called Woman* and *Hope*).

Schreiner's *Dreams* contains numerous points of interest for the Wattses, with its allegorical figures of Love and Life (Schreiner 2008: 3), and 'dream' titled 'The Artist's Secret' which tells of an artist who painted in his own blood so 'the work lived' after he died (Schreiner 2008: 25). Mary, with her increasingly strong interest in women's rights and suffrage, was perhaps particularly inspired by Schreiner's vivid imagery that came to form part of an early feminist discourse: the liberation of caged birds; woman's struggle to rise; 'woman . . . seeking for the land of Freedom' (16); open windows and doors; mothers and angels; and references to mountain tops, breaking day and the rising sun (36). Schreiner's 'inexpressibly beautiful parable[s] of life' (M. Watts 1891: 14 July) 'anticipated and indeed inspired many of the feminist ideas of the early twentieth century' (Showalter 1982: 104). Her treatise *Woman and Labour* (1911, dedicated to Constance Lytton) was one of the first to investigate the relationship between the position of women and capitalist economy. The Wattses and particularly Mary shared her interest in women's work and female freedom.

The Wattses' discussions about 'Miss Schreiner' and thoughts on the feminist significance of her work are detailed in Mary's diary. Mary writes,

> I never read a line of hers without its staying with me for long. . . . Her dreams are full of hope, of discontent with man's wrongs, but great hopes in powers for right, great hopes of woman – I should like to write & tell her how much Signor & I care for her book. (1891: 23 July)

Mary's favourite 'solemn beautiful "Dream"' by Schreiner titled 'The Sunlight Lay Across My Bed' states, '[w]hen one man and one woman shine together, it makes the most perfect light' (36), seeming to encapsulate the Wattses' creative partnership in a vision of gender equality. When its protagonist, standing atop a mountain with God, sees a figure but cannot tell 'whether it were man or woman', God says, 'In the least Heaven sex reigns supreme; in the higher it is not noticed; but in the highest it does not exist' (40). This union of – and elimination of distinctions between – the sexes apparently appealed to Mary as it did to other early feminists, and androgynous angels can be found in the works of the Wattses as well as of Evelyn De Morgan.

Recording Schreiner's profound effect on her, Mary writes that every 'line or word' of her favourite 'dream' is 'pregnant of some great suggestion – the conception so large & grand; the hope of it so full of real light & joy – I do not remember a happier evening in my life' (1891: 16 September). When Mary returns from a wintery walk later that year, she immediately reaches for '[her] preacher – Olive Schreiner'. After re-reading some of the 'dreams', she writes,

> new beauties appear each time I read them – surely she is a noble woman, & will take her place among the foremost teachers yet . . . she had a real message . . . the language of the bible almost! One comes up from her dream to desire better things. (1891: 13 December)

Mary clearly revered Schreiner as a feminist visionary and 'genius' (1891: 11 January), and saw her work as having almost sacred importance (despite her unorthodox life). This reveals Mary's deep preoccupation with the 'woman question' as well as her shared dream of female liberty.

The Wattses also greatly admired male writers who addressed gender-related or woman-centred issues, and particularly the writer and women's suffrage supporter George Meredith. Though George Watts knew Meredith from the late 1850s, when they bonded over similar views on art, literature and society, the Wattses became more intimately acquainted with him when he sat for his portrait to be painted at Limnerslease for the 'Hall of Fame'; Meredith stayed with friends nearby so that five sittings could be arranged. The Wattses formed a close friendship with Meredith during this year, and Mary's diary of 1893 contains a striking number of entries dedicated to him, including records of their private conversations, reflections on his literary works and commendations of his character. The Wattses became 'intensely interested' (M. Watts 1893: 31 March) in Meredith's literary works, and Mary's entries about them become increasingly detailed, complimentary and celebratory as she reads his novels alongside George in their 'niche'. She lists Meredith as one of 'the great preachers' along with Ruskin, the Brownings, George Eliot and Tennyson (1893: 23 August). An exploration of Mary's relationship with Meredith through a reading of her diaries not only reveals their allied feminist views but also how Meredith significantly strengthened feminist feeling in Mary.

Mary shared Meredith's strong sympathies with women and was moved to write down her reflections on his work in her diary. She particularly praises his 'great thought', 'incisive, & delicately descriptive' writing, and ability to paint 'men and women in flesh and blood' in his New Woman novel *Diana of the Crossways* (1885); she concludes, 'it is real and great. Art' (1893: 31 March). She appreciates the tension and struggle embodied by the passionate and intelligent female protagonist trapped in an oppressive marriage (a popular theme of the time), since she is 'so weak & so strong', and 'it is so easy to draw up a pretty heroine & carry her thro' the book without a fault' (1893: 6 April). Mary praises Meredith's 'subtle observations upon women especially' in his novel *The Egoist* (1879), writing, 'he seems to understand [women] better than any other man & he has blown the trumpet of greater freedom for them for many years – he is a leader of his times' (1893: 29 April). Indeed, a newspaper article on 'Women and the Vote' states, 'At one time George Meredith seemed the only great writer who consistently upheld that woman had a soul and individuality of her own and the magnificent women of his novels are the result' (*Berwickshire News and General Advertiser* 21 March 1911).

On another occasion, Mary writes,

> Mr Meredith read to me . . . I was deeply grateful, for a poet interprets himself to you as he reads . . . Mr Meredith was kind enough to say that he felt he could talk to me from the first moment that he saw me. (1893: 5 April)

This diary entry marks a shift from Mary's reflections on Meredith's texts to a record of her interactions with him. The references to feelings on both sides, as well as to the intimacy involved in Meredith's reading his own poetry to Mary, indicate their closeness and fondness for each other. Mary's most explicit expression of her progressive position in relation to the feminism of her time can be found in her 1893 diary, where she discloses the powerful feelings she experienced during a discussion with Meredith, which had a profound effect on her physically, emotionally and psychologically. Deeply inspired by his revolutionary vision of gender equality and female liberation, Mary documents their conversation in significant detail:

> My morning was one of <u>intense</u> enjoyment – I felt myself trembling from head to foot, & had to steady myself as I sat, by holding onto my chair – I cant [*sic*] say why. The pleasure of it perhaps was so great – & the essence of that pleasure lies in finding this mind [of Meredith's. . .] absolutely sympathetic with the whole direction of [George Watts's], His faith is in the adjusting of the balance . . . a better knowledge of one another, to bring about the wide sympathy, <u>at least</u> to reach the universal brotherhood – the perfect equality of man & woman – 'We want to be more naked' he said – women especially, circumstances have so moulded them they are seldom themselves. The male mind has so dominated them – he went on to say that woman is sometimes herself for just ten minutes, about midnight! The hope of the future lies greatly in the fact that woman is now beginning to take her place – He hopes to see a free intercourse between men & women, & would have boys & girls educated together at the same schools! (1893: 4 April)

Mary is moved by these progressive ideas even to the point of physical instability, and this retrospective 'writing of her body' (in which she recalls the uncontrollable 'trembling' induced by a distinctly feminist vision of female liberation) can be read as a kind of proto-*écriture féminine* as conceptualised by Cixous. Mary's multiple dashes, commas, underlinings and exclamation marks not only convey her enthusiasm about the progressive content of the stimulating conversation she relates, but also suggest that the memory of the event re-excites her as she writes. The excited physical state she describes is paralleled by her punctuation; the writing of her body is reflected by the body of her writing. She can be seen to represent the 'trembling body' of the 'ebullient' woman who writes, who feels a 'funny desire stirring inside her' as she dares to 'bring out something new' (Cixous 1976: 876, 881). Mary's powerful physical feeling that was a positive force of '<u>intense</u> enjoyment' and 'pleasure . . . so great' is perhaps one of the earliest examples of Cixous's notion of feminine *jouissance*.[2] While this term is often defined as sensual pleasure experienced by the female body, it is not simply a sexual ecstasy or orgasm (which would be a reductive oversimplification) but a term denoting 'enjoyment' with '*simultaneously* sexual, political, and economic overtones' (Betsy Wing qtd. in Cixous and Clément 1986: 165 [original emphasis]); it is a word that carries a range of meanings which include 'enjoyment in the sense of a legal or social possession [of certain rights or privileges]' (Stephen Heath qtd. in Susam-Sarajeva 2006: 180). Indeed, Mary's pleasure here seems to lie in her recognition of the potential for greater gender equality and freedom for women. This entry is significant in revealing '*the emergence* of an experience that has been located or noticed for the first time' (Blyth and Sellers 2004: 84 [original emphasis]) – specifically female experiences (feelings, thoughts, epiphanies) and the emergence of feminist ideas.

Mary's diary entry explicitly expresses her strong emotional connection and mental affiliation with Meredith's – in addition to Schreiner's – notion of a post-patriarchal and even utopian world of 'perfect' gender equality. Indeed, 'woman' was 'beginning to take her place' in art schools, institutional education, political debates and public spheres as cultural producers and creative partners, achieving greater independence and empowerment. Meredith's support of an ambitious educational project resonated with Mary, who, as we have seen, received formal training at a coeducational art school. There seems to be a recognition on behalf of Meredith and the Wattses that the masculinist (im)balance of Victorian society needs to be 'adjusted', the sexes need to develop a 'better knowledge of one another', and society needs to foster a 'wide sympathy' with women in order to achieve gender equality. Mary's other, similarly spirited and politically charged diary entries echo Meredith's ideas and optimism about the future of humanity: she expresses excitement at the prospect of breaking down the 'strictest barriers between the sexes', and writes that she supports the progression 'towards that splendid goal when we shall set about looking for all the points that unite us – & dropping those that disunite us' (1893: 4 April, 28 June). The passage concerning Meredith is particularly important on a personal as well as political level, since it marks a kind of epiphany or a pivotal point in Mary's feminist thinking that is rarely so strongly and explicitly evinced. Mary's entry shows how (even the most private) writing is a 'space that can serve as a springboard for subversive thought, the precursory movement of a transformation of social and cultural structures' (Cixous 1976: 879).

Meredith's recognition that 'circumstances have so moulded [women and . . .] the male mind has so dominated them' implies his awareness of prevalent patriarchal ideologies, from which he separates himself by advocating co-education, gender equality and, most significantly, female 'nakedness' (M. Watts 1893: 4 April). While the word 'naked', used by Meredith, seems to imply the kind of biological essentialism historically used to justify female oppression, the 'nakedness' that he advocates represents a form of liberation from male domination. Meredith's notion of nakedness, 'the stripping away of sartorial protection' (Peterson 1999: 34) or removal of restrictive feminine costume in a moment of self-discovery, has emancipating and empowering implications for women. Meredith envisions the transformation of woman from objectified body to embodied subject, liberated (if momentarily) from oppressive social constraints and feminine dress in an unveiling of her true identity or most authentic self. Moreover, he implies that, since gender is performative and socially constructed (that is, when a woman is not 'herself', she is performing a culturally constructed gender and conforming to male ideals of femininity), gender can be de/re-constructed to liberatory effect. The notion that femininity is a matter of artifice (as some suffragists and suffragettes argued) and can be deconstructed to a state of 'nakedness' implies that it could be constructed differently (as Judith Butler argues), with greater agency. This represents the potential for women – historically defined by, imprisoned in, restricted and reduced to their bodies – to renegotiate their relationships to their bodies and re-present themselves.

Of course, this entry can be read and interpreted in alternative ways to suggest that Mary was seduced not only by Meredith's views but also by his presence or personality. Mary's 'I can't say why' (M. Watts 1893: 4 April) might suggest not the freedom of *écriture féminine* so much as the shame of embarrassment or the discipline of self-censorship. Linda Peterson draws attention to a similar claim made by Mary Robinson in her memoirs of 1826, when she recalls a visit from the playwright Richard Sheridan:

> I was overwhelmed with confusion: I know not why; but I felt a sense of mortification when I observed that my appearance was carelessly *dishabille*, and my mind as little unprepared for what I guessed to be the motive of his visit. (qtd. in Peterson 1999: 33)

Peterson dismisses Robinson's claim 'I know not why' as duplicity, in that Robinson knows retrospectively that her '*dishabille*' aroused Sheridan's sexual desire (which induced her sense of 'confusion' and 'mortification'). This can be compared with Mary's encounter with Meredith: her disavowal designed to disguise the sexual nature of their connection and of her enjoyment of their private discussion. Meredith's proposal that woman should 'be more naked' and are 'only themselves' for 'just ten minutes, about midnight' (perhaps during sexual intercourse) is highly suggestive and even, for the time, salacious – especially since Meredith said this to Mary, a married woman, alone. That she struggles to stand and requires support during their discussion implies a swooning or sexual excitement induced by Meredith and his words.

Reading between the lines or rather beyond her apparent delight in his socio-political ideas, Mary writes that Meredith 'understand[s] [women] better than any other man' (note: she does not say 'except for my husband'), and that he speaks differently to her in a 'delightful voice' when they are alone, implying a secret flirtation. Meredith is known to have had many friendships with younger women, and Mary – referring to portrait sitters – writes, 'the long hours of tete a tete [*sic*] make one very intimate' (1891: 23 September). By the time George painted Meredith, he was too deaf to hear what his sitters said, and Mary would talk with them (sometimes working in the same studio) to 'break the monotony' of the silence (1891: 22 August). In this light, it would certainly not be prurient to propose that there was a romantic or sexually charged connection (as well as an evident bond over a common aesthetic and socio-political view) between the widowed Meredith and the married Mary. Mary's diary entry may suggest cross-currents of (sexual and political) enjoyment, freedom (of expression) and shame (of extra-marital feelings) without any necessary contradiction. Given its provocative nature, it is curious that this was not one of the many pages later torn out of Mary's diaries, allegedly by her ward Lily, in an attempt to preserve the family's reputation. Perhaps this entry was mild compared to those removed.

Perhaps Lily (assuming that she was the editor) failed to perceive its sexual subtext, or perhaps she did but thought that it was right to retain it. A retrospective reading of Mary's diaries reveals how she blurred the boundaries of accepted feminine behaviour, supported feminist ideas to an extent that is not widely recognised and formed a close relationship with Meredith.

Testifying to the longevity of their close bond, Mary produced the terracotta casket for Meredith's high-profile funeral in Dorking, where NUWSS and other suffrage society members paid tribute to the famous novelist 'in reverence and gratitude to one who to women was ever critic, counsellor, and friend', quoting his feminist poem 'A Ballad of Fair Ladies in Revolt' (1876) (*London Daily News* 24 May 1909). This poem presents contrasting male responses to women's 'revolt' against Victorian sexism in an exploration of contemporary debates, and ultimately suggests Meredith's support for feminists. Mary's close association with pioneering suffragist writers like Meredith and Schreiner reveals her private support of women's rights and her interaction with a widening feminist circle of writers and artists long before she publicly promoted the suffrage campaign in later life.

George's Social-Realist Paintings: Working and 'Fallen' Women

The Wattses' shared interest in social reform, belief in the benefits of philanthropy and deep concern about female oppression inspired, and was inspired by, their evening readings. The Wattses' readings of texts on these topics in turn influenced George's visual work. Sharing Josephine Butler's feminist impetus, George created art that conveyed his concerns about the destructive effects of male greed and the lack of concern for female suffering in the modern world. He addressed the topics of prostitution, sexual exploitation and Mammonism in his art to shock the viewing public into a recognition of the corruption beneath the respectable veneer of Victorian society. *The Minotaur* and *Monster and Child* (both 1885) were painted by George in appalled response to W. T. Stead's exposé of the child prostitution rife in Victorian London, titled 'The Maiden Tribute of Modern Babylon' (*Pall Mall Gazette* 1885).

George's earlier four large-scale social-realist paintings, all produced between 1848 and 1850 – long before he married Mary, evidencing his early interest in woman-centred social issues – all depict destitute or outcast female figures. These were remarkable

Figure 6.2 *Found Drowned*, George Watts, 1848–50, Watts Gallery Trust.

for their time not only as pioneering works of English social realism portraying oppressive scenes of modern life, depicting the miserable poverty of the working classes and condemning social ills, but also for their portrayal and condemnation specifically of female oppression. Each painting places an oppressed gender Other centre stage: a dead 'fallen woman' in *Found Drowned* (Fig. 6.2); a starving mother and her family in *The Irish Famine*; a homeless beggar-woman in *Under a Dry Arch*; and an impoverished seamstress in *The Song of the Shirt* (Fig. 6.3). George's social-realist paintings reflect his progressive socio-political position; his focus on dispossessed women was at the centre of his feminism. While these works would have been seen by studio visitors beforehand, they were first exhibited at the Grosvenor Gallery in 1881–2, when feminism was on the rise and they would have acquired greater political significance.

Mary notes that she 'made a sad wall' (1893: 7 June) of these social-realist paintings when redesigning Watts Gallery, enhancing their powerful visual impact by hanging them together. Her diaries reveal her similarly strong sympathy with 'the poor Laundresses, who have their grievances & very hard & long hours at heavy <u>disgusting</u> work' (1891: 14 July). She laments the 'abominable injustice' of prostitution that 'sacrific[es] the woman <u>entirely</u> and make[s] her only the outcast' (1893: 30 January); 'that social evil – the woman

Figure 6.3 *The Song of the Shirt*, George Watts, 1850, Watts Gallery Trust.

who is daily sacrificed in our streets' (1893: 21 May). The gender inequity and sexual double standard in Victorian society which punished only women angered and energised her to the extent that she felt she should abandon her husband in order to dedicate herself to women-centred social reform (1893: 30 January). In the same year, she writes of her disgust when she sees 'that wretched man who ruined the maid we like so much'; she writes, 'I gave him a cold greeting & he hung his head sheepishly, I fancied – When will opinion give its blame more justly? – He flourishes. She is dishonoured & has to support the child' (1893: 1 April). Mary perceives the injustice of the situation and implies the need for social and moral reform in her diaries, which convey her strong sympathy with 'fallen women'. This was strengthened by her close friendship with Josephine Butler in 1895.

The Wattses had a shared sense of obligation and duty to the less fortunate. Mary assumed an active role alongside her husband as a high-profile social reformer. They became council members for the

South London Fine Art Gallery and part of a free library founded to educate the poor through art. They supported the work of another conjugal partnership of social reformers, Samuel and Henrietta Barnett, who aimed to bring art to the deprived areas of London, believed in women's rights and were active in the HAIA (promoting women's craftwork). Mary also extended her support independently. In 1902 Mary attended the fourth Founder's Day of Lady (Daisy) Warwick's 'flourishing' hostel – a Horticultural and Agricultural College for Women – at Reading. Daisy was a socialist and supporter of women's rights, education and employment, and her hostel trained women in horticulture and the lighter branches of agriculture as an alternative to industrial 'sweated work'. Horticulture and landscaping were 'subjects in which women excelled in this period' (Sullivan 2012: 20), further evidenced by the creation of gardens and/or garden ornaments by suffragists Julia Chance, Margery Horne, Gertrude Jekyll and Mary herself. Mary was involved in communities of women meeting or working together in garden clubs and colleges which spawned suffrage activity. She was also later involved in organising an exhibition of sweated industries accompanied by a suffrage societies' arts and crafts exhibition (Paterson 2005: 719–20). In declaring open an exhibition as part of the celebration, 'Lady Warwick said the work was going forward steadily and prospering, and new posts and new professions were being opened up for the vast army of educated women, who were making for themselves a distinct place in the world' (*St. James's Gazette* 17 July 1902: 7). Mary similarly offered women new employment opportunities in her commercial potteries, born out of a voluntary community project, which was Mary's own point of access to professional practice.[3] Her HAIA projects and philanthropic work overlapped with her suffragist interests and had a feminist function in their empowerment of female citizens.

Newspaper reports of the early twentieth century show Mary's dedication to feminist-driven philanthropic endeavours even after George's death. In 1915, Mary and suffragist Iona Davey attended a meeting in Godalming where the secretary of the National Vigilance Association (the most prominent organisation to take on the fight against sex trafficking in turn-of-the-century Britain) gave a lecture on 'A Romance of Philanthropy' (*Surrey Advertiser* 4 October 1915: 4). The establishment of this society in 1885 was the result of W. T. Stead's articles. Mary's attendance at such lectures after her husband's death reveals the exploitation of women to be a personal concern of hers as well as one they both shared. While George expressed his concern in paint within the walls of his studio, Mary attended controversial public events alongside prominent local feminists and members of wider organisations fighting for legislative and social reform. Philanthropy (which was socially acceptable for women due to its voluntary nature and frequently religious motivation) legitimised Mary's entrance into the public sphere, where she could actively support the women's cause and build her own public profile.

George's social-realist paintings trace his transition from an aspiring painter of grand history painting to a poet–painter of allegory and symbol, although his consistent focus on serious social issues made him a very different poet–painter to Aestheticism pioneer Rossetti. Poetry inspired much of George's work, and he tells Mary 'how much he longed for a poetic power' (M. Watts 1887: 10 March). An interviewer notes the strong appeal of his 'painted poetry' (Friederichs 1895: 79), and Mary refers to George's painting of the original 'fallen woman' *Eve Repentant* as a 'poetic picture' in her diary (1893: 25 February). His social-realist paintings are arguably 'poetic' not only because some of them were inspired by poetry, but also because they are insightful, poignant, elegiac and full of pathos, and were designed to express something meaningful and significant. George promotes a reading of the visual in his article *What Should a Picture Say?*: 'roughly speaking, a picture must be regarded in the same light as written words. It must speak to the beholder and tell him something' (1894: 1). He also wrote,

> I paint primarily because I have something to say . . . my intention is not so much to paint pictures which shall please the eye, as to suggest great thoughts which shall speak to the imagination and to the heart, and arouse all that is best and noblest in humanity. (G. Watts 1905: 20)

He felt a moral obligation as an artist to 'tell [the viewer] more about [a subject] than he had before seen', to '[teach] others to see', and to '[arouse] pity for human refuse' (G. Watts 1894: 1, 4) – for the working and 'fallen woman', the poor and outcasts of society. He saw painting as a discourse for communicating moral messages, and his social-realist paintings can be seen to have a socio-political purpose in that they 'speak' the unspoken stories of historically silenced gender Others. These paintings aimed to represent the real social struggles of women who were so often idealised in art, and to reveal the reality of female oppression in Victorian society.

As the Aesthetic movement became increasingly associated with 'art for art's sake' in the late nineteenth century, George – for whom ethics and aesthetics were inextricably linked – stood out as a believer that art should have a moral purpose, although the feminist functions of his moral messages have been largely overlooked. There is an emotional intimacy in George's 1840s politically charged social-realist paintings that is absent from Rossetti's 1860s paintings of richly clothed, beautiful women lounging listlessly in luxurious interiors. George's paintings depicting poverty, deterioration and decrepitude are disturbing rather than decorative. They were designed not as objects to gratify the male gaze but rather as mediums to convey the plights of female subjects for the purpose of social edification, to inspire empathy and compassion rather than horror and disgust for outcast female figures like 'fallen women'. While the conjunction of early feminism and Victorian moralism may seem incongruous, there are surprising and illuminating parallels and points of contact between the two. The agenda of George's social-realist art arguably overlapped with, supported and visually promoted the agenda of the women's rights movement that emerged around the 1850s and escalated over the second half of the nineteenth century.

George's social-realist paintings, with their focus on suffering and working women, are comparable with early feminist propaganda (posters and postcards) produced by the Suffrage Atelier and ASL, highlighting the oppression of women's industrial labour. George's painting *The Song of the Shirt* (1850) is comparable with the 'Votes for Workers' poster designed by W. F. Winter (joint winner of the ASL poster competition in 1909) showing a seamstress at a machine, behind which is a dark gridded prison-like window. Following Thomas Hood's popular ballad 'The Song of the Shirt' (published in *Punch* 1843), the 'sweated seamstress had been sentimentalised in the press, paintings and popular prints as the most oppressed (but womanly) of female workers' (Tickner 1989: 51). Winter's sturdy and independent, if impoverished, middle-aged outworker is a departure from the 'consumptive heroine' (Tickner 1989: 51) and the more sentimental traditions of British art, which George drew on in order to inspire sympathy with the seamstress. Yet both images made the exploitation of domestic servants visible to the middle and upper classes that depended on them, and helped to promote the improvement of their working conditions through legislation. Between 1847 and 1901, from around the time George painted his social-realist series until just before his death, eleven acts were passed regulating the hours and conditions of women's work in factories and workshops.

Protective legislation was designed to be in working women's own interests but suffragists argued that without the vote women had no say in the laws that affected their livelihoods (Tickner 1989: 51). The 'Factory Acts' ('They've a Cheek I've Never Been Asked') pro-suffrage poster designed by Emily Ford (published by the ASL in 1908) portrays a mill girl in a shawl and clogs, standing in a cobbled industrial cityscape. This is somewhat comparable with George's *Under a Dry Arch*, which shows an older impoverished woman wrapped in a shawl with the cityscape in the background. Ford's image highlights the oppression of powerless women employed in factories as 'sweated labour', and comments on the fact that women were not consulted in the drawing up of the laws. A major aim of the suffrage movement was to improve the conditions of working-class women by achieving representation for them in Parliament and trade unions. The plight of the 'sweated worker' was at the forefront of national consciousness at the height of the women's suffrage campaign. Constance Lytton recalls how militant suffragettes' speeches raised the subject to incite stone-throwing: 'Think of the women who work with a sweated wage, who have not the energy to rebel, who are cloaked with poverty' (Lytton 1914: 208). Both George's work and early feminist work depicted women 'exploited by individual men or [in] subordination to the legislature framed to meet the interests of men' (Tickner 1989: 51), and were motivated by the social and economic problems of the day. This exemplifies the intersections between the Wattses' social-realist concerns and the women's suffrage campaign, and allows George's work to be reclaimed as part of a wider conception of early feminist art.

A consideration of George's art in more detail, and in relation to the poetry on which it is based, further reveals its feminist significance. George's *The Song of the Shirt* – which draws on and dialogises with Hood's poem of the same title – illuminates female exploitation in the textile industry. The solitary, thin, pale female figure sits beside a window (symbolic of freedom), covering her face with a 'weary hand' (Hood 1890: l.56) while the other holds her needlework that has dropped to her lap in a moment of tearful 'Grief' (l.76). It captures this moment of exhaustion and perhaps existential crisis in a pause from the monotonous 'Work! work! work!' (l.9). The contrast between the darkness surrounding her and her own deathly paleness mirroring the white garment on which she works evokes Hood's lines: 'In poverty, hunger, and dirt, / Sewing at once, with a double thread, / A Shroud as well as a Shirt' (ll.30–2). The small cell-like setting emphasises the enslavement of the seamstress

– explicitly referred to as a 'slave' (l.13) and a 'prisoner' (l.52) in contrast to the sunny-backed swallows and open sky in Hood's poem – as well as sweated workers and women more widely.

The barrenness of the room in George's painting, a stark contrast to the decorative interiors of Rossetti's 1860s paintings (themselves intended as room decoration), illustrates Hood's description detailing the seamstress's pitiful 'wages', poverty and poor working conditions: 'this naked floor – / A table . . . a wall so blank' (ll.45–7). The emaciated frame of the seamstress in George's painting visualises the 'Phantom of grisly bone [. . . and] terrible shape' (ll.34–5) of the woman in Hood's poem. It also prefigures later representations of suffragettes' 'ghostly bodies' – ill and weakened from fasting and forcible feeding – which 'stitch[ed] together a [political] community via [domestic] sentimentality' (Green 1997: 25) in the last phase of the campaign. Emmeline Pankhurst's final polemical speeches 'depended upon her weakened frame to give them power' (Green 1997: 141), and the partnership of sacrifice and sentiment in the suffrage period was crucial to the cause. Suffragettes gave harrowing accounts of their attempts to support themselves as seamstresses (Green 1997: 209), illuminating female exploitation in the textile industry and testifying to George's visual message.

The pathos of George's picture, designed to inspire sympathy in viewers, reveals his own; his social-realist series shows his dedication to representing the plight of the unprivileged, drawing attention to the harsh reality of life for working women along with suffrage art and crusading journalism. Needlework was one of the few ways that women could earn money respectably in the early nineteenth century, and yet exploitative employers paid woman workers so little (despite long hours) that they faced the choice between starvation and prostitution. George's two paintings inspired by Hood's poetry – *The Song of the Shirt* and *Found Drowned* – can be seen to represent this when viewed together. Nonetheless, women achieved greater economic empowerment through employment as embroiderers in the Arts and Crafts industry, and it was particularly the 'under-paid, despised and anonymous woman worker . . . who grasped the opportunity craft skills presented' (Cockroft 2005: 6). As we have seen, out of the handicraft that became a metaphor for Victorian women's domestic captivity (that is, needlework), suffrage artists produced propaganda including embroidered silk banners; they drew on a traditionally female vocation in order to produce feminist images.

George's painting *Found Drowned*, which presents the result of a woman's metaphorical and literal 'fall', was inspired by Thomas Hood's popular poem 'The Bridge of Sighs' (1939) – one of the most influential presentations of the drowned woman as a victim of Victorian society which lent itself well to visualisation.[4] The title of George's *Found Drowned* – a 'legal term indicating suicide' (Gould 2004b: 48) – was taken from a daily column in *The Times* newspaper which published lists of women, mostly prostitutes, found drowned in London (Errington 1984: 207).[5] *Found Drowned* parallels 'The Bridge of Sighs' not only thematically in its poignant portrayal of a woman who drowned herself but also in its sympathetic rather than misogynistic treatment of the 'fallen woman'. Although female prostitution, promiscuity and adultery was widely perceived as 'evil behaviour' (Hood 1939: l.104) – and suicide was seen as a sin and a crime – in Victorian society, the speaker of Hood's poem urges a 'Loving, not loathing' (l.14) and 'mournful' (l.16) rather than 'scornful' (l.15) approach to the 'fallen woman' who is apparently left purified and beautified by death. This is similarly suggested by George's portrayal of an almost angelic 'fallen woman' in *Found Drowned*, which draws attention to her not in order to condemn her immorality as a warning to women, but rather to sensitively and sympathetically re-present a female figure that was widely shunned in Victorian society according to patriarchal prejudices (even though she may have been sexually abused or forced into prostitution in times of hardship, and indeed, at a time when society offered few employment opportunities for women). In George's painting, the fair-skinned woman is illuminated by a seemingly celestial light in stark contrast to the dark background in which the star of redemption shines; her arms are outstretched in a cruciform pose (referencing Christ-like self-sacrifice) and her golden dress floats in the murky polluted waters of the River Thames.

Significantly, the Thames was then effectively an open sewer into which around 250 tons of sewage was dumped daily and which smelled so foul near Westminster Bridge that the House of Commons was forced to adjourn in 1858 (Nicoletti 2004: NP). That the female figure lies washed up on the banks by these waters in George's work, still semi-submerged, seems to symbolise Victorian society's perception and cruel treatment of the 'fallen woman' as filth, human waste, an outcast and Other (a double Other as both woman and 'fallen'). As the 'abject' she is an 'excremental polluting object' (Kristeva 1982: 71); she is representative of the 'second sex' relegated to

London's polluted netherworld. Yet Kristeva argues that the 'potency of pollution is . . . not an inherent one; it is proportional to the potency of the [sexual/moral/social] prohibition that founds it'. She explains that the social 'ritualization of defilement is accompanied by a strong concern for separating the sexes, and this means giving men rights over women'. The abject 'fallen woman' reflects – while representing a threat to – the strictures placed on women by Victorian society in which the phallocentric order is 'a device of discriminations, of differences' (Kristeva 1982: 69–70). Prostitution constituted an 'invisible danger' and inspired fear of contamination in the middle and upper classes, as it established a link 'between slum and suburb, dirt and cleanliness, ignorance and civilization, profligacy and morality: the prostitute made it impossible to keep the categories apart' (Nead 1988: 121). The 'fallen woman', carrying connotations of prostitution, thus embodied the (hidden) power to destabilise the separate spheres that underpinned the regulatory and discriminatory binary order of Victorian society.

Hood's 'The Bridge of Sighs' holds representatives of patriarchal power responsible for the death of the 'Unfortunate' (1939: l.1) victimised and marginalised 'fallen woman': namely, society – a 'whole city full' (l.47) of 'cold inhumanity' (l.97); the church – 'the rarity / Of Christian charity' (ll.43–4); and 'Dissolute Man' (l.77). In 'The Song of the Shirt' too, Hood specifically appeals to – and seems to indict – men: 'Oh, Men, with Sisters dear! / Oh, Men, with Mothers and Wives! / It is not linen you're wearing out, / But human creatures' lives!' (1890: ll.25–8). George's *Found Drowned* similarly seems to shift the blame from the illuminated foreground female figure onto the social ills of the sullied, dark and distant industrial city skyline, which can be seen to represent a 'polluted' masculinist world over which hangs an ominous smog. George painted *The Minotaur* specifically to signify man's bestiality and male lust, condemning exploitation of girls and women, and holding depraved man rather than prostitutes culpable. St Paul's Cathedral which looms behind the beggar in *Under a Dry Arch* is representative of formal, patriarchal religion which, in George's view, ignored the problem of 'fallen women'. Like Josephine Butler, George re-presented the 'fallen woman' as a victim of Victorian society's larger cultural and economic problems. His moral message is not directed at woman but rather at the patriarchal perceptions and Victorian values he apparently saw as responsible for her 'fall'; his work thus has a feminist function. His painting of the corpse presented male viewers with a disturbing vision of a subject-turned-object which had been violently cast out from culture;

his aim was not to gratify the male gaze but to force viewers to recognise the discrimination against – and reassess the cruel treatment of – 'fallen women' in Victorian society.

George's and Hood's images of angelic, passive, 'slender', 'young' and 'fair' (Hood 1939: ll.7–8) female figures can be seen to some extent as 'classic' male representations of femininity which merely replace the Victorian stereotype of the 'stain[ed]' fallen woman with that of the 'pure' angel woman (Hood 1939: l.18, l.20). Yet George's realistic portrayal of the poor drowned woman (possibly a servant-girl) is a subversion or 'pointed perversion' (Stewart 2004: 39) of the sensuous, merely decorative, idealised images of passive, sleeping women by his contemporaries. These include Edward Burne-Jones's *The Sleeping Princess* (1886–8), Albert Joseph Moore's *Jasmine* (1880), and Frederic Leighton's paintings *Summer Moon* (*c.*1872), *Cymon and Iphigenia* (1884), *Summer Slumber* (*c.*1894) and *Flaming June* (*c.*1895). Despite the beauty of colour and form in these works, they neglect and even totally reject the 'human dimensions of meaning . . . and morality' (Gould 2004b: 71) which were hugely important to George. As David Stewart argues, 'in word and in paint Watts attacked the sleeping beauties that lined the walls of the Royal Academy', and nowhere is this more evident than in *Found Drowned* in which 'sensuousness collapses into decay' (Stewart 2004: 39), sleep becomes death, and beauty is overshadowed by implicit brutality (that is, undermined or complicated by the implications of prostitution and/or abuse that drove the woman to suicide). George reacted against popular male ideals of sumptuous, flawless feminine beauty and resisted 'art for art's sake'. Rather than 'lull us into complacency' like Leighton, George attempts to 'jar us into motion' (Stewart 2004: 39), forcing viewers to recognise female suffering and reassess female stereotypes through his harrowing, poignant and thought-provoking portrayal of female suicide.

Although Hood's poem and George's painting primarily present the drowned woman as a passive victim, as a committer of suicide she is also an active perpetrator of death who embodies a tension between passivity and activity, powerlessness and powerfulness. While Hood's poem predominantly focuses on the female corpse, the analepsis around the middle of the poem effects her resurrection and paints a powerful 'Picture' (Hood 1939: l.76) of an active female figure taking control of her situation by deciding to take her own life: 'In she plunged boldly – / No matter how coldly / The rough river ran' (ll.72–4). The use of the adverb 'boldly' in addition to the verb 'plunged' rather than 'dropped' or 'fell' evokes the sense that this act of suicide is an active assertion of female agency and autonomy. That Hood's female protagonist does not 'tremble and shiver' (l.64) emphasises her bravery and stoicism rather than her 'weakness' (l.103) and 'meekness' (l.105). The speaker's voice morphs into the suicidal woman's voice in the line, 'Anywhere, anywhere / Out of the world!' (l.71), which offers the reader a fleeting insight into the subject's state of mind and articulates her ardent desire for somewhere beyond a patriarchal society. Rather than a romanticised portrait of a dead woman with her dress draped shroud-like around her, this is a passage of action: the actual taking of life. Hood's shift from the image of a passive corpse to that of a solitary, active and autonomous woman who has found for herself a form of liberation in suicide transforms the female figure from an ornament into an instrument of change.

A reading of Hood's poem in relation to George's painting illuminates the latter's subversive elements. Though George depicts the woman after her 'bold plunge' as a cold corpse, the small and faint but foreground image of the chain and heart-shaped locket that the woman clutches is a token indicative of her suicide which suggests female agency, leading the viewer to imagine a narrative. Like Hood's poem, George's painting implies the woman's admirable bravery: her cruciform pose suggests a martyrdom that not only has religious connotations but also connotations of feminist courage and heroism. The representation of the 'fallen woman' as martyr not only elevates her in respectability in the eyes of prejudiced viewers, but could also be seen in retrospect to represent the militant activists who resorted to dangerous measures and died in the fight for women's rights. It evokes the militant suffragette Emily Davison who protested at the Derby against the denial of votes to women and died after 'falling' or rather throwing herself beneath the king's horse in 1913. Indeed, on the front cover of the Emily Wilding Davison memorial issue of *The Suffragette* newspaper (No. 35, Vol. 1, 13 June 1913), which hails her as a martyr who died for women, she is depicted as an angelic, haloed figure with her arms outspread in a cruciform pose similar to the 'fallen woman' in George's painting.

Female 'fallenness' does not merely denote feminine victimisation but is also the result of woman's deviation from feminine norms and rebellion against patriarchal order. Rather than an object of pity who has been seduced or abused and discarded by men, the 'fallen woman' could be seen as a subversive sexual Other who threatens Victorian ideals of femininity; she is the antithesis of the 'angel in the house' and her nearly sexless purity, and of what Kristeva calls the 'clean and proper body' (1982: 72). This 'sexual Other' – defying and threatening patriarchal law and order with its 'uncontrollable power' – 'becomes synonymous with a radical evil that is to be suppressed' (70), hence the disgust directed at 'fallen' women in Victorian society. In George's painting, the composition and use of light and shadow draws the viewer's attention to the billowing skirts draped across the woman's stomach, suggesting she is 'with child' out of wedlock. It thus represents not only the abject 'fallen woman' but also the taboo of the unmarried pregnant woman in Victorian society.

As a committer of suicide (illegal at this time), the 'fallen woman' is a sinful self-murderer, breaking the law, disturbing order, disregarding 'borders, positions, rules' (Kristeva 1982: 4). Kristeva claims that 'that leap is drawn toward an elsewhere as tempting as it is condemned', and argues that 'there can be grandeur in . . . crime that flaunts its disrespect for the law – rebellious, liberating, and suicidal crime' (1, 4). Similarly, Cixous – who emphasises the subversiveness of 'turbulent . . . flying or diving' – urges women to 'take the plunge . . . *Gain* your freedom . . . shake off the Law' (1991: 40 [original emphasis]). In this sense, the leap of the suicidal woman – explicit in Hood's poem and implicit in George's painting – can be seen as a subversive act through which she defies or escapes patriarchy and achieves liberation. While the fatal leap of the 'fallen woman' was often prescribed by male artists and authors as a cure for her immorality and deviation from feminine norms, in George's and Hood's works it can be seen as a reiteration or reinforcement of her deviance, defiance and transgression.

While images of drowned women became hegemonic in Victorian art and typically featured female protagonists who were shown as 'passive icons of suffering' (Treuherz 1993: 38), Hood's poem and George's painting can be seen to re-present 'fallen women' as active participants as well as passive objects in Victorian death culture; while much critical material on nineteenth-century art focuses on the latter, the former has been comparatively neglected. A reading of George's painting and Hood's poem in conjunction shows how the former can be seen to illustrate (elements of) the latter, and how the latter provides a narrative for the former. They reinforce each other's moral messages, calling for social reform, and this intertextuality illuminates the feminist significance of their portrayals of 'fallen women'. What are ostensibly conventional, simple or straightforward representations of female passivity are imbued with subtly subversive elements that create more complex visions of femininity. The 'fallen woman' who has jumped to her watery grave in Hood's poem and George's painting is both passive and active, victim and perpetrator, objectified body and embodied subject.

An evolution of the representation of women is traceable in George's work: from the largely dispossessed, disempowered women of his 1840s social-realist canvases to the powerful and even omnipotent female Angels of Death in his later symbolist paintings of the mid-to-late 1880s. This movement – elevating dead, dying or destitute woman to mysterious, omniscient, (all-)powerful personifications of death – can be seen to reflect the socio-political progression of women towards female empowerment and emancipation over the second half of the nineteenth century. George worked within the Victorian tradition of associating femininity and death to create strikingly unconventional images of women that focus on the power, rather than the passivity, of women in conjunction with death. The following chapter develops a discussion of women and water in art and feminism, moving from George's social-realist painting of a drowned prostitute to Evelyn's symbolist paintings of mermaids; both artists use literary allusion and allegory to express their similar views on socio-political, moral and spiritual issues.

Notes

1. 'Reform' featured on suffrage posters and postcards produced by the Suffrage Atelier (The Women's Library Suffrage Collection, 1909–14: TWL.2002.703).
2. Hélène Cixous uses this term in 'Sorties' (1975): 'jouissance' translates as 'bliss', denoting 'pleasure' or 'enjoyment', and also having sexual connotations (relating to orgasm); it is a 'sensual pleasure', a bond or analogy between a woman's libidinal economy and writing, literal and linguistic *jouissance*.
3. The Compton Pottery established around 1900 was renamed the Compton Potters' Arts Guild in 1904, and continued up until *c.* 1955. Mary taught clay-modelling classes to the poor in Whitechapel in 1884.
4. Mary points out the link between Hood's poem and her husband's painting in the Catalogue of George Watts's works, p. 58, WG. A smaller version of George's painting *Found Drowned* was entitled *The Bridge of Sighs – 'Take her up tenderly, lift her with care'*, which is quoted directly from Hood's poem.

5. Hood's poem was published just weeks after 'fallen woman' Mary Furley was sentenced to be hanged in London in 1844 for infanticide after her desperation to avoid the workhouse led to her failed suicide attempt and the drowning of her illegitimate child. This infamous case caused great public debate, and Hood's text – which was inspired by and drew attention to the case – also influenced Charles Dickens's short novel *The Chimes* (1844) and Augustus Leopold Egg's painting *Past and Present No. 3* (1858). These literary and visual texts, as well as editorials and articles, protested against and helped fuel public outcry about Mary Furley's death sentence and the treatment of 'fallen women'.

Chapter 7

The Metamorphic Mermaid in Fairy Tales and Feminism

Sea Changes

Evelyn's diary and juvenilia reveal her avid interest in 'seriously reading' (E. De Morgan 1872: 19 August). Throughout her painting career she drew upon a remarkable variety of literary sources and subjects for inspiration: from the ninth century BC to the early twentieth century, including classical, biblical, Latin and European texts; there seem to be 'relatively few [paintings] that did not have some literary reference' (Yates 1996: 59). A striking number of Evelyn's paintings depict literary materials such as books or scrolls of poetry or prose, and several depict them in conjunction with women. This chapter investigates how her readings inspired and influenced her artworks. It focuses on Evelyn's series of oil paintings *The Little Sea Maid* (1880–8) (Fig. 7.1), *The Sea Maidens* (1885–6) (Fig. 7.2) and *Daughters of the Mist* (1900–9) (Fig. 7.3), based on Hans Christian Andersen's popular tale *The Little Mermaid* (1836–7), and shows how she 'seizes the narrative' as a suffragist (Mancoff 2012: 85).[1] Evelyn wrote her own fairy tales, and her paintings use narrative devices, showing female figures in defining moments of conflict or metamorphosis. Her art illustrates how 'a new twist on an old tale can be an act of transgression, as well as one of transformation' (Mancoff 2012: 85), giving a voice to the voiceless.

In Andersen's fairy tale noir, with which Evelyn's male and female contemporaries would have been familiar, the Sea King's daughter longs to explore beyond her underwater domain and sells her voice to a sea-witch in exchange for legs in order to become human, hopefully marry the prince and thus gain an immortal soul. Andersen visited England in 1847 and 1857, when translations of his works were already being made, and it is likely that the story's first translation into

Figure 7.1 *The Little Sea Maid*, Evelyn De Morgan, 1880–8, © De Morgan Collection, courtesy of the De Morgan Foundation.

Figure 7.2 *The Sea Maidens*, Evelyn De Morgan, 1885–6, © De Morgan Collection, courtesy of the De Morgan Foundation.

Figure 7.3 *Daughters of the Mist*, Evelyn De Morgan, 1900–9, © De Morgan Collection, courtesy of the De Morgan Foundation.

English in 1872 – when Evelyn was a teenager, undergoing her own transition into womanhood, and acutely aware of her own domestic captivity – inspired the idea for her understudied yet fascinating trilogy. Andersen also contributed to *Good Words for the Young* (1868), for which Mary Watts produced illustrations. Testifying to the cultural importance and continued relevance of fairy tales, and comparing his own work to them, George Watts stated, 'Fairy-tales keep their place very much because all the extravagant and impossible feats are woven about and upon some really great truth of human nature; their teaching is generally good' (qtd. in M. Watts 1912: 2.213).

Patricia Yates claims Andersen's story 'would have attracted the artist because the mermaid longed, not just for earthly love, but for an immortal soul' (1996: 61); in a similar focus on spirituality, E. L. Smith argues 'the fairytale as a whole served for [Evelyn] as an allegory of the spiritual development' (2002: 161) that was central to her work. Yet while *The Little Mermaid* may have resonated with Evelyn's spiritual beliefs and interests, as a female artist and suffragist she also almost certainly found the story moving and compelling because the mermaid longs for more knowledge and freedom, ventures into the unknown and forbidden, renegotiates her relationship to her body and redefines herself in relation to society. Feminism was arguably just as important as spiritualism in Evelyn's life and art despite the dominant critical focus on the latter. While Evelyn's three paintings can be seen to trace a 'spiritual transformation from constraint to freedom' (E. L. Smith 2002: 17), they also trace a specifically female, socio-political transformation from oppression to liberation, promoting the women's suffrage campaign that she so strongly supported.

The Little Sea Maid, *The Sea Maidens* and *Daughters of the Mist* place the plight of woman centre stage and anticipate the more explicit feminist significance of this union of women and the sea at the end of the nineteenth century and into the twentieth century. To summarise their feminist significance prior to close analysis: *The Little Sea Maid* – which depicts a dejected and (as the viewer learns through a reading of Andersen's story) suffering woman sitting alone on a rock in the sea which separates her from the distant Prince's Castle on the hill – represents the oppression, marginalisation and abjection of women by patriarchal society; *The Sea Maidens* – which depicts a line of interlinked female figures rising up out of the sea – represents the uniting of women in the fight for women's rights and the rise of feminism; and *Daughters of the Mist* – which depicts four expressive female figures elevated to the starred sky surrounded by opalescent swirling mists and shards of rainbow – symbolises female liberation. In all three paintings, the female figures are presented in liminal or transitional positions (on the shore, semi-submerged or airborne, moving from sea to land, mermaid to human, death to rebirth), reflecting the shifting socio-political position and evolving role of women in the nineteenth century.

This parallelism between Evelyn's (often neglected or dismissed) series of sea paintings and the progression of the contemporary women's rights movement is apparently unrecognised by critics. While it has been acknowledged that many of Evelyn's paintings draw upon neo-classical traditions, ancient symbolism, mythology, feminism and dramatic oceanic imagery, the link between the latter three has never been explored further. Referring to sirens and mermaids in art, Joseph Kestner claims mythology was used to foster misogyny in the nineteenth century, arguing that classical-subject myths constituted a symbolic language that perpetuated an ideology about women (as passive or mad) which delayed the cause of social reform (1989: 353–4). Yet while many nineteenth-century paintings of mermaids and sirens reinforce patriarchal notions of woman (as seductive or evil), Evelyn's mermaid paintings draw on myth in order to subvert patriarchal perceptions of women and support female emancipation. An exploration and analysis of these paintings in unprecedented depth – alongside their literary source, in relation to contemporary art and literature, and from more recent theoretical perspectives – reveals their relevance to nineteenth and twentieth-century feminism.

While Yates claims these paintings are 'able to stand apart' (1996: 60) from their literary source, the full extent of their feminist significance is only revealed through a reading of them alongside the story on which they are based. These literary and visual texts enhance each other's imagery and strengthen each other's subtexts to create distinctly feminist statements. Evelyn translates Andersen's work into a different medium in an artistic adaptation of his work, focusing on female figures embodying pivotal positions in the development of the narrative. She addresses the role and representation of women in late Victorian society through her art. Evelyn apparently recognised the relevance of Andersen's early nineteenth-century children's fairy tale – and the image of the potentially powerful, metamorphic mermaid – to the contemporary women's movement, and re-presented it for a late nineteenth-century audience. Her art featured a resurgence of the mermaid narrative as 'an apparent response to the changing status of women' (White 1993: 185) in Victorian culture. Thus the 'typical Victorian assumptions about the unimpeachable maleness of the art producer-audience relationship are subverted [. . . and] we are now presented with the possibility of a woman artist and a woman subject speaking directly to a woman viewer' (E. L. Smith 2002: 113) and a women's movement.

Evelyn's abundant representations of women and the sea continue, develop and refine her iconographic vocabulary foregrounding the tension between captivity and liberty. In this chapter I aim to show how Evelyn employed the metamorphic mermaid as a model for socio-political transformation from captivity to liberty, revealing the largely unrecognised feminist significance of these little-known works as well as Evelyn's status as a suffragist artist. Focusing on the mermaid series, this chapter explores the feminist significance of the sea; the representation of the female nude; the dynamics of the gaze; the subversive symbolism of the mermaid; and the significance of the dawn in early feminist iconography. It shows how Evelyn reappropriated masculine symbols and classical myths, re-presented the female body and re/de-constructed femininity in her art in order to engage with contemporary gender debates and early feminist issues.

> [In the nineteenth century, the sea was perceived as] a threat to masculine rationality and the order and culture that it constructed out of the dark chaos of nature. Water, traditionally aligned with the female principle, epitomized this primordial state: potent, fertile . . . mysterious, having symbolic associations with both birth and death. (E. L. Smith 2002: 160)

A consideration of Evelyn's trilogy in the context of the representation and symbolism of the sea in nineteenth and twentieth-century culture, and in comparison with contemporary literary and visual works, illuminates its feminist significance. The sea is conventionally female in Western culture and is traditionally associated with the feminine in mermaid mythology, which was popular in the Victorian period, as well as in stories of seductive sirens luring sailors to their death and oceanic metaphors for motherhood.[2] This was perhaps partly why the sea acquired such strong feminist significance in late nineteenth and early twentieth-century literary and visual texts. Though the hierarchy of mind/body has historically repressed the female by identifying woman and nature, the association of woman and the sea (active, dangerous nature) has potentially empowering implications for women. This was recognised by early feminist writers and artists. The sea embodies female liberation in Kate Chopin's proto-feminist novella *The Awakening* (1899), and Ernestine Mills's enamelled *The Octopus (Death of the Mermaid)* – exhibited at the Society of Women Artists in 1929 – depicts a mermaid entangled in the arms of an octopus. This can be interpreted as 'the establishment octopus that suppresses female initiative' and the 'ill treatment [of British women] by the government (the Establishment Octopus) throughout the years of suffrage campaigning' (Cockroft 2005: 29–30).

The votes for women movement was often depicted as a 'rising tide' or 'tide of change' sweeping the nation in early feminist iconography. The 'Mrs Partington: Rising Tide' (*c*.1910) postcard illustration designed and published by Ernestine Mills to promote the women's suffrage campaign depicts 'The New Mrs Partington (of the Anti Suffrage Society)' standing on the shore striving in vain to sweep back a rising tide of waves bearing the words 'liberal women', 'working women', 'medical women', 'professional women', 'socialist women' and 'mothers', and the accompanying quote reads 'somehow the tide keeps rising!' In this work, the sea represents the rising tide of feminist debate, agitation and progress: 'first-wave' feminism.

Partington was a Canute-like figure said to have tried to sweep back the ocean after a storm, whose story had already been used in debates on the 1832 Reform Bill to suggest the futility of trying to stem the tide of social progress (Tickner 1989: 41). In the background, the sun rises over the sea with the words 'votes for women' radiating from the emerging orb. This work influenced Mary Branson's recent tidal-controlled light installation *New Dawn* (2016) in the Houses of Parliament to commemorate the women's suffrage campaign; this shows the continued relevance of early feminist insignia and visual culture in the campaigns for gender equality that continue today.

Evelyn's paintings of female figures in oceanic settings not only engage with early feminist discourse but also prefigure the inextricable link between the female body and the body of the sea in Cixous's twentieth-century concept of *écriture féminine*, which privileges sea-like flux and fluidity. Her writing overflows with sea imagery that embodies the 'fantastic tumult' of women's drives and energies (1976: 876, 889), and she uses the ocean as a metaphor for female subjectivity in her 1975 essay 'Sorties' in her discourse of 'seas and mothers' (Cixious and Clément 1986: 88–9). The sea embodies female freedom in the work of Cixous, who urges women to 'take to the open sea . . . swim . . . take the plunge' (1991: 40). The mermaid who becomes woman, 'really experiencing metamorphosis', embodies the liberating fluidity, constant movement and subversive turbulence privileged by Cixous. The mermaid 'belongs to the race of waves. She arises . . . flows . . . takes pleasure in being boundless . . . very far from the "hearth" to which man brings her so that she will tend his fire' (Cixous and Clément 1986: 90–1). Cixous's writing stresses the subversiveness, the 'seemingly limitless possibilities and the sense of freedom that comes about with the total, instantaneous immersion into extreme otherness' (Blyth and Sellers 2004: 80) represented by the sea. A wider feminist lens encompassing more recent theory allows for a radical reconsideration of Evelyn's paintings.

The sea, which was an 'endless fascination' (M. Watts 1887: 21 November) to the Wattses and an inspiration to their works, was a recurring theme in the work of the De Morgans; they shared a passion and fascination for it that influenced one another's art. Ceramic works by William (engaged to Evelyn while she was working on *The Sea Maidens*) include merpeople designs, scale patterns, other fantastical sea creatures and ships. Reginald Blunt notes William's preoccupation with the sea in his 'lustred bowls . . . turquoise tiles . . . fishes, and the sea life, the . . . sweeping forms of limb and fin and wing . . . the transparencies of atmosphere, the swirl of wave, the shimmer of watery deeps' (1918: 190). The mythical sea monsters and reptilian creatures surrounding the female figures in many of Evelyn's paintings, including the dragons in *The Captives* (*c*.1888) and the sea serpents in *S.O.S.* (1914–16), are reminiscent of William's designs. Yet Evelyn almost invariably depicts the sea and its creatures – which can be seen as 'fearsome demons of patriarchy' (Marsh 1987: 152) – in conjunction with women. Through this imagery she developed a distinctly female voice that engaged with, and contributed to, an early feminist iconographic vocabulary.

Though not as prevalent as in Evelyn's works, the theme of the sea in conjunction with the female body features in William's novels. In *An Affair of Dishonour* (1910), he writes,

> Lucinda was on the side of the stones [. . . she] stoop[ed] at the water's edge to catch up the foam and run it through her fingers . . . [Sir Oliver] stood watching the girl's figure against the restless silver of the sea below the moon. The music of her laugh . . . its rich and joyous expression as she sprang back, drenched, from a rush the sea made to embrace her feet . . . had such power over him that he in a manner feared or resented its mastery. (68–70)

Despite the presence of a voyeuristic male gaze, the emphasis on the active female body immersed in the 'rush[ing]', 'restless' sea – which parallels her energetic movements and ebullience – subverts the prevalent image of passive femininity in paintings of seated, supine, languid women in littoral settings. The liminal space of the seashore (between sea and land; the water's edge) is itself suggestive of transition or transgression, while the 'rich and joyous expression' of Lucinda's laughter signifies a freedom that threatens Sir Oliver's patriarchal power. This passage can be read as a rare example of male-authored antiphallocentric writing, which uses the trope of women and the sea to represent female liberty and 'mastery' over man.

Evelyn's literary as well as visual work can be seen to draw on and contribute to early feminist oceanic symbolism. The sea is a recurring and persistent theme of Evelyn's early unpublished poetry, where it is specifically associated with freedom:

> I hear the ocean – whose ceaseless swell
> To me, of beauty, and grandiour [*sic*] tell.
> It chaunts [*sic*] forth an anthem to the free
> And the wild waves answer whisperingly

> That hope, blessed hope, still still remains
> To free me some day of my chains.
> (untitled 1869: ll.7–12)

These enjambed rhyming couplets mimic the fluidity and double motion (flow and ebb) of the sea, which speaks of hope and freedom to the oppressed, and prefigures the 'chants' and 'anthems' of suffrage supporters in propagation of their campaign. The 'whispering' reassurance of liberation resonates in the sibilance ('ceaseless swell'), alliteration ('wild waves') and repetition (of 'hope' and 'still' in the same line) of the poem, which seems to express a desire for the sociopolitical emancipation of women. The image of 'chains' parallels that in her later paintings of female captivity. The wildness of the waves contrasts with the (metaphorical or literal) captivity of the speaker while promising future freedom. The sea is a symbol of power and unrest in Evelyn's poetry: 'Restless sighed the swelling ocean / Rolling, tossing, tumbling' (untitled, *c.*1869). The 'roughly tossing' and 'swelling waters' of the 'mighty ocean' ('To the Swallow', undated) has the power to 'drag [man] down to lasting night' (untitled, undated) – a line which seems to allude to the deadly power of the mermaid. Evelyn's poetic images of 'graceful nymphs dancing / In the wild waves foam' and 'mermaids too with / Their fishlike tails' (untitled, 1868–9) prefigure her more politically charged paintings.

The Little Sea Maid

Andersen's little mermaid embodies a complex tension between feminine and feminist, passive and active, powerless and powerful, shedding new light on Evelyn's *The Little Sea Maid*. Andersen's protagonist is described as conventionally feminine and even the epitome of feminine beauty: 'the youngest was the prettiest of all, her skin was as soft and delicate as a roseleaf, her eyes as blue as the deepest sea' and her hair was 'long [and] thick' (2002: 1, 16). Through these very visual literary images, Andersen constructs a traditional male ideal of feminine beauty that parallels the 'stunners' of Rossetti's paintings in prose. A doll-like model of feminine beauty was prevalent in – and dictated by – Victorian art and society, as illustrated by Rossetti's idealised women with glassy-eyed stares and the fashion for tiny corseted waists. The row of uncannily similar female figures in Evelyn's painting *The Sea Maidens* – with their distant gazes, impassive faces, porcelain-white skin, long, thick hair and unnatural, stylised poses – are reminiscent of Rossetti's 1860s Aesthetic works. However, Evelyn's five figures were all taken from the same model (Jane Hales) which accounts for their striking similarity and reflects the limited access of Victorian women artists to professional adult life-drawing models. They can be seen from a feminist perspective to symbolise in order to satirise the oppressive Victorian norms of feminine beauty which systematically reduced women to pretty, passive, voiceless living dolls or objects to be purchased or played with by men – just as the prince in Andersen's tale 'played with [the little mermaid's] long hair' and 'kissed her rosy mouth' (19).

Andersen's detailed description of the process of feminisation following the little mermaid's fifteenth birthday can be seen to reflect and critique the construction of femininity in Victorian society, in which young upper-middle-class women were often dressed up like dolls and paraded like puppets around social events in order to attract husbands. The mermaid's grandmother the 'old queen dowager' heavily adorns her in preparation for the upcoming court ball, saying, 'now we shall have you off our hands' (6). Her grandmother tells her she must 'endure the pain for the sake of the finery' and bear this heavy burden of feminine beauty as silently, 'lightly and airily as a bubble through the water' (6). This value of feminine beauty over female liberty is precisely what George Watts objected to in his written condemnation of ornamental and oppressive feminine fashions – which seem symbolised by the mermaid's restrictive decorated tail. Andersen offers the reader insight into the mermaid's internal struggle, revealing her private desire for freedom: 'But oh! how gladly would she have shaken off all this splendor, and laid aside the heavy wreath . . . but she did not dare to make any alteration' (6). While this passage highlights the oppression of women incarcerated in feminised bodies to which they are restricted and reduced, it also draws attention to the female protagonist's rebellious, non-conformist attitude and desire to 'shake off' the shackles of femininity. In this sense, there are striking parallels between Andersen's protagonist and Evelyn herself, who shunned bourgeois feminine conventions and refused to be presented at Court and at balls.

Andersen's descriptions of the mermaid's progressive ideas and departure from feminine conventions allow her to be read as a proto-feminist protagonist: she 'wanted information' about 'so many things' and was 'so full of longings' (3); she ventured far beyond any of her sisters and 'swam much nearer the land than any of the others dared', longing to live among mankind because 'their world seemed so infinitely bigger than hers' (10). Her aspirations and ambitions are comparable with those of New Women like Evelyn, who ventured beyond the confines of the home in pursuit of knowledge, independence, autonomy, adventure and freedom (traditionally denied to them by patriarchal society). Andersen suggests the 'masculine' and even superhuman strength of the female protagonist as she 'dived like a swan' through the 'black waves' of the 'angry sea . . . [which] rose like mountains, high enough to overwhelm her' (7) to save the prince from drowning (instead of luring him to his death). Similarly, in William De Morgan's novel *Somehow Good*, the young heroine Sally, famous for her swimming prowess, saves the life of the main male character (Cain 2013: 19). Andersen's description of the weak, passive prince 'drifting about on the waves, half dead' emphasises the subversion of traditional gender roles: 'he was becoming unable to swim any further . . . and he must have died if the little mermaid had not come to the rescue' (2002: 10, 8). Though these scenes are not shown by Evelyn, a reading of *The Little Sea Maid* in relation to the text on which it is based infuses her painting with feminist subtext and her seemingly delicate seated protagonist with otherwise unseen subversive dimensions.

Andersen's focus on female suffering and strength in *The Little Mermaid* is consistent with Evelyn's focus in *The Little Sea Maid*. Andersen's protagonist is subjected to a variety of tortures throughout the text: her tongue is cut off and voice traded as payment to the sea-witch in exchange for legs which are so painful that walking feels like stepping on 'sharp knives and spikes' (16). She has to bathe her bleeding, 'burning feet' in the cool seawater to soothe them at night and 'at such times she used to think of those she had left in the deep' (17). Significantly, Evelyn chose to depict this particular scene in *The Little Sea Maid*. Separated from its literary context, Evelyn's painting might seem to depict nothing more than a woman peacefully paddling her feet in the sea under a pink evening sky – a picture of passive femininity. Yet a reading of the text on which it is based illuminates its feminist significance. In Andersen's tale, the mermaid's physical and emotional agony is dramatised in detail, and this is implicit in Evelyn's painting: she paints the female figure sitting dejected, desolate and naked on a rock, staring sadly down into the sea in which her family dwells and to which she can never return. Evelyn's subdued and introspective figure, depicted in a state of sadness and solitude as a symbol of female suffering, stands out from the plethora of highly eroticised, titillating, light-hearted or merely decorative images of mermaids and sirens more typical of the Victorian period. These include images by Evelyn's husband, who depicted mermaids in his ceramic work for their 'lively, graceful potential' (E. L. Smith 2002: 160) with no hint of the feminist significance that Evelyn found in the subject.

Evelyn's choice of scene in *The Little Sea Maid* which alludes to the 'agony Andersen shows to be involved in acquiring and occupying a woman's body' is an acknowledgement rather than erasure of the 'many pains involved in constructing the proper woman's body' (White 1993: 188) according to patriarchal perceptions of femininity. While Evelyn's painting could be perceived as a continuation of the male artistic tradition of painting female nudes that conformed to male ideals of feminine beauty and gratified the male gaze, the transformed mermaid's nudity 'should be read not as a sign of sexuality . . . but as a recognition of her sacrifice: entrapment in the voiceless body' (E. L. Smith 2002: 161). Although this classically posed nude female figure is comparable with that in paintings by Evelyn's male contemporaries, its allusion to specifically female experiences of loss and 'painful "growth" experiences' (White 1993: 186) makes it unique and significant from a feminist perspective. Andersen's and Evelyn's texts can be read in conjunction to form an allegorical story of the voicelessness and oppression of women in patriarchal Victorian society as well as the struggle for greater female empowerment and emancipation.

That Andersen's little mermaid must become voiceless in order to enter the 'man's world' on land can be seen to represent the silencing of women by a patriarchal society which is a primary focus of feminist critique. Yet the little mermaid's choice to sell her voice – the loss of which is 'voluntary and *explicitly* active' (White 1993: 191 [original emphasis]) – undermines 'the passivity of her voiceless state' (E. L. Smith 2002: 161) and a perception of her simply as a victim. It can be interpreted as her deliberate decision to depart from the male Logos or deconstruct phallocentric discourse and reconnect with a pre-linguistic, pre-patriarchal realm. She finds other, new ways to speak specifically with or through the medium of her body in her 'speaking eyes' (Andersen 2002: 15) and expressive dancing. The little mermaid's silent state which leads her to explore new forms of language (specifically, body language) can be seen to signify her liberation rather than oppression. Andersen's story can be read from a feminist perspective to reflect the struggle of women to find a voice – or rather to discover an alternative discourse – in patriarchal society.

A consideration of Evelyn's art in the context of the Victorian nude further illuminates its subversiveness and feminist significance. Evelyn painted numerous nudes at a time when the exposure of the body through images of the nude was one of the most controversial issues in Victorian art, and was regarded as a highly inappropriate if not forbidden subject for women artists. As Alison Smith explains, the bourgeois ideology of femininity informed the assumption that nudes were offensive, embarrassing and even potentially danger- ous to the delicate feminine sensibility (1996: 39–41).[3] By painting female nudes, Evelyn defied prevailing notions of propriety, overtly transgressed feminine norms and challenged conventional notions of womanhood. She ambitiously determined to study and master what was considered the highest ranks of art – the representation of the human figure – and her mastery is widely acknowledged and admired by critics. Evelyn's oil painting *Cadmus and Harmo- nia* (1877), an unconventional portrait of husband and wife based on Ovid's *Metamorphosis* painted ten years before her marriage, was one of the first nudes painted by a woman to appear in public. Depicting a full-frontal female nude standing on the shore with a snake coiling around her, it 'open[ed] up new psycho-sexual per- spectives on the body' (A. Smith 2001: 212), and it was on the basis of this daring submission to the Dudley Gallery that Evelyn received recognition and invitations to more exhibitions. She employed mer- maid iconography to explore 'sensual and sadistic treatments of the nude, testing the boundaries of what was permissible in high art without actually transgressing into the area of explicit violence or sexuality' (A. Smith 2001: 210).

Evelyn's use of Andersen's story as a source in addition to mythol- ogy legitimised and justified her portrayal of the nude Little Sea Maid. Her mermaid narrative and iconography was a strategy that enabled her to participate in the male tradition of painting female nudes whist protecting her reputation as a respectable woman art- ist. Evelyn's plethora of nudes is particularly impressive in the light of women's limited access to life-drawing classes and models in the nineteenth century. While women were accepted at the Slade School of Art to study fine art alongside men, women's study of the figure was still often limited to the antique and to decently draped nudes in segregated life classes. Women's access to adult professional models was restricted not only in accordance with strict Victorian notions of propriety but also with the patriarchal ideology of separate spheres which held that fine art and figure painting were male domains. Life drawing for female painters became a 'polemical political issue' (A. Smith 1996: 44), and women's struggle for equal rights in art institutions formed part of a wider fight for greater independence and autonomy.

While 'the majority of women artists, lacking experience working from the model, resorted to painting landscapes or still-lives'
(E. L. Smith 2002: 20), Evelyn appointed her sister's nursemaid Jane
Hales as her model. Jane, a similar age to Evelyn, features in many
of Evelyn's paintings including *Flora*, *Aurora Triumphans*, *Cadmus
and Harmonia* and *The Sea Maidens*. This one figure dominates Evelyn's work in various different forms as beautiful but robust women
in contrast to the delicate, waif-like Pre-Raphaelite model Elizabeth
Siddal. Unlike the overt sensuality of Rossetti's femme fatales, Evelyn's female figures have more depth in that they display inner and
physical strength. She can be seen to work within the male artistic
tradition of painting the female nude to radically different effect:
her nudes undermine patriarchal perceptions of women as essentially
passive sexual objects and support a feminist agenda to reveal or
display female power. Her persistent depiction of strong female figures can be seen to represent the growing body of resilient women
fighting for greater empowerment over the second half of the nineteenth century. Her skilled studies of the female body express a deep
appreciation and celebration of it: her art can be seen as an early
example of '*la peinture féminine*' (Wolff 1990: 68), or a painting and
reclamation of the female body by a woman at a time when women
were driven away from their bodies.

The Sea Maidens

Evelyn's painting *The Sea Maidens* – a sequel to *The Little Sea Maid*
(although it may have been painted first) – is not only a technically
accomplished 'tour-de-force of painting sea and half-nudes' (Yates
1996: 61) but also a subversive representation of women. The female
figures it depicts embody a subtle yet radical departure from traditional femininity. Though their long hair and rosy mouths visually
parallel Andersen's description of the little mermaid's typically feminine physical attributes that attract the prince, Evelyn's Sea Maidens are arguably 'rather heavy and quite different from their delicate
sister': their upright, robust or thick figures are juxtaposed with the
drooping figure of the Little Sea Maid. The stronger stature of the Sea
Maidens is reinforced by the unbroken chain formed by their bodies
as they stand bound in a strong sisterly bond with interlocked arms,
hands and fingers, creating a 'graceful but emphatic barrier that precludes any suggestion of invitation or allure' (E. L. Smith 2002: 159).
The rows of undulating wavelets surrounding them emulate their

interlinked limbs, reinforcing a sense of their solidity and unification. In contrast to the solitary female figure in *The Little Sea Maid*, in *The Sea Maidens* Evelyn uses a discourse of sisterhood, which can be seen to represent, support and promote the growing female community of nineteenth-century suffragists united in the fight for women's rights. This 'sisterly twinning', which is used as a recurring trope in various 'woman-as-nature images' by male artists to imply 'group orgies' (E. L. Smith 2002: 122), can alternatively be seen to suggest women's solidarity and communal strength in Evelyn's work.

Contradicting E. L. Smith's claim that there is 'no energy or emotion flowing through the connection' (2002: 159), the Sea Maidens can be seen to actively join forces to form a united female front and powerful all-female presence, holding hands and wrapping their arms protectively around each other as they rise out of the sea together straight towards the viewer in a manner more confrontational than seductive. The open pose of the mermaid who looks straight back at the viewer with both arms outstretched seems to invite combat or a solemn (rather than seductive) fatal embrace. *The Sea Maidens* alludes to the scenes in Andersen's text when the little mermaid's 'five sisters interlacing their arms would rise above the water together' to visit her, on one occasion bringing a sharp knife which they entreat her to 'plunge . . . into the prince's heart' (2002: 5, 21). They are not passive and docile but pernicious and deadly. This female activity which explicitly poses a threat to man is suggested by the united frontal figures dominating the centre foreground of Evelyn's painting, which suggests that they have approached or are approaching the (traditionally male) viewer; this undermines Smith's interpretation of their 'lassitude' and 'lax inertia' (2002: 159). They seem to approach boldly without the conventional coyness or else seductiveness of many female nudes by male painters of the period. While Andersen's mermaid's 'speaking eyes . . . able to bewitch a human heart' play up to the prince's gaze and '[appeal] more deeply to the heart than the songs of the slaves' (2002: 15, 17), the majority of Evelyn's Sea Maidens look slightly past and move beyond the definition of the viewer's sight; their gazes elude – and escape subordination by – the male gaze.

Analysis of the sexual politics of looking has long been central to feminist thinking, and further discussion of the dynamics of the gaze in Evelyn's art aids an understanding of its feminist significance. In Laura Mulvey's famous article (relevant to art of the Victorian period, which was strongly structured by sexual difference) she claims that

In a world ordered by sexual imbalance, pleasure in looking has been split between active/male and passive/female. The determining male gaze projects its fantasy on to the female figure, which is styled accordingly. In their traditional exhibitionist role women are simultaneously looked at and displayed, with their appearance coded for strong visual and erotic impact so that they can be said to connote *to-be-looked-at-ness*. (Mulvey 1999: 62–3 [original emphasis])

In Evelyn's painting, one particular Sea Maiden (the second figure from the right of the viewed painting) stands out and demands attention because she returns – and seems to stare down – the male gaze with a look direct, defiant and devoid of desire. This is the female gaze: the surveyed staring out of the painting straight back at her surveyor, challenging her role as spectacle. E. L. Smith overlooks this in her description of the Sea Maidens' 'repetitive, wistful expressions' and 'cool or distant' gazes (2002: 159–60). Evelyn subverts the traditional dynamics of the gaze along with patriarchal perceptions of women: the passive object of the male gaze has been transformed into the active subject bestowed with the power of the gaze that (according to myth) can lure men who gaze upon her to their deaths.

That this Sea Maiden in Evelyn's painting is 'seeing, not only seen . . . represented at the moment of her look' is remarkable for the time given that 'later nineteenth-century painting is characterised by an excess of unseeing female faces, female bodies swathed in or divested of drapery, female figures doing very little other than *looking* beautiful' (Cherry 1993: 190, 118 [original emphasis]) as exemplified by much of Rossetti's art. This female gaze can be seen to reflect the rise of female spectatorship in the second half of the nineteenth century as women increasingly produced, viewed and appraised art as a result of artistic education and professions which facilitated women's active looking. Women became spectators in and of visual texts, re-presenters of femininity and revisers of man-made myths, showing how women could look otherwise in and at art. Evelyn's sea paintings stand testimony to her viewing of and drawing from the forbidden subject of the female nude, deemed inappropriate for Victorian women to look upon. These works challenged Victorian prudishness while signifying Evelyn's disregard for, and defiance of, patriarchal notions of feminine purity and propriety which attempted to censor and control what women viewed. *The Sea Maidens* and *The Little Sea Maid* were exhibited at reputable galleries in 1906 and 1907 (respectively), when their relevance to the escalating women's suffrage campaign would have been particularly perceptible.

The shameless, cold, confrontational gaze of Evelyn's Sea Maiden evokes that of the nude female figure in Édouard Manet's controversial painting *Olympia* (1863), which shocked contemporary audiences in its departure from the conventional coy, alluring or averted gazes of nude women in more classical paintings such as Titian's *Venus of Urbino* (1538) and Giorgione's *Sleeping Venus* (1510). The look of the more demure, classically posed female nude in Evelyn's *The Little Sea Maid* – whose 'downcast gaze was considered a sign of feminine modesty' at the time – contrasts sharply with the unwavering, penetrating stare of the frontal, more subversive female nude in *The Sea Maidens* whose direct glance could be 'construed as an indicator of sexual deviancy' (Cherry 1993: 118) as well as denial.

This Sea Maiden who stares confidently back at the viewer with unusual assertiveness is a stark contrast to the looks of women in similar oceanic or littoral spaces in nineteenth-century paintings by men. Paul-Jacques-Aimé Baudry's painting *The Pearl and the Wave* (1862) shows a nude woman laying sluggishly on the seashore with her head turned to gaze backward and smile over her shoulder towards the voyeuristic viewer. This critically acclaimed painting – along with Alexandre Cabanel's *The Birth of Venus* (1863) depicting a nude woman posing seductively as she lays upon the waves – was painted by a man for male pleasure. Despite their semi-nudity, Evelyn's Sea Maidens are a striking contrast to the highly feminised and eroticised mermaids by male artists more typical of the period, such as J. W. Waterhouse's painting of *A Mermaid* (1900) busy combing and adorning her hair; Fred Appleyard's painting *Pearls for Kisses* (*c*.1900) depicting a mermaid with a silver tail and shiny hairpiece seducing a merman; and Frederic Leighton's painting *The Fisherman and the Siren* (1856-8) presenting a mermaid with streaming golden hair, plaited and entwined with pearls and coral, throwing her arms around a man's neck. In *The Sea Maidens*, there is no suggestion of feminine vanity, beautification or adornment typical of the charming, seductive mermaid images characteristic of the period which often featured motifs and ornaments such as mirrors, jewellery and hairpieces. It represents a radical departure from male artists' depictions of typically nude sirens and semi-nude mermaids placed in overtly erotic poses to gratify the male gaze. It can also be seen to signify Evelyn's move away from the classical subjects favoured by the Slade School of Art to explore her own style and ideas about roles and representations of women as a suffragist artist.

William De Morgan's illustration of a mermaid for a fairy tale ('Through the Fire') written by his sister Mary De Morgan (1877:

208) is similar in setting to Evelyn's *The Little Sea Maid* where the figure is seated on a rock, and physically similar to the long-haired, semi-nude mermaids in Evelyn's *The Sea Maidens*. However, the 'long bright' coiling tail and large harp held by the 'very beautiful maiden' with 'green eyes and long green hair' singing a 'beautiful' song in a 'sweet voice' (M. De Morgan 1877: 207–10) differentiate William's more conventional, decorative depiction from Evelyn's portrayal of transformed or enigmatic mermaids. Mary De Morgan's sinister description of a mermaid conveys the danger embodied by Evelyn's Sea Maidens (as they allude to Andersen's text):

> That is a mermaid . . . and she is singing to a ship . . . she will gradually lead it down into a whirlpool, and there it will be swallowed up, and the poor sailors will never return to their wives and little children. (1877: 208–9)

The mermaid thus poses a threat to the patriarchal family model which restricted women to the domestic sphere, representing a challenge to the stability, order and culture constructed by 'masculine rationality out of the dark chaos of nature'. However, while Evelyn's mermaids embody pernicious and predatory potential when read in relation to Mary De Morgan's and Andersen's fairy tales, *The Sea Maidens* are not depicted with instruments, singing open-mouthed to ships as in many contemporary images of seductive and dangerous mermaids or sirens (such as Rossetti's *Ligeia Siren* [1873]).

Evelyn's representation of mermaids is distinctive: she presents them neither as overtly aggressive sexual predators nor innocent, passive decorative objects, eschewing the typical Victorian stereotyping and 'dualistic fin-de-siècle conception' (E. L. Smith 2002: 121) of woman as angel or demon, victim or femme fatale, icon of danger or beauty. *The Sea Maidens* departs from the strong eroticism and heavy feminisation of many *fin-de-siècle* images of mermaids, instead focusing on the (inner and physical) strength of these female figures. She employed, entered into and engaged with this iconographic vocabulary, drawing on classical myth in order to re-present the female figure: not as conceived by the patriarchal imagination, 'produced for and productive of viewing positions for masculinity' (Cherry 1993: 118–19) but as a woman artist who apparently recognised the mermaid's feminist significance, subversive connotations and empowering implications for women. Evelyn presented a more complex image or symbol of femininity that defied convention and disrupted or complicated prevalent male ideals of – and misogynistic ideas about – women. She drew on the Pre-Raphaelite femme fatale and the (male artists') language of mermaid mythology as well as 'seizing the narrative' of Andersen's tale in order to make powerful if implicit socio-political statements; she reinterpreted and appropriated visual and literary narratives by men in order to contribute to early feminist discourse.

While Evelyn's *The Sea Maidens* predates the period around the turn of the century when mermaid imagery was most prevalent, it was painted around the same time as – and almost certainly influenced by – her good friend Edward Burne-Jones's painting *The Depths of the Sea* (1886). This was 'one of the most horrifying of the femme fatale genre', which (unlike John William Waterhouse's *The Lady of Shalott* or John Millais's *Ophelia* who die watery deaths) depicts a mermaid dragging a passive or perhaps futilely struggling male figure down through her walled, womb-like underwater domain to his death with a direct, eroticised gaze that made 'many a viewer . . . [feel] personally threatened' (E. L. Smith 2002: 160). Evelyn, like Burne-Jones, makes much of the gaze, and the direct stare of her Sea Maiden who challenges the objectifying male gaze is perhaps just as subversive. The other Sea Maidens have disconcerting penetrative or other-worldly stares, seeming to possess an omniscient or prophetic blindness; they thus become subtly ominous rather than simply titillating figures. Burne-Jones's murderous mermaid is strong, active and powerful, a smile of satisfaction or victory playing on her lips. In this painting, it is not the male but the female figure that is the aggressive sexual predator. Burne-Jones's visual image is reinforced by his statement that 'once [woman] gets the upper hand . . . she's the devil . . . as soon as you've taken pity on her she's no longer to be pitied. You're the one to be pitied then' ([1884] qtd. in E. L. Smith 2002: 160). Although this text perpetuates dichotomous views of woman (as angel/devil), it acknowledges female power.

The portrayal of the wicked siren who lured men to their deaths reinforced the patriarchal Victorian stereotype of women as descendants of Eve who were potentially evil manipulators of men; the many male representations of sirens as young women with legs suggest that 'the destructive allure of these sea-monsters is in fact a property of "ordinary" women' (A. Smith 2001: 219). Despite to some extent fuelling misogyny, the explicit portrayal of woman's power over man in mermaid imagery challenged and subverted prevalent patriarchal views of women as essentially passive or submissive, powerless and inferior. This is perhaps why the image of the mermaid was employed by suffragist artists as visual propaganda in their fight for female empowerment. Burne-Jones's painting seems to be a warning to men not to perceive women as innately weaker vessels, like Andersen's prince who treats the little mermaid like a helpless, pretty pet and calls her his 'sweet, dumb foundling' (2002: 19). Ironically, it is man's objectification and eroticisation of the mermaid – and male weakness for feminine beauty – that leads him to his death; man is thus fatally punished for perceiving woman merely as a passive or erotic object. Burne-Jones's image of man being dragged to his death by woman is a striking contrast to the plethora of contemporary images of women being driven to their watery deaths by men or masculinist society, such as George Watts's painting *Found Drowned*. While the drowned were typically victimised 'fallen women' in Victorian visual culture, an alternative parallel visual culture of mermaid imagery emerged in the nineteenth century which presented men as the victims of women in a subversion of traditional power relations between the sexes.

The fact that Evelyn's mermaids do not have legs is integral to the subversiveness of *The Sea Maidens* even as it seems to adhere to prevalent Victorian notions of social propriety which held that the depiction of female genitalia was indecent and should be masked or covered in paintings. More recent theoretical perspectives reveal the unsettling connotations of Evelyn's image of women with fishtails, showing how Evelyn challenges while seeming to cater to the male gaze. Though Evelyn's bare-breasted, semi-nude figures might titillate in another context – like many other mermaid images designed to gratify the male gaze – a glimpse of the '"phallic" tail's "otherness"' (White 1993: 186) (its scales; its fishiness) through the water, which Evelyn skilfully and deliberately makes partially visible, undermines any straightforward perception of these figures as erotic objects designed for male pleasure. The scaly shaft, which precludes male penetration and any potential for sexual gratification, repels the male gaze that travels down from the attractive feminine face and upper torso, and incites revulsion. The phallic dimensions of the tail may reveal how female desire has almost always been read in Western (and especially Victorian) culture as masculine or improperly feminine (White 1993: 186). The mermaid can be seen to embody a complex, uncanny fusion of familiar and unfamiliar that is simultaneously reassuring and disturbing for the male viewer: her female form represents both familiarity as man's '(oceanic) place of origin' and unfamiliarity as a sea-creature inhabiting a 'no-man's-land' of dark internal depths that is the symbolic 'abyss of the feminine' (White 1993: 186, 192). She embodies both the phallic dimensions of the tail and the breasts of the M/Other, seemingly both male and female, human and animal, defying binaries.

While the mermaid's body is uncanny from a psychoanalytic perspective, it can be seen as a progressive and subversive amalgamation of binary opposites when viewed in relation to Judith Butler's gender theory. As an embodiment of both phallic and feminine attributes, the mermaid blurs the boundaries of the traditional sex and gender binaries, representing a convergence, disorganisation and destabilisation of the oppressive oppositional binary and the 'rules that govern sex / gender / desire' (Butler 2006: 32). The anatomical ambiguity or hermaphroditism of the mermaid, and this apparent free-play or fusion of attributes, confuses the conventional correlation between sex and gender. The mermaid who undergoes a transformation to change her body – losing her 'phallic' tail and acquiring the legs of a woman which carry the implication of female genitalia – can be seen to embody Butler's argument that sex is just as constructed as gender, as well as Simone de Beauvoir's argument that 'one is not born but rather becomes a woman' ([1949] qtd. in Butler 2006: 11). Indeed, the mermaid has become a 'symbol of the girl's difficult rite of passage to womanhood' (White 1993: 186), to which Evelyn's teenage diary testifies. Butler's theory seems implicit in the juxtaposition of Evelyn's Sea Maidens and Little Sea Maid which, when read in relation to the text on which they are based, can be seen to trace the construction of the woman's body and the physical and emotional changes it entails.

Butler's argument that sex and gender are constructed is further attested to by Andersen's little mermaid who not only undergoes a transformation to 'become a woman' but also subsequently crossdresses, temporarily assuming another gender identity in a further disruption of the traditional gender binary so that she can participate in 'masculine' activities with men: '[the prince] had a man's dress made for her, so that she could ride about with him' (Andersen 2002: 17). The mermaid's transformation into an anatomical woman and oscillation between the components of the traditional gender binary reveal its boundaries to be fluid rather than fixed, and sex and gender to be 'regulatory fictions'. That sex and gender are constructions which can be 'constructed differently' (Butler 2006: 10) represents the potential for women to renegotiate their relationships to their bodies and re-present themselves, breaking out of the oppressive norms of femininity and deconstructing traditional perceptions of womanhood. The transformed mermaid depicted by Andersen and Evelyn deconstructs the notion of a fixed, natural or essential body in defiance of the 'biology-is-destiny formulation' (Butler 2006: 8). *The Little Sea Maid* thus not only represents the suffering of women confined to and defined by their bodies in Victorian society but also the emancipating and empowering implications of the mermaid's metamorphosis for women: she symbolises the potential for change, for greater freedom of self-representation, and for the transgression of apparently impermeable binary boundaries. Evelyn's figure of the mythical mermaid appears to be distant from the realities of Victorian society, and yet it reflects aspects of the 'confusion of sexual identity that emerged as a result of the changing political and legal situation of women' (Kestner 1989: 353) over the second half of the nineteenth century.

Daughters of the Mist: the Dawn of a New Era

The final painting in Evelyn's trilogy based on Andersen's text, *Daughters of the Mist* (1900–9), alludes to the conclusion of his narrative. In the story, the little mermaid throws herself into the sea and her body dissolves into foam, but instead of ceasing to exist she turns into a spirit and joins the 'daughters of the air' (Andersen 2002: 22) who can attain immortal souls and a place in paradise by doing good deeds. Andersen's interest in and ideas about spirituality are aligned with those expressed in *The Result of an Experiment*, published just after Evelyn completed *Daughters of the Mist*. The evolution towards emancipation in her painting is echoed by numerous 'spirit messages' in this text: for example, 'I am a spirit of Light . . . My path is upwards . . . I once was on Earth, fettered in the prison of the body. Now I am free' (De Morgan and De Morgan 1909: 70). Her images of 'Angel forms . . . brightly beaming, / Thronging in the dewy morn' with its 'tints of dawn' (untitled, undated) in her early verses are also manifest in *Daughters of the Mist*. The transition from one state to another is emphasised by Evelyn in both word and image. Evelyn's series of sea paintings tracing the metamorphosis of the mermaid exemplifies how she employed the female body as a model for socio-political as well as spiritual transformation from constraint to freedom. While the Little Sea Maid and Sea Maidens are bound to the world below, the Daughters of the Mist are elevated to an ethereal realm of female freedom in the sky. The triangular composition suggests an upward movement or a liberating ascent into light, and freedom is visualised by the floating forms, expressive poses and loose diaphanous draperies.

Evelyn envisions not only a spiritual rebirth but also a socio-political awakening for women. The 'harmonious accord' of the touching or overlapping buoyant airborne female figures in conjunction with the rainbow, shards of light and pink clouds of dawn was perhaps not only 'intended to be read as spiritual fruitfulness' (E. L. Smith 2002: 164) but also as a utopian future of female liberty. Unlike Arthur Hacker's painting *The Cloud* (1901) in which a female nude lays seductively upon a fluffy cumulus, and Herbert Draper's painting *Clyties of the Mist* (1912) in which the female figures seem to be shielding themselves from (and at the mercy of) the elements, Evelyn's figures are 'joyous, free, strong, fully in control, and unhampered by social conventions of dress or pose' (E. L. Smith 2002: 164). Their active, dynamic postures signify transformation, moving from seated to upright positions, unlike the languid female nudes reclining in sexually inviting poses in Hacker's and Draper's paintings. Evelyn's *Daughters of the Mist* arguably serves as an allegory of release from the fetters of female (rather than non-gendered human) embodiment and its socially defined roles. The ease and relaxation of the poses combined with the powerful motion and extension of the figures (E. L. Smith 2002: 121) represents a renewed female energy and freedom from restraint, envisioning a liberated future specifically for women.

Evelyn's *Daughters of the Mist* combines the delicate translucency of the ethereal swirling mists and draperies with the tangible execution of the robust physical female forms beneath these thin veils. Its suggestion of female strength beneath surface delicacy is reminiscent of George Watts's *She Shall Be Called Woman*, and yet his painting *Dawn* (undated, showing the back view of a semi-draped standing female figure with her breast slightly exposed by her lifted arm) is comparatively static. Similarly, his painting *Undine* (1835), comparable with Evelyn's work in its mythological subject, shows a half-length draped female figure holding a harp in a lost profile, emphasising her exposed white neck. Evelyn's painting is more comparable with Emily Ford's strong, flying figures such as her 'feminist painting' (Crawford 1999: 226) *Towards the Dawn* (undated). It is also comparable with the exquisite illustrations by little-known artist Rosie Pitman for Friedrich De La Motte Fouqué's fairy tale *Undine* (1897) and for Hans Christian Andersen's tale 'The Snow Queen' (*c.*1896). The former illustrations depict female figures rising dramatically from the ocean into the air, surrounded by swirling winds and waters, and the latter illustration depicts a trio of angels in a starred sky. These women artists drew on male-authored fairy tales to produce feminist images; Evelyn was part of a wider female-produced visual culture.

The 'narrative destiny of female characters in [nineteenth-century] fiction . . . was either marriage and social integration or death/disaster and social alienation' (Evans 1997: 78). The latter is apparently the woman's fate in Andersen's text after the prince marries another woman and the little mermaid (having refused to kill the prince to save her own life) throws herself overboard into the waves in an act of self-sacrifice. The crimson robe beside the Little Sea Maid arguably symbolises not only love and blood (bleeding feet; menstruation) but also martyrdom (as it also does in Evelyn's *Ariadne in Naxos*), signifying her heroic dimension hinted at in Andersen's tale. The pink sky in Evelyn's *The Little Sea Maid* and *Daughters of the Mist* alludes to Andersen's description of the 'pink tinted dawn; the first sunbeam, she knew, would be her death' (2002: 21). Edmund Dulac's illustration for this passage of Andersen's story – which depicts a deathly pale female figure floating in the sea with her arms outstretched in a cruciform pose – not only reinforces the idea of the mermaid's martyrdom evoked by Evelyn's painting but is also strikingly similar to the cruciform pose of the semi-submerged 'fallen woman' in George Watts's *Found Drowned*. George and Evelyn's art often overlaps in its focus on female suffering and strength, reflecting the contemporary female struggle for socio-political freedom. Although the story on which Dulac and Evelyn draw is a fairy tale, their artworks can be seen to dialogise with the social reality of female suicide in a fusion of fact and fantasy; George's social-realist paintings and Evelyn's symbolist paintings are thus more similar than they might seem.

However, physical death is not synonymous with spiritual death for the mermaid in Andersen's text:

> dawn was spreading fast . . . Now the sun rose from the sea and with its kindly beams warmed the deadly cold foam [into which she had dissolved], so that the little mermaid did not feel the chill of death. She saw the bright sun and above her floated . . . the daughters of the air. (Andersen 2002: 22)

This regeneration or rebirth is represented by Evelyn's painting *Daughters of the Mist*, in which the dawn sky not only prefigures spiritual afterlife or the 'dawning of a new life promised by the happy twist of the story's conclusion' (E. L. Smith 2002: 161) but can also be seen to represent 'the dawn of a new age of equal opportunity' fervently hoped for by many Victorian women including herself. In her discussion of New Dawn Women whose careers were in the ascendancy at the dawn of the twentieth century, Cockroft claims that the 'sunrise over the ocean' signifying dawn – implied by the pink sky in *The Little Sea Maid* and the sunrise in *The Sea Maidens* as well as the morning mists and rays of light in *Daughters of the Mist* – 'reflected womanhood's international aspirations' (Cockroft 2005: 5). Dawn – with its connotations of beginning, re/birth, emergence, enlightenment and up/rising – became an incipient feature of early feminist iconography with which Evelyn dialogised. The slogan 'Rise Up Women' was famously shouted before suffragettes rushed the House of Commons, and many of Evelyn's paintings show rising women or women suspended over the sea, including *Evening Star over the Sea* (*c*.1905–10); her paintings *Night and Dawn*, *Twilight* and *Eos* also focus on the dawn.[4]

New Dawn Women worked against the 'dawn of phallocentrism' (Cixous and Clément 1986: 100), challenging male traditions, structures and ideologies, and reappropriating traditionally masculinist motifs, placing them into new contexts and creating new significations. The image of the rising sun, often viewed as the quintessential symbol of masculinity and traditionally gendered masculine in literary imagery, was reappropriated by early feminist artists and writers. In their discourses, it became an icon of the dawn of female empowerment, female enlightenment and greater gender equality that coincided with the early twentieth century. A 1908 WSPU banner designed by Sylvia Pankhurst (featuring the self-sacrificing pelican and inspired by George Eliot's verse) bore the phrase, 'Strong souls live, like fire-hearted suns, to spend their strength [in furthest striving action]' (Tickner 1989: 261). A postcard published by the Suffrage Atelier, titled 'The Anti-Suffrage Ostrich "The Sun is Not Rising"', depicts an ostrich with its head in the sand inscribed with 'ignorance, stupidity', and the sun shining over mountains in the background inscribed with 'women's freedom'.

Images of the sun and dawn also resurface in Mary Watts's work: in her winged sun motif; the sunrays radiating from the inner wheel of her Compton Potters' Arts Guild trademark; and the Guild's *Sunrise Wave Bookends* (*c*.1930). In the chapel interior, the angelic figures lead the eye up towards the 'Eternal Circle of the sun' (Gould 1998: 56), and Freedom (panel IV) is depicted as an angel with a sunburst behind it. On the chapel doorway is a circular symbol for 'Light, Twilight, and Night' suggestive of the words 'The morning cometh' (M. Watts 1905: 13). Cixous prioritises the 'twilight' as a time of intense female creativity (2006: 8), and Rich describes the 'awakening consciousness' of woman writing at dawn (1980: 34).[5] Indeed, Mary writes her diary before or at dawn (from 4am), while George and Evelyn trained themselves to rise with the dawn to make the most of the daylight for painting.

In Evelyn's painting *Aurora Triumphans [The Dawn]* (1886), the Roman goddess of dawn Aurora's bonds fall away as Night flees and three trumpeting figures, their wings glowing with the red of the rising sun, herald the triumph of dawn in an overt transition from darkness to light, captivity to liberty. This has striking similarities with Sylvia Pankhurst's 'Angel of Freedom' logo (1911), featuring a trumpeting winged angel with 'Freedom' written on a banner above her head, which appeared on WSPU 'Votes for Women' propaganda. Evelyn's angels prefigure the trumpeting, forward-stepping 'Bugler Girl' (designed by Caroline Watts of the ASL, originally on banners for the NUWSS procession of 13 June 1908), who became an enduring symbol of the suffrage movement. Although the NUWSS and its artists generally avoided Militant Woman iconography, in the Bugler Girl they adopted a rousing allegorical image: 'the Amazon who stands on the battlements of the fort may be said to be heralding the new day of which the sun is just seen rising' (Tickner 1989: 211). In November 1913 – when Mary hosted her suffrage meeting at Limnerslease – the Bugler Girl (inspired by Elizabeth Barrett Browning's 'Now press the clarion to thy woman's lip') made her debut on the front page of the *Common Cause*. Tickner explains, 'it is the definitive account of . . . "constitutional militancy"; the National Union's response to the stakes as they had been raised by the WSPU, and its use of the same crusading rhetoric' (1989: 211). The NUWSS's Bugler Girl – a young woman in military dress with a (sheathed) sword, bugle and banner – was an image of female heroism not dissimilar to the WSPU's Joan of Arc. Suffragists were accused of adopting similar iconography and ideology to suffragettes. The NUWSS's emphasis and insistence on the symbolism of the Bugler Girl's spiritual armoury (Tickner 1989: 51) could not disguise her socio-political potency; this is also perceptible in Evelyn's and Mary's symbolism and powerful allegorical female figures.

A dramatic sunrise over the ocean is depicted on the illustrated cover of the first issue of the liberal-feminist newspaper *Shafts* (3 November 1892), accompanied by the words 'Light Comes to Those Who Dare to Think' – praising thought or knowledge as the instrument of socio-political emancipation – and by lines of poetry:

> Oh, swiftly speed, ye Shafts of Light
> All round the shadows fly;
> Fair breaks the dawn; fast rolls the night
> From woman's darkened sky.

The image of the rising sun symbolises the dawn, and the verse parallels this passage from dark to light, representing a progression towards female emancipation. The opening lines of a poem titled 'The New Woman' published in *Shafts* seems to describe Evelyn's many strong female figures in transitional or newly liberated positions:

> Pausing on the century's threshold,
> With her face towards the dawn,
> Stands a tall and radiant presence;
> In her eyes the light of morn.
> (unknown February 1895: 378)

Matthew Beaumont's description of the woman on the front cover of the first issue of *Shafts* as 'quietly triumphant, at once authoritative and calmly combative' with 'neither the languid sexuality associated with decadent images of women at this time, nor the sexless aggression associated with caricatures of Amazonian feminists' (Beaumont 2006: 2) evokes Evelyn's figures in *The Sea Maidens* and *Daughters of the Mist*. In the latter painting, the first rays of sunrise appear as shafts of light behind the liberated female figures rising up into the air. The female archer on the cover of *Shafts* embodies a composed energy as she draws the string of her bow and takes aim with the arrow while stepping forward, just as Evelyn's female figure of Lightning in *The Storm Spirits* steps forward as she emits bolts from her hand, and the figures in *Aurora Triumphans* stand poised or step forward as they sound trumpets heralding the dawn; they assume the stances of winged heralds and militant female figures in suffragette iconography. In these works, traditionally masculine images and phallic symbols – 'shafts' of light, arrow shafts, trumpets and lightning bolts, in addition to the sun – are reappropriated by women and acquire feminist significance.

Evelyn's sea paintings depicting the pink sky of dawn and the rising sun can thus be seen to draw on and contribute to the emergent early feminist iconographic vocabulary of the time. In painting the sunrise at dawn, Evelyn paints a picture of the potential for and imminence of female emancipation. While the movement from darkness to light is traditionally used in religious rhetoric, it also pervades the language of early feminism; the imagery and chiaroscuro are imbued with suffrage significance in Evelyn's paintings. These images and artistic details are visual clues that suggest how Evelyn's paintings promote female liberation, narrating or tracing the progression of the women's movement towards the achievement of its goals. Evelyn repeatedly depicted the dawn in her paintings of women not only for its 'spiritual connotations of rebirth' but because this transitional time between the 'shrouded dimness of night' and the 'developing light of day' (E. L. Smith 2002: 126) suggests new beginnings and a progression towards a brighter future for women. Andersen may have intended to use the story of *The Little Mermaid* to express the ideals of Christian faith and redemption, but Evelyn seems to recreate this story to express feminist ideals of female empowerment and emancipation. Evelyn translates Andersen's spiritualist story into a suffragist story, drawing on, engaging with and supporting the women's movement in her art.

Evelyn's three paintings based on Andersen's tale focus on specifically female experiences of suffering and freedom, and – when viewed in conjunction, from more recent theoretical perspectives and in relation to contemporary works – can be seen to trace a transformation from female oppression to liberation. Evelyn's deliberate depiction of female figures at pivotal points in Andersen's story not only affords her paintings a narrative quality but also traces a progression that visually paralleled – seemingly with a purpose to promote – the women's suffrage movement as it gained momentum over the late nineteenth and early twentieth centuries. Evelyn thus employed the female figure and specifically the metamorphic mermaid as a model for socio-political transformation from constraint to freedom, from disempowerment to empowerment. The mermaid image seems to have acquired deeper meaning and relevance specifically for women at a time when women were fighting for greater social, political and economic power. In Evelyn's art, the ancient image and classical myth of the mermaid – which provided a primary source for the male mythologisation of women – becomes a symbol of female autonomy and power. She appropriated the man-made mermaid myth in a feminist reclamation of an image historically used either to objectify or denounce women. The final painting in Evelyn's trilogy, visualising female emancipation, can be seen to have the most overtly feminist function, and perhaps best illustrates her role as a suffragist artist.

Notes

1. Andersen's tale was first written in 1836, first published by C. A. Reitzel in Copenhagen in *Fairy Tales Told for Children* in 1837 and first translated into English by H. P. Paull in 1872. While there is no known direct information from Evelyn about her influences for these three paintings, they are mentioned in catalogues of Old Battersea House compiled by Mrs Stirling (DMF); she states that the first two are from Hans Andersen's tale, and the third is linked by association. Andersen's name, summaries of and quotations from his text accompany the names of Evelyn's paintings as explanations for the scenes they depict. The frame for *The Sea Maidens* bears a Danish quote attributed to Andersen.
2. In Western culture, 'water was a traditional symbol of the feminine' (E. L. Smith 2002: 22), associated with sea-nymphs, Nereids, kelpies, harpies and undines. However, the sea is not always imagined as feminine: see Poseidon and Neptune.
3. However, the perception and reception of the nude in art was very much dependent on the figure, viewer and context (A. Smith 2001: 210).
4. Evelyn also develops traditional female or feminine lunar imagery in a feminist direction in her paintings: *Lunar* (1885), *Moonbeams Dipping into the Sea* (1918) and *Sleeping Earth and Waking Moon* (1905–10) reappropriate that in Edward Burne-Jones's *Luna* (1870) and Frederic Leighton's *Summer Moon* (1872).
5. Women writers including Toni Morrison and Sylvia Plath are known to have written at dawn before their children awoke and they had to return to domestic maternal duties during the day in which time was not their own.

Conclusion

This book identifies and rectifies important omissions in the existing public material on the Wattses and the De Morgans in its focus on the historically neglected female figures, its exploration and comparison of their largely unexplored creative partnerships, and its feminist analysis of their understudied works. It shows how Victorian women repositioned themselves in relation to men as successful professional writers and artists as well as creative partners and 'significant others' rather than servile wives, secretaries or muses. It thus challenges ideologically dominant images, ideals and stereotypes of Victorian women – and specifically, longstanding misperceptions of Mary and Evelyn – as submissive or subordinate. These women achieved and promoted greater social, political and economic freedom, empowerment and equality through their professional creative practices and anti-patriarchal partnerships, transgressing, subverting and deconstructing oppressive masculinist binary structures which served to sustain sexual difference through separate spheres and gendered activities. This book shows women – traditionally the 'repressed of culture' (Cixous 1976: 878) – to have been active and assertive participants in the cultural production of art and literature as well as in progressive political movements that developed over the later nineteenth and early twentieth centuries, revealing a rich female and early feminist culture of the time.

While Elaine Showalter identifies 'feminine' (about 1840–80) and 'feminist' (about 1880–1920) as phases in the evolution of women's literature (1979: 35–6), these can also effectively be applied to the evolution of women's art, and the chronological limits can be redefined to show how the 'feminist phase' began before 1880 – as women began to enter artistic and literary professions en masse for the first time as well as public debates about the place of women through artistic and literary discourses. During the second half of the nineteenth century, the 'feminist content' of (that is, the protest against patriarchy in) art and literature was not just 'oblique, displaced' (1979: 35) and subtextual (as in the 'feminine phase') but also increasingly overt and direct. The creative practices and works of the women discussed in this book were innovative rather than imitative (imitation being associated with the 'feminine' phase in Showalter's theory).[1] The tension between 'feminine' and 'feminist' – and a (by no means straightforward) transition from the former to the latter – can be traced through a re-view of the lives and works of Mary and Evelyn, who can themselves be reclaimed as early feminists who challenged male supremacy and patriarchal assumptions in their literary and visual texts, professional creative practices, partnerships and positions as cultural producers. Artistic and literary activity was for Victorian women a strategy of self-empowerment through which they redefined themselves in relation to femininity, masculinity and society.

Through an analysis of unpublished and neglected texts, this book shows how nineteenth-century male and female figures were interested and involved in the women's rights movement, addressing the place of women and supporting women's liberation in their artistic and literary work. An exploration of the parallels and dialogues that took place between nineteenth-century figures and texts shows how they were influenced by, and contributed to, feminist discourse at the *fin de siècle*. The female figures developed a shared politically charged iconographic vocabulary primarily concerned with female figures and liberty – prioritising, for example, images of the female body (in active states, liminal spaces or processes of transformation); avian and oceanic imagery; sunrise and the dawn; life, death and rebirth; saints and angels; mother figures; windows, doors and openings; bonds and bond-breaking – which dialogised with contemporary, and prefigured more recent, feminist discourse. An application of Cixous's – and to a lesser extent, Kristeva's and Butler's – theory to their literary and visual works illuminates the subversiveness of these nineteenth-century texts, which can be seen to challenge phallo(go)centrism, re/de-construct gender, and embody elements of *écriture féminine*. Mary and Evelyn re-viewed, re-presented and reclaimed the female body, employing it as a model for socio-political transformation from captivity to liberty (often represented by closed spaces, locks and bars in contrast to open spaces, horizons and wings). They depict women as energised, ebullient, empowered, embodied subjects in contrast to representations of women as passive, powerless, objectified bodies.

The evolving role of Victorian women has been traced specifically through the lives and works of the female figures who can be seen to embody increasingly progressive socio-political positions, reflecting the rise of feminism over the second half of the nineteenth century and the development of the women's movement that escalated over the course of their careers. This can be clearly perceived in their responses to the feminist and anti-feminist petitions of their time: while their contemporary Christina Rossetti signed the anti-suffrage petition, Mary refused to sign the anti-suffrage petition, and Evelyn signed the women's suffrage petition. Their increasingly progressive positions are also revealed through an exploration of their practices and works: Mary combined private and public, philanthropic and commercial, art and craft in her creative practice; Evelyn overtly transgressed traditional female spheres in her professional fine art practice and produced politically charged paintings carrying conspicuous pro-liberation messages (while Mary undermined Victorian concepts of gender in more subtle or implicit ways). Yet, while Evelyn put her name to the women's suffrage movement as it was emerging in the late nineteenth century (as an early petition signatory), Mary put her name to it as it was escalating in the early twentieth century (in a presidential role, in speech and procession). Evelyn announced her allegiance before Mary, but Mary assumed a more active and radical role in the movement in later life. Evelyn promoted female emancipation through the bodies in her art; Mary did so with her own body: both made the feminist body visible. Both women were pioneering suffragists in different ways, at different times, fusing artistry and activism. An analysis of their works shows Mary and Evelyn had strong feminist convictions and presented a challenge to the status quo of Victorian England.

This argument is reinforced by the views and positions of the men with whom these women formed partnerships. They were open-minded, independent thinkers who had strong sympathies with women. George supported women's suffrage, perceiving it as just, natural and beneficial to socio-political progression; he publicly called for reforms in restrictive feminine fashions, and produced artworks that highlighted female suffering and condemned female oppression as well as paintings that re-presented women as active and (all-)powerful. William publicly and privately promoted (and apparently financially supported) women's suffrage, expressing his strong views about women's rights in press articles and letters as well as his novels. This book thus shows how Mary's and Evelyn's formation of partnerships with these like-minded, liberal, artistic men was strategic; the men supported and facilitated their creative practices and helped them to promote the women's cause – although the women in both partnerships showed their support for this cause in more sustained and independent ways. These pairs represented a model for a new, egalitarian form of artistic marriage, which provided new opportunities for women and men. The women forged their own careers in companionship with men while challenging male dominance; they developed distinctive styles and specifically female and feminist voices.

The nineteenth century offers a number of other examples of familial and marital creative partnerships ripe for further study, including Robert and Elizabeth Barrett Browning, Charlotte and Patrick Branwell Brontë, Jane and William Morris, Mary and Percy Shelley, and Dorothy and William Wordsworth. The study of partnerships could also be applied to, or extended to encompass, female/female or male/male as well as male/female relationships, international artistic and/or literary partnerships, partnerships involving more than two individuals, and periods preceding and/or succeeding the nineteenth century. This could offer a broader understanding of sexual relations and roles of women in artistic and literary contexts, allowing larger patterns or shifts to emerge, and opening up possibilities for further original comparisons and contrasts between partnerships. There is also scope for further comparison of women's roles within and pre- or post-partnerships – that is, after the deaths of husbands or separation from male partners – in order to investigate if and how their practices and focuses changed. Comparisons of a figure's familial and romantic partnerships, or marital and sibling relationships, and a figure's first and second marriages to creative women could highlight similarities and differences in dynamics and gender roles in these relationships. Such comparisons could serve to consolidate and reinforce my findings, contrasting more traditional male/female relationships with those involving gender-role inversions. The many nineteenth-century partnerships that failed, or in which women's creative careers were curtailed upon marriage or childbirth, could be contrasted with this book's discussion of atypical nineteenth-century partnerships that facilitated and developed (rather than impeded) women's creative careers.

This book has drawn together links between the Wattses and the De Morgans, and highlighted new connections between individuals, couples, circles and movements. These figures bonded with each other and their contemporaries over art, literature and politics; at the same time, they drew out, supported, inspired and strengthened each other's feminist views. They were part of a growing late-Victorian creative feminist community (connected in various if not immediately obvious ways to more prominent suffragists and suffragettes), and they contributed in word and image to early feminist culture. Individually and collectively, publicly and privately, in their visual, literary or social work, they supported and promoted the women's rights movement that gained momentum over the second half of the nineteenth century. This book offers a more comprehensive understanding of these figures as well as the rise of early feminism through artistic and literary discourses, practices and partnerships in Victorian–Edwardian England.

Note

1. Mary's and Evelyn's works can also be seen to display features of what Showalter calls the 'Female phase, ongoing since 1920', in which women turn to 'female experience as the source of an autonomous art' (1979: 36). Their works thus blur and break down the boundaries between Showalter's categories.

Bibliography

Aaron, Jane (1991), *A Double Singleness: Gender and the Writings of Charles and Mary Lamb*, Oxford: Clarendon Press.

Ahlquist, Dale (2008), 'Introduction', in G. K. Chesterton, *G. K. Chesterton on G. F. Watts*, Compton: Watts Gallery, pp. 9–12.

Andersen, Hans Christian [1837] (2002), 'The Little Mermaid', in Janet Baine Kopito (ed.), *The Little Mermaid and Other Fairy Tales*, New York: Dover Publications, Inc., pp. 1–23.

Anon. (1970), *EDM* exhibition booklet, London: Hartnoll & Eyre Ltd, De Morgan Foundation Archives.

A. R. A. (Associated Member of the Royal Academy) (1888), 'Woman, and Her Chance as Artist', in *The Magazine of Art*, p. xxv, De Morgan Foundation Archives.

Armstrong, Isobel (1993), *Victorian Poetry: Poetry, Poetics and Politics*, New York: Routledge.

Barrington, Emilie Isabel Russell (1905), *G. F. Watts; Reminiscences*, New York: The Macmillan Company; London: G. Allen.

Barrington, Emily Russell (c.1922), *William De Morgan: The Potter as I Knew Him*, Unpublished Manuscript, De Morgan Foundation Archive Box 2, MS_0047.

Bashkirtseff, Marie (1884), 'Author's Preface' in *The Journal of a Young Artist, 1860-1884*, trans. Mary J. Serrano, New York: Cassell & Company, Ltd, pp. iii–viii.

Bashkirtseff, Marie (1889), *The Journal of a Young Artist, 1860–1884*, trans. Mary J. Serrano, New York: Cassell & Company, Ltd.

Bateman, Charles T. (1901), *Bell's Miniature Series of Painters: Watts*, London: George Bell & Sons.

Beaumont, Matthew (2006), 'Influential Force: Shafts and the Diffusion of Knowledge at the Fin de Siècle', *Interdisciplinary Studies in the Long Nineteenth Century*, 19:3, pp. 1–19.

Bills, Mark (2010), *Watts Chapel: A Guide to the Symbols of Mary Watts's Arts and Crafts Masterpiece*, London: Philip Wilson Publishers Ltd.

Bills, Mark (2011), '"Two artists who are of just the same mind concerning their ideals of art": George Frederic Watts (1817–1904) and Mary

Seton Watts (1849-1938)', in Mark Bills (ed.), *An Artists' Village: G. F. Watts and Mary Watts at Compton*, London: Philip Wilson Publishers Ltd, pp. 9–23.

Bills, Mark, and Desna Greenhow (eds) (2012), *The Word in the Pattern: A Facsimile With Accompanying Essays on Mary Watts's Cemetery Chapel Drawn from the Watts Gallery Symposium 2010*, The Society for the Arts and Crafts Movement in Surrey.

Black, Ros (2010), *A Talent for Humanity: The Life and Work of Lady Henry Somerset*, Chippenham and Eastbourne: Antony Rowe Publishing.

Bloom, Lynn Z. (1996), '"I write for myself and strangers": Private Diaries as Public Documents', in Suzanne L. Bunkers and Cynthia A. Huff (eds), *Inscribing the Daily: Critical Essays on Women's Diaries*, Amherst: University of Massachusetts Press.

Blunt, Reginald (1918), *The Wonderful Village*, London: Mills and Boon.

Blunt, Wilfrid (1989), *England's Michelangelo: A Biography of George Frederic Watts*, London: Columbus Books Ltd.

Blyth, Ian, and Susan Sellers (2004), *Hélène Cixous: Live Theory*, London: Continuum.

Boreham, Louise (2013), 'Cumnock to Compton', *Northern Ceramic Society Journal*, 29, pp. 79–96.

Bryant, Barbara (2012), 'G. F. Watts's *'The All-Pervading'*: Before the Altarpiece and After', in Mark Bills and Desna Greenhow (eds), *The Word in the Pattern; A Facsimile*, The Society for the Arts and Crafts Movement in Surrey, pp. 32–43.

Burne-Jones, Georgiana (1906), *Memorials of Edward Burne-Jones*, New York: Macmillan Co.

Butler, Judith (1990), 'Bodily Inscriptions, Performative Subversions', in Sara Salih (ed.), *The Judith Butler Reader*, Oxford: Blackwell, pp. 90–118.

Butler, Judith (2004), *The Judith Butler Reader*, ed. Sara Salih, Oxford: Blackwell.

Butler, Judith (2006), *Gender Trouble*, New York: Routledge.

Cain, Felicity (2013), *The Crime or Folly of Writing a Novel: William De Morgan, Accidental Novelist*, University of Lancaster: MA Dissertation.

Cain, Felicity (2012), 'Notes on William De Morgan's Women Characters', Word document, sent via personal email attachment, 31 December 2012.

Caine, Barbara (1992), *Victorian Feminists*, New York: Oxford University Press.

Casteras, Susan P., and Linda H. Peterson (1994), *A Struggle for Fame: Victorian Women Artists and Authors*, New Haven: Yale Center for British Art.

Chapman, Ronald (1945), *The Laurel and the Thorn; A Study of G. F. Watts*, London: Faber and Faber Limited.

Cherry, Deborah (1993), *Painting Women: Victorian Women Artists*, London: Routledge.

Cherry, Deborah (2000), *Beyond the Frame: Feminism and Visual Culture, Britain (1850–1900)*, New York: Routledge.

Chesterton, G. K. (2008), *G. K. Chesterton on G. F. Watts*, Compton: Watts Gallery.

Chrisman, Laura (1990), 'Allegory, Feminist Thought and the Dreams of Olive Schreiner', *Prose Studies*, 13:1, pp. 126–50.

Cixous, Hélène (1976), 'The Laugh of the Medusa', trans. Keith Cohen and Paula Cohen, *Chicago Journals*, 1:4, pp. 875–93.

Cixous, Hélène (1991), *Coming to Writing and Other Essays*, ed. Deborah Jenson, Cambridge: Harvard University Press.

Cixous, Hélène (2006), *Dream I Tell You*, trans. Beverley Bie Brahic, Edinburgh: Edinburgh University Press.

Cixous, Hélène, and Catherine Clément (1986), *The Newly Born Woman*, trans. Betsy Wing, Manchester: Manchester University Press.

Cockroft, V. Irene (2005), *New Dawn Women: Women in the Arts & Crafts and Suffrage Movements at the Dawn of the 20th Century*, Compton: Watts Gallery.

Cowman, Krista (2009), 'What Was Suffragette Militancy? An Exploration of the British Example', in Irma Sulkunen, Seija-Leena Nevala-Nurmi and Pirjo Markkola (eds), *Suffrage, Gender and Citizenship – International Perspectives on Parliamentary Reforms*, Newcastle upon Tyne: Cambridge Scholars Publishing.

Cowman, Krista (forthcoming 2018), 'Suffragette Attacks on Art 1913–1914', in Miranda Garrett and Zoe Thomas (eds), *Suffrage and the Arts: Visual Culture, Politics, and Enterprise*, London: Bloomsbury.

Crawford, Elizabeth (1999), *The Women's Suffrage Movement: A Reference Guide, 1866-1928*, London: UCL Press.

Crawford, Elizabeth (2006), *The Women's Suffrage Movement in Britain and Ireland: A Regional Survey*, Oxford and New York: Routledge.

Delafield, Catherine (2009), *Women's Diaries as Narrative in the Nineteenth-Century Novel*, Farnham: Ashgate.

De Morgan, Evelyn (1869–70), *The Reader* (January 1869), *Nora de Brant* (1869), notebooks and books of verses (*c.*1869–70), De Morgan Foundation Archive Box 1: DMF_MS_0023, DMF_MS_0022, DMF_MS_0006, DMF_MS_0008.

De Morgan, Evelyn (1872), Personal Diary, De Morgan Foundation Archive Box 1: DMF_MS_0010.

De Morgan, Evelyn (1904), Letter to Kate Holiday, 3 June, De Morgan Foundation Archive Box 2: MS_0293.

De Morgan, Mary (1877), *On a Pincushion and other Fairy Tales*, London: Seeley, Jackson, & Halliday.

De Morgan, Sophia (1882), *Memoir of Augustus De Morgan*, London: Longmans, Green, and Co.

De Morgan, William (1910), *An Affair of Dishonour*, London: William Heinemann.

De Morgan, William (1913), letter to Mr Lansbury, 12 January, pp. 1–2, De Morgan Foundation Archive Box 2: MS_0018_1.

De Morgan, William, and Evelyn De Morgan (1909) [published anonymously], *The Result of an Experiment*, London: Simpkin, Marshall, Hamilton, Kent & Co.

De Morgan, William, and Evelyn De Morgan (1919), *The Old Madhouse*, London: William Heinemann.

De Morgan, William, and Evelyn De Morgan (1920), *The Old Man's Youth and the Young Man's Old Age*, New York: H. Holt and Company.

Errington, Lindsay (1984), *Social and Religious Themes in English Art 1840–1860*, New York: Garland Publishing.

Evans, Mary (1997), *Introducing Contemporary Feminist Thought*, Oxford: Blackwell Publishers Ltd.

Festing, Sally (1991), *Gertrude Jekyll*, London: Penguin Books Ltd.

Foster, Shirley (1990), 'Speaking beyond Patriarchy', in Helen Wilcox et al. (eds), *The Body and the Text: Hélène Cixous, Reading and Teaching*, Hemel Hempstead: Harvester Wheatsheaf, pp. 66–77.

Fowle, Frances (2000), Summary of George Watts's *'The All-Pervading'* for the Tate website, NP, <http://www.tate.org.uk/art/artworks/watts-the-all-pervading-n01687/text-summary> (last accessed 23 April 2014).

Fraser Tytler, Christina (1869), *Sweet Violet, and Other Stories*, London: Hatchards.

Friederichs, Hulda (1895), 'An Interview with Mr. G. F. Watts, R.A.', *The Young Woman: A Monthly Journal and Review*, 39, pp. 73–82.

Gilbert, Sandra (1986), 'Introduction', in Hélène Cixous and Catherine Clément, *The Newly Born Woman*, trans. Betsy Wing, Manchester: Manchester University Press, pp. ix–xviii.

Gilbert, Sandra, and Susan Gubar (1979), *The Madwoman in the Attic*, New Haven: Yale University Press.

Gordon, Catherine (ed.) (1996), *Evelyn De Morgan: Oil Paintings*, London: De Morgan Foundation.

Gould, Veronica Franklin (1993), *The Watts Chapel: An Arts and Crafts Memorial*, Compton: Privately Published.

Gould, Veronica Franklin (1998), *Mary Seton Watts (1849–1938): Unsung Heroine of the Art Nouveau*, London: Lund Humphries.

Gould, Veronica Franklin (2004a), *G. F. Watts: The Last Great Victorian*, New Haven: Yale University Press.

Gould, Veronica Franklin (ed.) (2004b), 'The Catalogue', in Veronica Franklin Gould (ed.), *The Vision of G. F. Watts*, Compton: Watts Gallery, pp. 45–90.

Granby, Marchioness of (1900), *Portraits of Men and Women*, Westminster: Archibald Constable.

Grand, Sarah (1894), 'The Modern Girl', *The North American Review* (University of Northern Iowa), 158:451, June, pp. 706–14.

Green, Barbara (1997), *Spectacular Confessions: Autobiography, Performative Activism, and the Sites of Suffrage 1905-1938*, Basingstoke: Macmillan Press Ltd.

Greenhow, Desna (ed.) (2016a), 'Introduction', in *The Diary of Mary Watts 1887–1904: Victorian Progressive and Artistic Visionary*, London: Lund Humphries, pp. 9–14.

Greenhow, Desna (ed.) (2016b), *The Diary of Mary Watts 1887–1904: Victorian Progressive and Artistic Visionary*, London: Lund Humphries.

Halberstam, Judith (1998), *Female Masculinity*, Durham, NC: Duke University Press.

Harris, Ann Sutherland, and Linda Nochlin (1976), *Women Artists 1550–1950*, Los Angeles: Los Angeles County Museum of Art.

Hartman, Kabi (2003), '"What Made Me a Suffragette": The New Woman and the New (?) Conversion Narrative', *Women's History Review*, 12:1, pp. 35–50.

Hood, Thomas [1843] (1890), 'The Song of the Shirt', *The Poetical Works of Thomas Hood*, London: Frederick Warne, pp. 223–6, ll.1–89.

Hood, Thomas [1844] (1939), 'The Bridge of Sighs', in Arthur Quiller-Couch (ed.), *The Oxford Book of English Verse 1250–1918*, Oxford: Clarendon Press, pp. 776–80, ll.1–106.

Housego, Molly, and Neil R. Storey (2012), *The Women's Suffrage Movement*, Oxford: Shire Publications Ltd.

Hunter, Jane H. (1992), 'Inscribing the Self in the Heart of the Family: Diaries and Girlhood in Late-Victorian America', *American Quarterly* [The Johns Hopkins University Press], 44:1, March, pp. 51–81.

Ibsen, Henrik (1992), *A Doll's House*, New York: Dover Publications.

Jacobs, Mary (ed.) (1979), *Women Writing and Writing about Women*, London: Croom Helm Ltd.

Jefferies, Richard (2006), *Watts Gallery: A Personal View by Richard Jefferies*, Compton: Watts Gallery.

Jekyll, Francis (1934), *Gertrude Jekyll: A Memoir*, London: Jonathan Cape.

Jenkins, Lyndsey (2015), *Lady Constance Lytton: Aristocrat, Suffragette, Martyr*, London: Biteback Publishing Ltd.

Jones, Ann Rosalind (1985), 'Inscribing Femininity: French Theories of the Feminine', in Gayle Greene and Coppélia Kahn (eds), *Making a Difference: Feminist Literary Criticism*, London: Routledge, pp. 80–112.

Jones, Ann Rosalind (1993), 'Writing the Body: Towards an Understanding of *l'écriture féminine*', in Stevi Jackson, Karen Atkinson, Deirdre Beddoe et al. (eds), *Women's Studies: A Reader*, Hemel Hempstead: Harvester Wheatsheaf, pp. 454–8.

Kaplan, Cora (1979), 'The Indefinite Disclosed: Christina Rossetti and Emily Dickinson', in Mary Jacobs (ed.), *Women Writing and Writing about Women*, London: Croom Helm Ltd., pp. 61–79.

Kestner, Joseph A. (1989), *Mythology and Misogyny: The Social Discourse of Nineteenth-Century British Classical-Subject Painting*, London: Wisconsin University Press, Ltd.

Kristeva, Julia (1982), *Powers of Horror: An Essay on Abjection*, trans. Leon S. Roudiez, New York: Columbia University Press.

Lee, Hermione (2008), *Body Parts: Essays on Life-Writing*, London: Pimlico.

Lewis, Jane (1983), 'Re-reading Beatrice Webb's Diary', *History Workshop* [Oxford University Press], 16, Autumn, pp. 143–6.

Lytton, Constance [Jane Warton] (1914), *Prisons and Prisoners: Some Personal Experiences*, New York: George H. Doran Company.

Macmillan, Hugh (1903), *The Life-Work of George Frederick Watts*, London: J. M. Dent & Co.

Mancoff, Debra N. (2012), *Danger! Women Artists at Work*, London: Merrell.

Marsh, Jan (1987), *Pre-Raphaelite Women: Images of Femininity in Pre-Raphaelite Art*, London: Weidenfeld & Nicolson.

Marsh, Jan (ed.) (1994), *Christina Rossetti: Poems and Prose*, London: Everyman.

McMahon, Mary (ed.) (2013), *The Making of Mary Seton Watts*, Surrey: Watts Gallery.

Meaney, Gerardine (1993), *(Un)Like Subjects: Women, Theory, Fiction*, London: Routledge.

Michie, Helena (2006), *Victorian Honeymoons: Journeys to the Conjugal*, Cambridge: Cambridge University Press.

Millim, Anne-Marie (2010), 'The Victorian Diary: Between the Public and the Private', *Literature Compass*, 7:10, Blackwell Publishing Ltd, pp. 977–88.

Milne, James (1922), 'The Romance of the De Morgans', *The Graphic*, 24 June 1922, p. 808, De Morgan Foundation Archive Box 23, MS_0589.

Mulvey, Laura (1999), 'Visual Pleasure and Narrative Cinema', in Sue Thornham (ed.), *Feminist Film Theory: A Reader*, Edinburgh: Edinburgh University Press, pp. 58–69.

Naughton, Gail (2011), 'Lilian Abbott Macintosh (1879-1972)', pp. 1–4, Watts Gallery Archive.

Nead, Lynda (1988), *Myths of Sexuality: Representations of Women in Victorian Britain*, Oxford: Basil Blackwell Ltd.

Nicoletti, L. J. (2004), 'Downward Mobility: Victorian Women, Suicide, and London's "Bridge of Sighs"', *The Literary London Journal: Interdisciplinary Studies in the Representation of London*, 2:1, March, NP.

Nunn, Pamela Gerrish (1987), *Victorian Women Artists*, London: The Women's Press Ltd.

Ormond, Leonée and Richard Ormond (2012), *G. F. Watts: The Hall of Fame; Portraits of His Famous Contemporaries*, Compton: Watts Gallery.

Overton, Jenny, and Joan Mant (1998), *A Suffragette Nest: Peaslake, 1910 and After*, Surrey: Hazeltree Publishing.

Paterson, Elaine Cheasley (2005), 'Decoration and Desire in the Watts Chapel, Compton: Narratives of Gender, Class and Colonialism', *Gender and History*, 17:3, November, pp. 714–36.

Peeters, Nic (2002), 'Pre-Raphaeladies', in Serena Trowbridge (ed.), *The Review of the PRS*, X:2, pp. 17–27.

Peterson, Linda H. (1999), *Traditions of Victorian Women's Autobiography: The Poetics and Politics of Life Writing*, Charlottesville, VA and London: University Press of Virginia.

Phelps, William Lyon (1917), 'William De Morgan', *The North American Review*, 205, 1 March, pp. 440–6.

Pitcher, Harvey (2013), 'The Flower-Girl's Story', pp. 1–16, Watts Gallery Archives.

Regan, Tom (1986), *Bloomsbury's Prophet: G. E. Moore and the Development of His Moral Philosophy*, Eugene: Wipf and Stock.

Rich, Adrienne (1980), 'When We Dead Awaken: Writing as Re-Vision', *On Lies, Secrets, and Silence: Selected Prose 1966–1978*, London: Virago Press Ltd, pp. 33–50.

Ritchie, Anne Thackeray (1924), *Letters of Anne Thackeray Ritchie*, ed. Hester Ritchie, London: John Murray.

Rossetti, Christina (1994), *Christina Rossetti: Poems and Prose*, ed. Jan Marsh, London: Everyman.

Rossetti, William (1911), 'Memoir', in William Rossetti (ed.), *The Poetical Works of Christina Rossetti*, London: Macmillan & Co. Ltd, pp. xlv–lxxi.

Rubinstein, David (1977), 'Cycling in the 1890s', *Victorian Studies*, 21:1, pp. 47–71, <http://www.jstor.org/stable/3825934> (last accessed 20 August 2014).

Ruskin, John (1916), 'Of Queens' Gardens' (Lecture II), *Sesame and Lilies*, ed. C. R. Rounds, New York: American Book Company, pp. 81–113.

Schreiner, Olive [1890] (2008), *Dreams*, Biblioteca Virtual Universal, pp. 1–42, <http://www.biblioteca.org.ar/libros/167741.pdf> (last accessed 10 November 2016).

Sharp, Frank, and Jan Marsh (eds) (2012), *The Collected Letters of Jane Morris*, Woodbridge: The Boydell Press.

Shattock, Joanne (ed.) (2001), *Women and Literature in Britain, 1800–1900*, Cambridge: Cambridge University Press.

Shore, Emily (1891), *Journal of Emily Shore*, London: K. Paul, Trench, Trübner & Co.

Showalter, Elaine (1979), 'Towards a Feminist Poetics', in Mary Jacobs (ed.) *Women Writing and Writing About Women*, London: Croom Helm Ltd, pp. 22–41.

Showalter, Elaine (1982), 'Review of *Olive Schreiner: A Biography* by Ruth First and Ann Scott', *Tulsa Studies in Women's Literature*, 1:1, pp. 104–9.

Smith, Alison (1996), *The Victorian Nude: Sexuality, Morality and Art*, Manchester: Manchester University Press.

Smith, Alison (ed.) (2001), *Exposed: The Victorian Nude*, London: Tate Publishing.

Smith, Elise Lawton (2002), *Evelyn Pickering De Morgan and the Allegorical Body*, London: Associated University Presses.

Smith, Elise Lawton (forthcoming), '"A Rising Stream of Life": Nature as Ground and Spirit in the Art of Mary Watts', in Judith W. Page and Elise Lawton Smith, *Women, Literature, and the Art of the Garden in Early 20th-Century England*.

Steinitz, Rebecca (2011), *Time, Space, and Gender in the Nineteenth-Century British Diary*, New York: Palgrave Macmillan.

Stewart, David (2004), 'Watts, the Royal Academy and Leighton in Conflict', in V. F. Gould (ed.), *The Vision of G. F. Watts*, Compton: Watts Gallery, pp. 35–40.

Stirling, A. M. W. (1922), *William De Morgan and His Wife*, New York: Henry Holt and Company.

Stirling, A. M. W. (1924), *Life's Little Day*, London: Thornton Butterworth Ltd.

Sullivan, Sarah (ed.) (2012), *Phillips Memorial Park: An Arts and Crafts Movement Tribute to a Hero of the Titanic*, Surrey: The Society for the Arts and Crafts Movement in Surrey.

Susam-Sarajeva, Sebnem (2006), *Theories on the Move: Translation's Role in the Travels of Literary Theories*, Amsterdam: Rodopi.

Tennyson, Alfred [1863] (1987), 'Flower in the Crannied Wall', *The Poems of Tennyson*, ed. Christopher Ricks, Harlow: Longman, Vol. II, p. 693, ll.1–6.

Thirlwell, Angela (2003), *William and Lucy: The Other Rossettis*, New Haven: Yale University Press.

Thomas, Zoe (2015), 'At Home with the Women's Guild of Arts: Gender and Professional Identity in London Studios, c. 1880–1925', *Women's History Review*, 24:6, pp. 938–64.

Thomas, Zoe (2016), 'Mary Seton Watts and the Women's Guild of Arts', conference paper for *Mary Watts: Victorian Progressive and Artistic Visionary*, Compton: Watts Gallery.

Tickner, Lisa (1989), *The Spectacle of Women: Imagery of the Suffrage Campaign 1907–14*, London: Chatto & Windus.

Tong, Rosemarie (1992), *Feminist Thought: A Comprehensive Introduction*, London: Routledge.

Treuherz, Julian (1993), *Victorian Painting*, London: Thames & Hudson Ltd.

Tromans, Nicholas (2011), *Hope: The Life and Times of a Victorian Icon*, Compton: Watts Gallery.

Tromans, Nicholas (2016), 'Foreword', in Desna Greenhow (ed.), *The Diary of Mary Watts 1887–1904: Victorian Progressive and Artistic Visionary*, London: Lund Humphries, pp. 6–8.

Unwin, Melanie (2004), 'Significant Other: Art and Craft in the Career and Marriage of Mary Watts', *Journal of Design History*, 17:3, pp. 237–50.

Van Valkenburgh, F. K. (1992), 'A Victorian Woman's Response: Liberal Feminism in Evelyn Pickering's Paintings', *Tulsa Studies in Women's Literature*, pp. 1–11, De Morgan Foundation Archives.

Von Volkmann, Richard (1874), *Fantastic Stories*, trans. Paulina B. Granville, London: Henry S. King & Co.

Watts, G. F. (1883), 'On Taste in Dress', in Mary Watts (ed.), *George Frederic Watts: The Annals of An Artist's Life: Volume III: His Writings*, London: Macmillan and Co. Ltd., 1912, pp. 202–27.

Watts, G. F. (1894), *What Should a Picture Say?* London: Penny and Kull, Watts Gallery Archives.

Watts, G. F. (1905), The Royal Scottish Academy's *Memorial Exhibition of the Works of George Frederick Watts in the Royal Academy Galleries*, Edinburgh: T. and A. Constable, Edinburgh University Press.

Watts, Mary (1870–86, 1887, 1891, 1893, 1896, 1898, 1902, 1904, 1906–8), The Diaries of Mary Seton Watts, Compton: Watts Gallery Archives COMWG2008.4, MSW/1-10, Box A25.

Watts, Mary (1905), *The Word in the Pattern: A Key to the Symbols on the Walls of the Chapel at Compton*, London: W. H. Ward & Co. Ltd.

Watts, Mary (1912), *George Frederic Watts: The Annals of An Artist's Life* [Vols 1–3], London: Macmillan and Co. Ltd.

Watts, Mary, and Gertrude Jekyll (1913), *Jessie Godwin-Austen*, England: Privately Printed, National Art Library General Collection: G.28.DD.42: 38041990033672.

Weeks, Charlotte J. (1883), 'Women at Work: The Slade Girls', *The Magazine of Art*, De Morgan Foundation Archive Box 23: MS_ 0587_1-6.

White, Susan (1993), 'Split Skins: Female Agency and Bodily Mutilation in *The Little Mermaid*', in Jim Collins, Hilary Radner and Ava Preacher Collins (eds), *Film Theory Goes to the Movies*, London: Routledge, pp. 182–95.

Wilson, Shelagh (2004), 'Watts, Women, Philanthropy and the Home Arts', in Colin Trodd and Stephanie Brown (eds), *Representations of G. F. Watts: Art Making in Victorian Culture*, Aldershot: Ashgate Publishing Ltd., pp. 169–85.

Wingerden, Sophia A. Van (1999), *The Women's Suffrage Movement in Britain, 1866–1928*, Basingstoke: Macmillan.

Wolff, Janet (1990), *Feminine Sentences: Essays on Women and Culture*, Oxford: Polity Press.

Woolf, Virginia (1942), 'Professions for Women', in Leonard Woolf (ed.), *The Death of the Moth and Other Essays*, New York: Harcourt Brace & Co., pp. 235–42.

Woolf, Virginia [1933] (2008), *Selected Diaries*, ed. Anne Olivier Bell, London: Vintage.

Yates, Patricia (1996), 'Evelyn De Morgan's Use of Literary Sources in her Paintings', in Catherine Gordon (ed.), *Evelyn De Morgan: Oil Paintings*, London: De Morgan Foundation, pp. 53–74.

Index

Printed and bound by CPI Group (UK) Ltd, Croydon, CR0 4YY

18/03/2025

01834110-0001